A Royal Life

A Royal Life

HRH The Duke of Kent
and Hugo Vickers

HODDER &
STOUGHTON

First published in Great Britain in 2022 by Hodder & Stoughton
An Hachette UK company

1

Copyright © HRH The Duke of Kent and Hugo Vickers 2022

The right of HRH The Duke of Kent and Hugo Vickers to be
identified as the Authors of the Work has been asserted by them in
accordance with the Copyright, Designs and Patents Act 1988.

A CIP catalogue record for this title is available from the British Library

Hardback ISBN 978 1 529 38970 8
Trade Paperback ISBN 978 1 529 38971 5
eBook ISBN 978 1 529 38972 2

Typeset in Janson Text by Hewer Text UK Ltd, Edinburgh
Printed and bound in Great Britain by Clays Ltd, Elcograf S.p.A.

Hodder & Stoughton policy is to use papers that are natural, renewable
and recyclable products and made from wood grown in sustainable
forests. The logging and manufacturing processes are expected to
conform to the environmental regulations of the country of origin.

Hodder & Stoughton Ltd
Carmelite House
50 Victoria Embankment
London EC4Y 0DZ

www.hodder.co.uk

To K, G, H & N
With my love
E

Contents

Key to the Contributors

Spoken Accounts

HRH The Duchess of Kent, GCVO
(born 1933)

Katharine Worsley, wife of the Duke, and daughter of Sir William Worsley, 4th Bt (1890–1973), Lord Lieutenant of the North Riding of Yorkshire. Taught at Lady Eden's School in London, married HRH The Duke of Kent in 1961. She converted to Catholicism in 1994. She withdrew from most royal duties in 2002 and later taught piano in a primary school in Hull. Involved with numerous charities, she is the co-founder of Future Talent, which helps young people on low incomes pursue a career in music.

HRH Princess Alexandra,
The Hon. Lady Ogilvy, KG, GCVO
(born 1936)

Princess Alexandra, sister of the Duke, has undertaken royal duties since her teenage years and still does today. In 1963 she married the (Rt) Hon. (Sir) Angus Ogilvy (1928–2004), younger son of the 12th Earl of Airlie. They had a son, James, born in 1964, and a daughter, Marina, born in 1966.

HRH Prince Michael of Kent, GCVO
(born 1942)

Prince Michael, brother of the Duke, was born shortly before his father's untimely death in 1942. He undertakes certain royal duties, and is a considerable expert on Russia, himself speaking fluent Russian. In 1978 he married Baroness Marie-Christine von Reibnitz. They have a son and daughter, Lord Frederick Windsor, born in 1979, and Lady Gabriella Kingston, born in 1981.

The Earl of St Andrews
(born 1962)

George, Earl of St Andrews, elder son of the Duke, is Chancellor of Bolton University and trustee of various charities. He married the Cambridge academic, Sylvana Tomaselli, in 1988 and they have three children, Edward, Lord Downpatrick, born in 1988, Lady Marina Windsor, born in 1992, and Lady Amelia Windsor, born in 1995.

Lady Helen Taylor
(born 1964)

Lady Helen Windsor, daughter of the Duke, was a Director of the Karsten Schubert Gallery at the height of the YBAs, and a fashion ambassador and muse for Giorgio Armani for twelve years, while also supporting CLIC Sargent cancer charity and more recently the Royal Marsden Cancer Charity, of which she is a Trustee. She married the art gallerist, Timothy Taylor in 1992. They have four children: Columbus, born in 1994, Cassius, born in 1996, Eloise, born in 2003, and Estella, born in 2004.

Lord Nicholas Windsor
(born 1970)

Lord Nicholas Windsor is the younger son of the Duke. He is a Roman Catholic, and involved with various Catholic charities. He married Paola Frankopan in Rome in 2006, and they have three children, Albert, born in 2007, Leopold, born in 2009, and Louis, born in 2014.

The Cousins

HRH Princess Elizabeth of Yugoslavia
(born 1936)

Princess Elizabeth, the Duke's cousin, is the only surviving child of Prince Paul of Yugoslavia (1893–1976), one-time Regent of Yugoslavia, and his wife, Princess Olga of Greece and Denmark (1903–97), eldest sister of Princess Marina. She is a member of the House of Karageorgevitch. She lives in Belgrade, and runs the Princess Elizabeth Foundation.

She was married to Howard Oxenberg, and had two daughters, Catherine (famous as the star of *Dynasty* in the 1980s), born in 1961, and Christina (a writer), born in 1962. Divorced in 1966, she was married to Neil Balfour between 1969 and 1978, and had a son, Nicholas, born in 1970. She was married in 1987 to Manuel Ulloa Elías, former Prime Minister of Peru. They separated in 1989.

Count Hans Veit zu Toerring-Jettenbach
(born 1935)

Hans Veit Toerring, the Duke's cousin, is the only son of Count Carl Theodor zu Toerring-Jettenbach (1900–67) and his wife, Princess Elisabeth of Greece and Denmark (1904–55),

elder sister of Princess Marina. He lives at Schloss Frauenbühl, Winhöring, in Bavaria, and oversees the family properties. He is a keen photographer and a considerable expert on his extended family.

In 1964 he married Princess Henriette zu Hohenlohe-Bartenstein, and they have three children, Clarissa, born in 1965, Ignatius, born in 1966, and Karl Theodor, born in 1969.

HIH Archduchess Helen of Austria
(born 1937)

Helen Habsburg, the Duke's cousin, is the only daughter of Count Carl Theodor zu Toerring-Jettenbach (1900–67) and his wife, Princess Elisabeth of Greece and Denmark (1904–55), elder sister of Princess Marina. In 1956 she married HIH Archduke Ferdinand of Austria (1918–2004), a descendant of Emperor Franz II of Austria (1768–1835), and nephew of Emperor Karl I (1887–1922), the last reigning Emperor of Austria and King of Hungary. They had three children, Maximilian, born in 1961, Elisabeth (1957–83), and Sophie, born in 1959. She lives in Austria and London.

The Household

Lieutenant-Commander Sir Richard Buckley, KCVO
(1928–2022)

Lieutenant-Commander Sir Richard Buckley was private secretary to the Duke and Duchess from 1961 to 1989. He was later an extra equerry. He lived with his wife at Coppins Cottage, formerly the home of Baroness de Stoeckl, in Coppins Lane, Iver.

Captain Nicholas Turnbull, MBE, QGM
(born 1962)

Nick Turnbull joined the Duke and Duchess as Private Secretary in 2018. He served with the Queen's Own Highlanders in Northern Ireland and Scotland, and subsequently with the Foreign Office, serving abroad in the Balkans, Afghanistan and West Africa.

Written Accounts

Sir Cecil Beaton, CBE
(1904–80)

Sir Cecil Beaton was well known as a photographer, illustrator, and designer of sets and costumes for opera, ballet, stage and films. He was responsible for some of the greatest photographs of the British Royal Family in the twentieth century. Princess Marina was one of his favourite photographic subjects and he became a personal friend of hers. An inveterate diarist, his account of the wedding of the Duke and Duchess of Kent in 1961 is published here for the first time.

Sir Charles Johnston, GCMG
(1912–86)

Sir Charles Johnston was variously a diplomat, translator and poet. He served as Ambassador in Jordan from 1956 to 1959, Governor of Aden from 1959 to 1963 and High Commissioner in Australia from 1965 to 1971. He is credited with having produced one of the finest translations of Pushkin's *Eugene Onegin*.

In 1944 he married Princess Natasha Bagration (1914–84), a member of the Georgian and Bagration royal dynasties. She

was a great-great-granddaughter of Emperor Nicholas I of Russia (1796–1855). She was a third cousin of Princess Marina, twice over [*see* Family Tree], and was close to her at the time of Prince George's death in 1942 and until Princess Marina died. Sir Charles's essay on Princess Marina has not been published before.

Baroness Agnes de Stoeckl
(1874–1968)

Agnes de Stoeckl, known as 'Auntie Ag' of the courts of Europe, was the daughter of William Barron. In 1892, she married Baron Alexander (Sasha) de Stoeckl, who served at the Russian Embassy, was equerry to Grand Duke Michael, and later comptroller to Grand Duchess George. A number of her books, written late in life, were published by John Murray. She and her family lived at Coppins Cottage.

Prologue

HV: Would you say that being a member of the Royal Family has given you a more interesting life than you would have had otherwise?

The Duke of Kent: It certainly gave me a lot of opportunities to meet people and to travel. I have done a great deal of travelling through the years. So, yes, I think it certainly gave me advantages of that kind.

HV: My theory is that working within the system is the right way to operate as a supportive member of the Royal Family. The system is easy to work with, and the Queen is the person you are helping in a general sense, and you can also do other things for the general good that interest you. Taking Prince Philip, he worked out whenever he was needed and when he wasn't he explored many different enterprises.

Duke: Exactly. I never felt I was locked into a system that was operating against me, or restricting me unduly. Far from it.

HV: The Queen needs so much support. She can't do everything she's asked to do in life.

Duke: I always felt I wanted to support her. That's by far the most important thing in life.

1

The Duke waiting with the Queen at the Grand Entrance to
Buckingham Palace when President Jorge Sampaio and his wife
Maria came to lunch on 13 February 2002. They are both in
mourning for Princess Margaret, who had died four days earlier

The Duke Today

The Duke of Kent is now eighty-six. He lives with the Duchess and her Labrador, Bramble, at Wren House, in the precincts of Kensington Palace, beyond the main palace buildings. Princess Eugenie and her family live in the house just beyond, and the Duke and Duchess of Gloucester, who used to occupy Princess Marina's apartment, are also in the vicinity. Nottingham Cottage, where variously Prince William and Prince Harry have lived, and which was once the home of Marion Crawford, governess to the Queen and Princess Margaret, almost adjoins Wren House.

PROLOGUE

The Duke and Duchess of Cambridge live in Princess Margaret's former apartment with their children. The Duke of Kent's brother, Prince Michael, lives with his wife in a small house, which is part of the main palace.

The Duke maintains an office in St James's Palace, opposite that of his sister, Princess Alexandra. His private secretary, Nicholas Turnbull, has his office in Friary Court. From there the Duke's official business is conducted.

Like everyone else, the Duke's activities were considerably curtailed during the Covid-19 pandemic. Normally he would have regular programme meetings each year to outline his planned engagements.

Duke: I have always done it like that. I would have one just before Christmas to map out what was coming in the next few months. These meetings would be conducted about every three or four months but, of course, that stopped in 2020. We haven't had a proper planning meeting for two years.

I used to receive a lot of invitations. I'm not sure there will be so many now. I looked at my old diaries and they were packed. There has recently been a bit of slacking off. But as things have been opening up, I have had a few engagements recently. For instance, I had one the other day [autumn 2021] to go down to Bristol. It just depends on the local Lord Lieutenant. Sometimes I have struck up a friendship with a Lord Lieutenant and then they keep asking me back. Sometimes I don't know them at all, but the one in Bristol has invited me several times. It is largely a matter of luck. That, combined with the fact that certain people know I have particular interests, which makes a difference, of course. As patron or president of a society or association, I will attend their events. I am occasionally asked to present the Queen's

Awards to Industry and spend a whole day doing that. Regiments also keep me occupied.

If a speech is required, the organisation suggests some points to make and we work with them on the final words.

The Duke has many responsibilities. He has 110 patronages, on top of which there are the honorary fellowships and his membership of a great number of organisations. The Duke of Edinburgh had a great many more and with the withdrawal from public life of other members of the Royal Family, there will be many patronages to be distributed.

Nick Turnbull: In terms of what the Duke is doing today, his regimental associations remain very strong, the Scots Guards, the Royal Scots Dragoon Guards, the Royal Fusiliers, the Rifles and the Lorne Scots in Canada. There are the Lord Lieutenancy visits, during which he might visit companies whose work the Lord Lieutenant would wish to highlight and who may have been awarded a Queen's Award for Enterprise. His musical patronages are important to him and numerous, such as the London Philharmonic Orchestra, the Hanover Band, the Wigmore Hall, Opera North, The Royal Choral Society, Trinity Laban College, the Royal Choral Society, the International Music Seminar (IMS) Prussia Cove, the Newbury Spring Festival, the King's Lynn Festival. Opera North and IMS regularly feature in Lord Lieutenancy visits to Cornwall and wherever Opera North might be performing. Other events may be in connection with patronages such as the RNLI, the Commonwealth War Graves Commission, Blood Cancer UK, the Stroke Association, the University of Surrey or the Edge Foundation. The Duke seems absolutely determined to continue to serve.

The Queen cannot undertake all the engagements that are asked of her, and therefore members of her family take on different areas, and step in where needed. As the Queen has grown older, we have seen her accompanied by other members of the family on her official visits. When from time to time Prince Philip was ill, and after he stepped down formally from public duties in 2017, the Queen has invited the Duke of Kent to be with her on the dais at Trooping the Colour, to represent her at prominent memorial services and to be at her side when required.

The Duke with the Queen at the Birthday Parade on 15 June 2013, at which the colour of the Welsh Guards was trooped. The Duke of Edinburgh was in hospital. The Queen wears the brooch of the Brigade of Guards

Lady Helen Taylor: When Prince Philip stepped down from doing royal duties like Trooping the Colour, the Queen brought him in to be at her side on the podium. He was so touched – touched beyond belief.

A key engagement in June 2021 was Trooping the Colour in the Quadrangle of Windsor Castle to mark the Queen's official birthday. The Duke was there as Colonel of the Scots Guards.

Duke: That Trooping was highly unusual because it was on a very reduced scale at Windsor with no crowds. Only a select number of people were there watching – mostly people connected with my regiment. It was their colour that was being trooped. I was the only Colonel to be there with the Queen. Normally it would be a proper full-scale Trooping, which I hope will happen this year [2022]. Until a few years ago Prince Philip was always there too. The other Colonels were all riding. I haven't ridden in the Trooping now for ten years or so.

Normally I would go there in a carriage, and when the Queen arrives, I join her. I never had to worry about a horse. In the days when I was riding I was given very good horses, always police horses.

The Queen was scheduled to join the Duke in Edinburgh in September 2021.

Duke: I was in Edinburgh on Friday night, 3 September, for the Royal Scots Dragoon Guards, formerly Greys – their fiftieth anniversary of amalgamation. It was remarkable to realise that it was already fifty years, and they produced a photograph of me as a serving officer standing in front of my squadron at the amalgamation parade in July 1971. Sadly out of the six officers in my squadron all but about two have gone. There were quite a few friends in that picture. On Saturday morning, they paraded through Edinburgh, marching down Princes Street,

which is quite a feat as it's a steep hill, with cobbles underfoot. Marching downhill in spurs, which some were, looked most alarming. Anyway, they managed it. It was especially difficult for those on horses, a little mounted group of about four people with the standard.

The Queen would have been there – she was coming for a little service and reception – but a message had come through that bad weather was on the way and the helicopter that was going to bring her down from Balmoral might not be able to land. The helicopter company cancelled the flight. That was it. She couldn't come. And then the weather was perfectly all right.

In September the Duke attended the memorial service for Lady Mary Colman in Norwich Cathedral. Princess Alexandra represented the Queen. He represented the Queen at the memorial service for Major General Jeremy Phipps in London. As Britain opened up after the long months of lockdown, the Duke's name once again appeared regularly in the Court Circular, as he undertook his engagements.

The Duke standing in for the Queen and saluting on the balcony of the former Home Office at the Cenotaph, 14 November 2021. Princess Alexandra is behind him

Of these, his most significant appearance took place on Remembrance Sunday on 14 November 2021. The Queen was due to attend the Remembrance Day parade at the Cenotaph. In November 2021 the Duke, who had laid his first wreath as long ago as 1961, was to be present on the balcony with her. When the Queen's doctors decided she should stay at Windsor Castle, he and his sister, Princess Alexandra, were on the central balcony in her place.

In their youth, the general public would have recognised them instantly, but it was clear that the BBC commentator, David Dimbleby, did not at first recognise that it was Princess Alexandra at his side, since the camera had to return to identify her later. The Duke wore his Field Marshal's greatcoat. A wreath was laid on his behalf by his equerry.

Nick Turnbull: The photographers at the Cenotaph were all set for Her Majesty to appear, until they were told two hours before that she would not be, which was a surprise. The Duke had always planned this year to be beside her on the balcony alongside his sister, Princess Alexandra, but given the Queen's absence he had a prominence he wasn't expecting. It reminded me of the photograph of the Duke as a young boy, with the Duke of Windsor, walking behind George VI's funeral cortège following his mother's instruction that it was his duty to serve and he's been quietly doing so ever since.

When he came out on the balcony at the Cenotaph, he immediately saluted. He's always done the right thing.

Shortly afterwards the Duke paid a two-day visit to Belgium for the burial of some Northumberland Fusiliers.

Duke: One of the characteristics of the Commonwealth War Graves Commission, of which I've now been the president for fifty years, is that of the 1.5 million war dead they commemorate and care for, about half are missing. They have no graves. Many people don't realise that. Almost every year further remains are uncovered, almost entirely in France or Flanders, and sometimes in quite large numbers. In 2009 some 250 bodies were found, and the Commission had to build a new cemetery for them in a place called Fromelles, west of Lille, and south of Calais. The battle in July 1916 had been a disaster and the Germans had buried 225 Australians and soldiers of other nationalities.

The last one I went to, in November 2021, was in the neighbourhood of Ypres: they had found nine bodies and all were from the same regiment, the Northumberland Fusiliers, which happens to be part of my regiment, so there was a double reason for me to be there. The Northumberland Fusiliers raised fifty-two regiments in the First World War, sent twenty-nine of them overseas and lost 16,000 men in action. They had five Victoria Crosses to their honour.

It was a very moving little ceremony. They had present-day soldiers from the regiment act as bearers, and one by one, they brought out coffins. They didn't bury all of them, but a smaller number to symbolise. It was all beautifully done, as a British military occasion, with perfect drill to very high standards. And those very young men lowered the small coffins into the graves that had been dug. The Last Post was sounded. Every dead soldier had some of their descendants there, and this was three generations on. Some of the relatives told me that it had come out of the blue to be contacted by the War Graves Commission to be asked whether they knew anything about Private So-and-so, who had died at Passchendaele in 1917. In many cases they had not heard that their great-grandfather or

great-great-uncle had died in that way. In some cases it was a
shock to learn this and in others it was a great solace. It meant
a great deal to them, because in many cases, so far as the
family was concerned, their relative was simply missing with
no confirmation of where he had died, or how, or where he was
buried. Even the minimal amount of information was valuable
to them.

If a missing soldier has no grave, their name is inscribed on a
memorial. When their remains are found and placed in a grave,
their name is removed from the memorial. So, the names you
see are all of those who died and had no grave. If you look at the
Menin Gate at Ypres, for example, there are something like forty
thousand names on it. The Thiepval memorial at the Somme, a
Lutyens-designed arch, a very fine memorial, includes at least
seventy-two thousand names, all of them missing, so it's an
astonishing business.

Nick Turnbull: The bodies were reburied at Tyne Cot, nine
soldiers who were discovered by some canal workers. There
were three elements to this programme. The Duke was wearing
two hats – as chairman of the Commonwealth War Graves
Commission, and Colonel-in-Chief of the Royal Fusiliers. He
went to Talbot House, where Toc H* was established, then to a
chapel service. He laid a wreath at Menin Gate where a memor-
ial is managed by the Commonwealth War Graves on which all
of the missing soldiers are listed. The next day was the burial
ceremony for the Northumberland Fusiliers. Of those nine
soldiers, seven were identified and two were not. About fifty
members of the families of the fallen were present and each

* Toc H, an international Christian movement, founded by the Reverend 'Tubby'
Clayton in 1915 as a soldier's rest and recreation centre.

family received the Union Flag and the forage caps, once the coffin had been laid in the ground. Of the two that remain unknown, one was a Northumberland Fusilier and the other from an unknown regiment. They gave the Union Flag and the forage cap of the Fusilier to the Duke. I liked this idea as it reminded me of King George V, after the First World War, laying his own wreath on the Unknown Soldier's coffin on its final journey into Westminster Abbey.

As 2021 came to an end, the Duke was looking forward to playing his part in the Platinum Jubilee of the Queen. Six years earlier, in October 2015, he had celebrated his eightieth birthday with a party at the Polish Club.

In his speech at the dinner, his old friend, Vincent Poklewski-Koziell, commended his sense of duty. The Queen was sitting next to the Duke and she said: 'Hear, hear.' His daughter Helen commented: 'He doesn't expect any praise or thanks, so when he gets it, it builds him up and it's just lovely to see.'

Introduction

This book is not a biography or a royal memoir. It is based on a series of conversations with His Royal Highness The Duke of Kent, first cousin of the Queen. He has been a frontline witness to the key events of this reign. Aged sixteen he walked with the royal dukes in the funeral procession of George VI in 1952, and the following year he was one of the three royal dukes to pay personal homage to the Queen at the Coronation. At an early age he was called upon to take a key role in state visits to Britain, and at the age of twenty-five, he presided over the first of many independence ceremonies in Africa. He was riding directly behind the Queen at Trooping the Colour when blanks were fired at her in 1981, and at the age of eighty-five, he was the oldest soldier on parade at the Cenotaph on Remembrance Sunday in November 2020. No major royal event has taken place in the present reign without him being there, as part of the inner circle.

The Queen attended his christening in 1935, and all these years later he is still actively supporting her. He was at her side as Colonel of the Scots Guards at Trooping the Colour at Windsor Castle in June 2021, and on the balcony of the former Home Office in her place for the Remembrance Day wreath-laying on 14 November.

Royal memoirs are extremely rare. In the present reign, there were books by Princess Marie Louise, Princess Alice, Countess of Athlone (both granddaughters of Queen Victoria, whom they knew well), and Princess Alice, Duchess of

Gloucester (widow of the Queen's uncle, Prince Henry). These were informative and of historical value. Most of the stories related to earlier reigns. No member of the Royal Family has spoken extensively of the present reign.

The Duke was born in the year of the Silver Jubilee of his grandfather, King George V, and christened Edward George Nicholas Paul Patrick. Hundreds of people flocked to Belgrave Square to see the first male prince to be born in the House of Windsor (created in 1917). He was the first prince to be born in thirty years, and he was seventh in line to the throne.

Of all the Royal Family, he and his siblings are the most thoroughly royal. Besides being a member of the House of Windsor, he has interesting descent through his mother, Princess Marina, from Greek and Danish kings. His grandmother, the formidable Grand Duchess Helen, was a descendant of Tsar Alexander II of Russia (1818–81). She married Prince Nicholas of Greece and was the grandest of the royal wives in Athens, looking down on her sisters-in-law. Helen's parents were larger than life characters in St Petersburg – Grand Duke Vladimir and Marie of Mecklenburg-Schwerin.* Helen was somewhat austere. Her sister-in-law Princess Alice, mother of Prince Philip, defined her philosophy as: 'God first, then the Russian Grand Dukes, then the rest.'

The Duke's Aunt Olga was married to Prince Paul of Yugoslavia, Regent in the early years of the war, who was exiled to Kenya and South Africa. The Duke speaks of his 'international cousinage'.

* Grand Duke Vladimir (1847–1909), general in the Russian army, historian and wit. Married to the formidable Princess Marie (1854–1920), daughter of the Grand Duke of Mecklenburg-Schwerin.

The Duke's father, Prince George, Duke of Kent, was killed in an air accident in Scotland in 1942, so he has been a duke for nearly eighty years. His mother was a war widow, raising her young family on her own. His early days were enlivened by exposure to her wide circle of friends, people like 'Chips' Channon, Noël Coward, Cecil Beaton, Douglas Fairbanks Junior, and Malcolm Sargent* – many of the most creative people of her generation. They were a tight-knit family – the Duke is particularly close to his sister, Princess Alexandra, and his younger brother, Prince Michael.

Briefly, he went to Eton but then to Le Rosey in Switzerland, so his education was international. Prince Philip, a cousin through his mother, took him to the Olympic Games in Helsinki in 1952. He accompanied his mother on a Far Eastern tour later that year and celebrated his seventeenth birthday in Singapore.

He was at Sandhurst, where he won prizes in foreign languages and interpretership. In 1955 he joined the Royal Scots Greys, a cavalry regiment, and this was his main career until 1976. Like Prince Harry, he suffered from his royal identity. In 1971 he was pulled out of Northern Ireland, as a target for terrorists, which was a blow: he realised that his prospects in the army were likely to be curtailed. From then on he had to balance his career with royal duties. He was known for an interest in fast cars, skied for his regiment, and developed a passion for Wagner. His marriage to a Yorkshire

* Sir Henry Channon (1897–1958), Conservative MP, social figure and diarist, whose unexpurgated diaries will run to three volumes, the size of bricks; Sir Noël Coward (1899–1973), playwright, composer, actor and singer; Sir Cecil Beaton (1904–80), photographer, designer, artist, diarist and writer; Douglas Fairbanks Jr (1909–2000), American actor and film star, sometimes known as 'Young Doug'; and Sir Malcolm Sargent (1895–1967), conductor and composer, sometimes known as 'Flash'.

girl, Katharine Worsley, at York Minster drew a crowd of seven thousand.

Today he is Colonel of the Scots Guards, a Field Marshal, a Knight of the Garter and Britain's senior Freemason. Until last summer, as President of the All England Lawn Tennis Club he presented the prizes at Wimbledon. In the Order of Precedence in Britain, he stands twelfth in the land. He has numerous patronages and presidencies, has undertaken extensive royal tours and often represented the Queen at home and abroad. He rose to Lieutenant-Colonel in the army, which he left in 1976, stating, 'Certainly I was restricted in the Army. But that was chiefly because of Ulster. It was, in a sense, my bad luck. I felt I was being restricted when it mattered most. There came a moment when all my colleagues, my contemporaries, were having to serve in Ulster and I was prevented from doing so.'

He became vice-chairman of the British Overseas Trade Board, working with no salary. Passionate about electronics, he became deputy chairman of the National Electronics Council. He was the first member of the Royal Family to visit China after the Cultural Revolution.

The Duke has been present at all of the great events of the reign, royal weddings, such as the Cambridges' in 2011, and royal funerals, such as Prince Philip's in 2021.

He is dutiful, modest, thoughtful and well-read. He loves music. He is one of the Royal Family's greatest assets, quietly supporting the Queen, who holds him in great affection and respect.

* * * * *

I first met the Duke in January 2001 when the Anglo-Hellenic League invited me to give a lecture on Princess Marina. They said they would invite King Constantine of Greece, who was

living in London, the Kents, and the Ogilvys, and I thought, Well, that's fine, none of them will come. As it happened, seven did come, including the King, the Duke, Princess Alexandra and Sir Angus Ogilvy. (It is the only time that I have ever had a completely sleepless night – the night before.) I had, of course, seen the Royal Family in my childhood and while growing up, and remember in particular the procession of eight of them before the State Opening of Parliament in April 1966, perhaps the first time I saw Princess Marina properly. On 13 December 1967 I found myself sitting directly behind her and her family in Her Majesty's Theatre, on what was to be her last birthday, for a performance of Dodie Smith's *Dear Octopus*. Princess Marina was such an iconic figure when I was growing up, much loved by the British public, who were aware of her as a brave young widow, bringing up her children on her own. I never met her, but at the lecture I confessed I had reached out and touched the back of her mink jacket.

Princess Marina died the following summer and, as I had connections with St George's Chapel, I was allowed to watch her funeral from the organ loft. It was the only time I ever saw the Duke of Windsor.

The Duke of Kent, Princess Alexandra and Prince Michael have attended other talks I have given over the years and, as keen readers, have read a number of my previous books. All three came to the launch of that surprise hit *The Quest for Queen Mary*. I suppose that somehow it had become clear that I knew a lot about their family. I have always thought that if I did *Mastermind* I would be fine on my specialist subject, though on more general questions would score nothing, with a considerable number of passes.

This book was essentially a lockdown project. Unable to

undertake his normal duties for his regiments and charities, the Duke had time. It seemed a good opportunity for him to reflect on his life. In 2021, the Duke and I began a series of Zoom conversations. The Duke was invariably at his home, Wren House, Kensington Palace, and I was at mine in Wiltshire. Through these, the pattern of his life developed, a mixture of reminiscence and comment. In preparing the text, I have largely dropped out, leaving the Duke to speak, while occasionally moving the story forward in a kind of recitative, so his voice and mine alternate in this story.

For me, it was a fascinating opportunity and a far cry from the first book I ever worked on back in 1972 – *Burke's Guide to the Royal Family* – when I was sent to see the private secretaries of the various members of the Royal Family. At that time the Royal Family were distant figures, operating through their private secretaries, and the only one I saw in person was Princess Alice, Countess of Athlone. Two such private secretaries survived into their nineties: Sir Simon Bland, who worked for the Gloucesters, and Sir Richard Buckley, who worked for the Kents. Normally the form is that you ask the private secretary if you can see the member of the Royal Family. This time the situation was reversed. I asked the Duke if I could see Sir Richard and, as a result, spent an enjoyable morning with him. Sadly, Sir Richard died before this book was published.

I am glad to report that the Duke himself has been much easier to talk to than some of those I have interviewed on royal matters in the past. When I was writing a book on Prince Philip's mother, Princess Alice, Sir Brian McGrath sent me to see Lady Katherine Brandram (the former Princess Katherine of Greece, sister of three Kings of

Greece) in 1997. She was obviously very nervous and had rehearsed what she intended to say: 'My aunt was very beautiful, very fair and a very nice person.' She folded her arms. That was all she wanted to say about her. I tried to veer off on another tack and asked her about another aunt, Princess Nicholas of Greece. 'Ah! Princess Nicholas! Anything you want to know about Princess Nicholas, you must ask the Duke of Kent, don't you see?' We chatted about other things and I went home.

I had not fared much better with Sir Philip Hay, Princess Marina's former private secretary, when I went to see him at Nottingham Cottage, at Kensington Palace, in March 1980. There had been an ill-fated idea that I might write a book on Prince George and Princess Marina but this was superseded by Cecil Beaton inviting me to be his biographer. I was fairly sure that Sir Philip would vouchsafe very little and I was not disappointed. I tried what I thought was a safe question: 'What did Princess Marina think of her native land, Greece?'

His lips pursed. He said: 'Now, anything that I might tell you about what Princess Marina thought of Greece might be read by the present King of Greece. Have you thought of that?' Well, no, I hadn't. I enjoyed the generous gin and tonic he served me and again made my way home.

The approach of the Queen's Platinum Jubilee, a remarkable seventy years on the throne, is a good time to focus on the life of one of her principal supporters. Many books will be published in Jubilee year, but who better than the Duke, who has played a prominent part in the Queen's reign from 1952 onwards? He is by nature self-effacing. He represents important values, not always shared by the present generation. A thoughtful tribute was paid to the Duke's uncle,

Prince Henry, Duke of Gloucester, by his private secretary, Sir Michael Hawkins, in 1974. He wrote in cricketing terms and in some respects his words could also apply to the Duke of Kent: 'He was an ideal twelfth man who was always ready to step into a breach but who was content that his side should win with or without his personal participation.'[1]

Following what the Duke said about his life in the Prologue, I asked his family what they would cite as his approach. His daughter, Lady Helen Taylor, said, 'I suppose loyalty is the first word that comes to mind but also duty and diligence. It's his reason for being, his purpose. He's never questioned it, I think, because he inherited the mantle so young that he had a long time to get used to the idea, and his mother would have definitely drummed it into him – what a privilege to be in this position and what a gift to be able to serve his Queen and country. He sees it as the greatest possible honour – being able to serve her. So all I've ever seen is this extraordinary sense of duty. For my part my heart swelled with pride whenever I saw him on duty – for example looking resplendent in his uniform at the Trooping or giving the trophy at Wimbledon. Outside of office hours though he has an enviable number of passions, chief among those being music and cars and on a more personal level he has a fantastic sense of humour, which I have always seen as my duty to invoke!'

His son George, Earl of St Andrews, agreed: 'He certainly takes his official duties very seriously, with a great sense of duty, discipline, responsibility and loyalty to the Queen, to support her, to help her. In a lot of things he's involved with, he has a strong sense of their significance, and when he goes to the Lord Lieutenants' days, visiting schools and factories,

he's getting to know different corners of the country, and showing the flag in areas that, maybe, don't get a lot of attention. I think that's important to him. And at the same time, when he's not doing things like that, he has a great love of music, a great love of the countryside, and reading. He has a passion for history.'

This was confirmed by his brother, Prince Michael: 'He is dutiful, but there was always a lot of humour behind it, a lot of laughter. He was probably less given to outbursts of hysterical laughter than I was.'

The Duke's younger son, Lord Nicholas Windsor, added: 'Duty is a bit of a dry word. It *was* the underpinning, but also he had huge interest in what he was doing, whether it was with the forces, or industry and science. He was very dedicated to all that. But I think he takes great pride in playing his part in supporting the Queen.'

George St Andrews also spoke of his father's sense of punctuality: 'He has taken to heart the saying that "l'exactitude est la politesse des rois" [punctuality is the politeness of kings], to such an extent that he always insists on arriving long in advance for any event he is attending, to the amusement of his family who would be happy simply to arrive on time. His concern for timekeeping even extends to keeping precise records of how long different conductors take for performances of every opera he sees.'

The Queen has always held the Duke in great affection and been grateful for his support. Lady Helen Taylor reminded me that the Queen was nine years his senior, 'so when he lost his father, she was old enough to understand that he was just a little boy, and she was always so kind and sweet, an older cousin, who kept an eye out for him, and I think she still does – really heart-warming'.

Studying the Duke's life, I have come away impressed by that quiet sense of duty, how important it is to the Queen to have a supporting Royal Family, aware of the sacrifices its members have made, and of how important and indeed possible it is to make a vital and significant contribution, working within the system. Prince Philip is an example of one who faced considerable opposition in his early years as the Queen's husband, and who compartmentalised his life into supporting her, while having time to pursue his own endeavours.

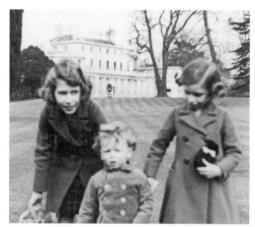

Prince Edward with his cousins Princess Elizabeth and
Princess Margaret in the garden at Frogmore

The greatest part of this book is a mixture of the Duke's words and my own, but I was also keen to talk to some of his relations. He has long been close to his sister, Princess Alexandra, who is only just over a year younger than he is. She came to Wren House to talk to me with her brother, the two sparking reminiscences between them. Later I spent an enjoyable hour and a quarter with Prince Michael.

The Duchess of Kent kindly offered to help with some memories, she having been an integral part of the Duke's life since 1957. On his mother's side, he has three cousins, all of whom have known him since childhood, and who remain in close touch with him today – Princess Elizabeth of Yugoslavia, Hans Veit Toerring and Archduchess Helen Habsburg. As mentioned, I was also able to speak to his children, George, Earl of St Andrews, Lady Helen Taylor, and Lord Nicholas Windsor.

Then, besides his former private secretary, Sir Richard Buckley, who was with him from 1962 till 1989, I was able to catch up on the present day with the present private secretary, Captain Nicholas Turnbull.

There were a few places where I relied on outside sources, who are no longer with us. Princess Natasha Bagration was a cousin of Princess Marina, and close to her when Prince George was killed in 1942. Her husband, Sir Charles Johnston, wrote perceptively about Princess Marina, and as his literary executor, I have drawn on his words. Agnes de Stoeckl, known as 'Auntie Ag' in the courts of Europe, wrote about the early years at Coppins from the vantage point of a close neighbour, her daughter Zoia being one of Princess Marina's closest friends. I have drawn on the diaries of people like Sir Cecil Beaton, Sir Noël Coward, and Kenneth Rose. I am also grateful to Tahir Hasanovic for his help with the Duke's visit to the Grand Lodge of Serbia in 2019, Allan Mallinson, Ian Brunskill, Mr and Mrs Ian Hamilton, Princess Katya Galitzine for letters from the collection of her parents, Prince and Princess George Galitzine, Cleeves Palmer, secretary of the Kandahar Ski Club and Lady Buckley and Peter Buckley, for permitting the interview with Sir Richard to be published. The book

also profited from the editorial guidance of Rowena Webb and Tom Perrin, the eagle-eyed copy-editing of Hazel Orme, and Elizabeth Vickers' help with photography.

I began by setting the scene and asking the Duke about his early days.

1

Early Life

The Duke of Kent (HRH Prince Edward of Kent) arrived in the world in 1935 towards the end of the reign of his grandfather, King George V. He was the first-born son of Prince George, Duke of Kent, who was the fourth son of the King, and of his mother, Princess Marina of Greece and Denmark, the youngest daughter of Prince Nicholas and his Russian-born wife Grand Duchess Helen.

His father, Prince George, was the most artistic of George V's sons. Born at York Cottage in 1902, he was one of the first princes to go to a preparatory school. He then passed through Osborne and Dartmouth, and entered the Royal Navy. During that time he served with the Mediterranean Fleet, attended the Royal Naval College in Greenwich and served as a lieutenant aboard HMS *Hawkins* in Shanghai. He left the navy in 1929. He was intelligent and quick-witted, had a keen eye for antiques, played the piano enthusiastically, shot well, rode bravely to hounds and was a keen golfer. Philip Ziegler wrote of him:'By temperament he was enquiring, adventurous, and dangerously ready to sample any delight that might be offered him.' The Duke commented, 'I think he was quite a naughty young man.' Queen Mary, though censorious of the Duke of Windsor following the Abdication, was always grateful to her eldest son for his kindness to Prince George.

Prince George, Duke of Kent

Duke: The Duke of Windsor – known as David by the Royal Family – and my father had been great friends. From what I've been told, my father felt terribly let down by his brother. They ended up on rather unfriendly terms at the time of the Abdication and after the Windsors went to France. And then they simply didn't see each other. My Uncle David had looked after my father, long before my father had married. He had a bad period – there were drugs involved. An American person had provided him with drugs and he got into quite a serious state. David rescued him and had him to stay at Fort Belvedere for a month or two, and pretty much pulled him out of it. My uncle took him to South America, and my father lived at York House with him at one point.

George's choice of bride in 1934 was immensely popular. Princess Marina was one of three beautiful sisters, dubbed by

Prince Michael of Greece* 'the Fabergé aunts'. Born in Athens in 1906, she was initially raised there and at the summer palace of Tatoi, and was brought up in the Greek Orthodox faith. Her paternal grandfather was King George I of Greece, giving her Danish blood, while her mother was the daughter of Grand Duke Vladimir of Russia, uncle of Tsar Nicholas II, and his formidable wife, Maria Pavlovna, described as 'the grandest of the Grand Duchesses', with a passion for jewels and for gambling. Life in Athens was comfortable, and well-run. Princess Marina had an English governess, Miss Kate Fox, who remained close to her in later life.

Duke: Miss Fox was a big figure in my mother's life. She was quite an old-fashioned lady and was known as 'Nurnie'. We used to see her, not very often, probably two or three times a year. She would sit us down and lecture us. She did not live at Coppins, our family home near Iver. She used to come and stay with my mother, maybe for quite long stretches.

There were occasional visits by the three sisters to the splendours of the Russian court. Princess Marina brought to the marriage considerable connection to royal cousins in Europe, and a mixture of Danish, Russian and German blood. She was fluent in Greek, French and English.

The Greek Royal Family were sometimes considered unwelcome foreigners in Athens. They were frequently driven into exile, King Constantine I departing for Switzerland in 1917, and returning briefly in 1921. All of the Greek Royal

* HRH Prince Michael of Greece (born 1939), son of Prince Christopher, and grandson of King George I of Greece. A first cousin of Princess Marina. He is a historian and author.

Family left again in 1922, after the ill-fated Asia Minor campaign (when the Greek Army was driven back by the Turks), then settled in Paris, where Prince Nicholas supported his family as best he could by painting.

Duke: It was not easy to be King of Greece, but my mother thought of herself as Greek. She was very conscious of her Greek roots. She spoke the language with her sisters and Greek friends, like Lilia Ralli, and she felt the pull of Greece, although she never lived there after the age of ten.

Princess Marina attended a finishing school run by Princess Meshchersky, an old friend of the family. Her eldest sister, Princess Olga, married Prince Paul of Yugoslavia in 1923, and her middle sister, Elisabeth, married the Bavarian Count Carl Theodor zu Toerring-Jettenbach in January 1934.

It was while staying with her sister in Bavaria that Princess Marina became engaged to Prince George, and they were married in Westminster Abbey on 29 November 1934. Like Queen Alexandra before her, she was a beautiful princess from across the water, and immediately found a place in the hearts of the British for her grace, beauty and elegance.

The present Duke was obviously too young to remember the events of the mid-1930s, but there was much to preoccupy his parents towards the end of 1935. King George V had been touched by the response the nation had shown to him during his Silver Jubilee celebrations. 'I didn't realise they felt like this,' he told his nurse, Sister Catherine Black, but he was tired and, although he was only seventy, he did not think he would survive very long, an expectation shared by those around him.

On 5 September the Duke and Duchess of Kent and her

sister, Countess Toerring, arrived back at London's Victoria station from a holiday in Yugoslavia and went to stay at Adsdean, near Chichester, which they borrowed from Lord and Lady Louis Mountbatten, returning to 3 Belgrave Square (the house they rented from Lady Juliet Duff) at the end of the month. On 1 October they lunched with the King and Queen and Lady Alice Montagu-Douglas-Scott, the fiancée of the King's third son, Prince Henry, Duke of Gloucester. On 4 October the Kents had a private viewing of Greta Garbo's latest film, *Anna Karenina*, which might have shown the Duchess how unmaternal a mother could be – she became quite the opposite.

Elisabeth Toerring was still with the Duchess when she gave birth to her son, Prince Edward, weighing six pounds twelve ounces, at 3 Belgrave Square at 2.15 a.m. on Wednesday, 9 October 1935. The Duke of Kent and his mother-in-law Princess Nicholas of Greece were present. Two doctors were in attendance, William Gilliat* and A. E. Gow,† and, as prescribed by a law introduced to prevent repetition of the famous warming-pan incident (in which Mary of Modena, wife of James II, was said to have swapped a stillborn child for a healthy boy), the glacial home secretary, Sir John Simon, was on the premises, arriving soon after the doctors. The King and Queen were informed at Sandringham.

* Sir William Gilliat (1884–1956), gynaecologist to the Duchess of Kent. He delivered all three of her children, and was also gynaecologist to the Queen, present at the birth of Prince Charles and Princess Anne. He died as the result of a car accident in Chertsey.

† Dr Alexander (Alec) Gow (1884–1952), consulting physician at St Bartholomew's Hospital, physician-in-ordinary to the Duke of Kent until 1942, and then to the Duchess. A man with 'a grave expression but a charming smile'. Impervious to cold, he never wore an overcoat or a hat.

'Chips' Channon hailed Edward as 'the sixth gentleman in the Kingdom, and seventh heir to the throne'.[2] Channon observed that the birth was fairly sudden. Forty-one-gun salutes were fired in Hyde Park and at the Tower of London. The Lord Mayor of London was informed and the baby was promptly elected 'a junior member of the Bath Club, so that in swimming and squash he may, we hope, continue the family tradition'.[3] As mother and child's condition advanced from 'satisfactory' to 'very satisfactory' to 'excellent', the Antique Dealers Fair gave Prince George a miniature wheelback Hepplewhite child's chair with an eighteenth-century silk-embroidered needlework cushion for his son.

Crowds in Belgrave Square before Prince Edward's
christening at Buckingham Palace in 1935

An early visitor was the Prince of Wales, who became one of his godfathers; on 20 October Princess Olga came to inspect the baby; the King and Queen visited on 23 October. Two days later a small crowd gathered to witness the infant prince's first outing. He was taken by his nurse to Buckingham Palace and carried around the grounds. Prince Nicholas sketched the infant prince when he was six days old.

Excitement over the royal birth was matched by interest in the forthcoming Gloucester wedding at Westminster Abbey. By the beginning of October, it was known that the bride would be given away by her brother, the Earl of Dalkeith, as her father, the 7th Duke of Buccleuch, was ill. The Duke languished at Bowhill in Scotland, suffering from cancer, and as his condition worsened, the Prince of Wales put his aeroplane at Lady Alice's disposal so that she could fly to him. On 19 October the Duke died, aged seventy-one. He was an old naval friend of King George V, having served with him in HMS *Bacchante* between 1879 and 1882. The funeral took place at Dalkeith and he was buried in the Buccleuch Memorial Chapel of St Mary's Episcopal Church. The Gloucester wedding took place quietly at Buckingham Palace on 6 November.

Deaths came thick and fast in the King's circle. Lord Sysonby (the former Sir Frederick Ponsonby) died the day after the Duke of Buccleuch, depriving George V of one of the mainstays of his reign. On 21 November the King recorded his 'profound sorrow' at the death of Admiral of the Fleet Earl Jellicoe, and then, on 3 December, his favourite sister, Princess Victoria, died at Coppins, her home near Iver. Court mourning in its various degrees was commanded until 14 January 1936. On 7 December, the Princess was lowered into the Royal Vault at St George's Chapel. The deaths kept

coming. On 12 December William Barker, the oldest surviving royal servant, who had wheeled Queen Victoria's mother (the Duchess of Kent) around her grounds for four years, died at Windsor aged ninety-one. So respected was he that the King and Queen had looked in on his Frogmore cottage when he turned ninety. Rudyard Kipling died on 18 January 1936.

In those early days, the young Prince Edward was frequently photographed emerging from 3 Belgrave Square, his perambulator pulled by a liveried footman, a detective in a bowler hat on duty alongside one or even two nannies. Sometimes his mother went with them, the press invariably noting her stylish hats. On the day of his christening, huge crowds gathered, discreetly held at a distance, to see the infant prince in the long robe made for Queen Victoria's christening over a century before. He was christened Edward George Nicholas Paul Patrick by the Archbishop of Canterbury in the Private

Young Prince Edward at Coppins

Chapel at Buckingham Palace on 20 November. The King and Queen came especially from Sandringham. The press was not allowed to photograph it, and, instead, commissioned a drawing of what they thought the scene might look like.

The godparents were the King and Queen, the Prince of Wales (uncle), the Princess Royal (aunt), the Duke of Connaught (great-uncle, represented by his son, Prince Arthur, as he was wintering as usual in Bath), Princess Louise, Duchess of Argyll (great-aunt), and his maternal grandmother, Princess Nicholas of Greece. Besides his parents, the others present were Princess Elizabeth, Princess Margaret, and Princess Arthur of Connaught. The choir of the Chapel Royal sang 'Around the Throne'.

Duke: One of my favourite pictures is by Winterhalter of Queen Victoria with Prince Albert just behind her, the Duke of Wellington next to her, and she is holding up a small child for the Duke to look at, because the Duke had become the godfather of this child – Prince Arthur, later Duke of Connaught. The child became *my* godfather. I have always felt a connection with Wellington.

Prince Edward was housed in a sunny nursery, painted in restful blues and whites, distantly overlooking the garden of Belgrave Square. Humphrey and Vera Joel of *Woman's Journal* were allowed in to photograph the elaborate cot (cream net over crêpe de Chine with rosettes), the baby basket and the embossed leather screen concealing empty bookcases, awaiting his first books.

The young Prince was inspected by King Haakon and Queen Maud of Norway and King Frederick VIII of Denmark when they

lunched at Belgrave Square on 8 December, the day after Princess Victoria's funeral.

The Duke and Duchess of Kent, with the young Prince Edward, the Prince of Wales, and Princess Alice, Countess of Athlone, arrived at Sandringham to join the King and Queen, the Gloucesters, Princess Elizabeth and Princess Margaret of York for a quiet Christmas.* Forbidding weather kept many at home that Christmas, and King George V refrained from braving the cold rain to distribute Christmas beef to the workers on the Sandringham estate. As usual he gave his broadcast on Christmas Day, and sent tons of logs from Windsor Great Park to the poor and unemployed in Windsor. Prince George presided over the Sandringham shooting parties in his father's absence. Britain was soon covered with thick snow. The young Prince Edward was lodged in the nursery previously used by Princess Elizabeth and Princess Margaret. He was photographed in the lap of Queen Mary, she adorned in pale lilac lace, a pearl choker and three rows of pearls, with Princess Elizabeth and Princess Margaret at either side of them.

On 14 January 1936, the Kent family returned to London, press photographers catching a glimpse of Prince Edward in the car with his nanny, 'looking wonderfully bonny ... a wide awake young man with an unfailingly sunny smile' at three months old.

By this time the King's health was causing concern. The following day, his doctor, Lord Dawson of Penn, arrived and the King took to his bed, remaining in his room thereafter awaiting, as it was revealed years later, his doctor's despatching needle.† Prince Edward was left at Belgrave Square,

* The Duchess of York, their mother, had pneumonia, and stayed with the Duke of York at Royal Lodge, Windsor.

† See Kenneth Rose, *King George V* (Phoenix Press, 2000), Postscript, pp. 407–8.

when his father and later his mother returned to Sandringham. A bulletin on the night of 20/21 January announced: 'Death came peacefully to the King at 11.55 p.m. to-night in the presence of Her Majesty the Queen, the Prince of Wales, the Duke of York, the Princess Royal and the Duke and Duchess of Kent.' *The Times* reported: 'This morning the death chamber is in darkness, but lighted rooms elsewhere bear witness to the many formalities attendant on the death of King George . . .'[4]

Court mourning, which had ended for Princess Victoria but a week earlier, was commanded for the next nine months.

The Duke and Duchess of Kent were present at every part of the funeral, following the coffin on foot in sleet and rain to Sandringham Church, accompanying the coffin to London, witnessing the lying-in-state at Westminster Hall, and attending the funeral in St George's Chapel, Windsor. And as the King followed his sister into the Royal Vault, Queen Mary noted: '. . . we left him sadly, lying for the present with his ancestors in the Vault'.[5]

* * * * *

We can follow the first year of the present Duke's life through contemporary press cuttings and the accounts of the diarist 'Chips' Channon, a neighbour and friend of his parents in Belgrave Square. Photographed at eight months, the young Prince was described as having a strong likeness to his cousins, the Princesses of York, and one commentator detected more of a resemblance to Queen Mary's family, the Tecks, than to the Windsors. Presently he was to be observed at Coppins, inherited by Prince George from Princess Victoria, where he took his first tentative steps.

Princess Victoria, who bequeathed Coppins to
Prince George, with Zoia Poklewska

He was sent to Queen Mary at Sandringham while his parents cruised in the Adriatic, spending time with Princess Marina's parents, sisters and their husbands. When he was one, he was photographed again, this time in the lanes at Coppins. It was noted that he possessed 'princely composure before a stranger' and waved politely to the photographer.

Lady Honor Channon, wife of Chips, had given birth to her son, Paul, on the same day as Prince Edward had arrived. The two would later become lifelong friends. On 14 May 1936, Channon was recording that Prince Edward now had one tooth: 'He is a lovely golden baby, a "Windsor" baby, just like the Queen and probably like the Duke of Kent at that age.'[6] Channon saw him at Coppins on 1 November, noting that the besotted father brought in the 'v. curly-haired, very red Prince Edward'[7] as the *pièce de résistance*.

On 16 December more happy photos were taken by the press, the young Prince blissfully unaware of the travails that were then assailing the Royal Family. He looked as happy as his parents seemed gloomy. That month changed the lives of Prince Edward's parents. While he was happily celebrating his first birthday, they were increasingly worried about Prince George's elder brother, King Edward VIII, and his developing relationship with Wallis Simpson. This matter did not become a crisis until Mrs Simpson instituted divorce proceedings against her husband. At that point there was serious concern that the King might wish to marry her. His dilemma was made the more urgent by the impending Coronation. Had he taken the Coronation oath, it would effectively have prevented him from marrying a woman with two husbands living. As it happened, when confronted with the choice of renouncing Mrs Simpson or the throne, the King chose to give up his throne. He abdicated on 11 December 1936 and set off into voluntary exile from which, as it turned out, he never permanently returned. Prince Edward became fifth in line to the throne.

Meanwhile Princess Marina gave birth to her daughter, Princess Alexandra, on Christmas Day 1936, again at Belgrave Square, a mere fourteen months after her brother's birth, which the doctors considered dangerous. Once again enthusiastic crowds gathered to witness her setting off for her christening, and in the course of the next year the photographs in newspapers invariably showed two prams going out. In the fullness of time, a clear bond formed between the two children, which would last a lifetime. Photographers captured moments of 'mischief'.

In the summer of 1937 King George VI and Queen Elizabeth were crowned in Westminster Abbey. The King

gave his nephew his first medal – the 1937 Coronation medal. That summer, the family enjoyed a seaside holiday on the sands at Lowestoft, then joined Queen Mary at Sandringham, and were back at Sandringham in December for Christmas with the Royal Family.

Duke: I can remember the arrival of my sister about a year after me when I was less than eighteen months old. I also vaguely remember my grandfather [Prince Nicholas]. I only saw him once, at Belgrave Square. He died in 1938.

2

Coppins

Coppins

Prince George and Princess Marina moved into Coppins in June 1936. In those days, the nearby village of Iver still retained quiet charm and a rural atmosphere, despite somewhat drastic alterations to its sixteenth- and seventeenth-century buildings and an encroachment from industry and housing development. Coppins was set in 130 acres of low-lying and well-watered countryside, surrounded by arable fields, woods and plantations. The house was built in about 1850, taking its name from Copynsfield, a name given to a manor in Iver in 1374. There were royal connections from the start. Its first owner was John Mitchell (1806–74), a theatrical manager for the St James's theatre in London, and a well-respected bookseller in Old

Bond Street, sometimes described as 'king of the ticket agencies'.[8] During the twelve years he ran the St James's, he lost a lot of money, gamely staging top French plays and operas. He used to arrange royal visits to theatres, Queen Victoria's mother, the Duchess of Kent, even attending a performance by the controversial Mademoiselle Rachel (1821–58). He organised command performances at Windsor Castle, and amassed a fortune by publishing portraits of the Royal Family.

On his death, Coppins was taken on by Baroness Churchill (1826–1900), a significant lady of the bedchamber to Queen Victoria. After the death of Queen Alexandra in 1925, her unmarried daughter, Princess Victoria, moved there, creating a model farm with pedigree cattle and other valuable livestock. Although members of her family have been disparaging about her, Queen Mary finding her Philistine, and the Duke of Windsor annoyed that she reported him to the King at every opportunity, she was considered something of a 'Lady Bountiful' in the Iver district. After her death in 1935, Coppins became the property of Prince George. The builders arrived in March 1936, and the Kents took up residence in June, having created a nursery for young Prince Edward.

In 1938 *Country Life's* correspondent G. C. Taylor was not wholly flattering about the house: 'The long, low, many-gabled Victorian house, with its cream-washed walls and green shutters, while having no pretensions to architectural merit, nevertheless fits in remarkably well in the quiet and attractive setting of lawns and trees.'[9]

Not unsurprisingly Princess Victoria's taste had been resolutely Victorian. The house was crammed with furniture of every period. The drawing room was full of glass-fronted cabinets and vitrines, tables were completely covered with framed photographs, objets d'art, miniatures and souvenirs,

collected by the Princess and her late mother, Queen Alexandra. Princess Victoria owned an extensive collection of Fabergé. Each room was crowded with sofas, occasional chairs and stands filled with palms and flowers.Her desk was covered with photographs of friends and relations. As Agnes de Stoeckl recorded, 'The Princess dearly loved these souvenirs and had a sentimental affection for every gift that her friends offered her, and as she refused to part with one, accumulation grew enormous.'[10]

The house was not palatial. There were lots of gables. Prince George modernised the interior and added a sun loggia to the house. He tackled the fifteen-acre garden, sweeping away a tangled mass of laurels, hollies, yew and other Victorian shrubbery, which had formed an almost impenetrable jungle around the house. He created attractive vistas through a park to the south and the west, bounded by the occasional high tree, leaving only the functional areas of the garden in their former state. Daffodils and narcissi abounded during the spring; there were beautifully mown lawns, a simple wooden garden house, rhododendrons, and other hybrids, and a rock garden in Westmorland stone. The west side was smaller, the east boundary wall clothed with cascades of aubretia. The short flight of steps was bordered with tulips in the spring, followed by summer flowers and an abundance of roses.

The kitchen garden was on the north side of the house, which was adorned with climbers and wall shrubs. A fine *Cydonia japonica* was trained on the south gable. There were borders of azaleas, lilacs, viburnums and forsythias, nearby Japanese cherries and crab apples, lilacs, and escallonias concealing the greenhouses. Wrought-iron gates terminated this vista and a pergola, covered with climbing roses, led in turn to a sunken garden. Pollarded and trained lime trees

formed a screen on the eastern boundary wall. The result was a discreet but colourful garden. In 1938 *Country Life* concluded: 'Though the Victorian scene has been swept away and the original design in some degree has been lost, the garden has gained that quality of human interest that is not easy to define but which clearly pervades and illumines the whole place and adds so much to its interest, beauty and charm.'[11]

In 1939, prior to his planned move to Australia as its Governor General, the Duke put the house on the market with two estate agents, but withdrew it when the war came and his appointment was cancelled.

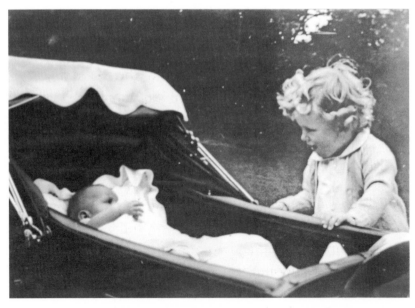

Prince Edward and his sister, Princess Alexandra,
in the garden at Belgrave Square

Duke: We were very fond of Coppins. The house contained briefly my parents and the three of us, as well as the nanny and other staff. Three were eight bedrooms, four bathrooms, four

reception rooms and a ballroom. There was a farm, which would continue to work all through the war. There were two cottages, which must have been empty by the time my parents moved in because they got to know and became great friends with a Polish couple called Poklewski. The father, Alik, was in the embassy in London and my father said, 'What are you doing? Do you have to go back to Poland,' and Poklewski replied, 'I have nowhere to go.' They were offered the cottages, so the parents and children moved into one and the wife's mother, Agnes de Stoeckl, moved into the other. The cottages were next door to each other, so there was quite a crowd in the relatively small Poklewski cottage. The cottage was only a hundred yards away from Coppins.

The arrival of the Poklewskis was a significant moment. Agnes de Stoeckl and the Poklewski family moved into Coppins Cottage in 1940, and remained there for the rest of their lives, the Baroness de Stoeckl dying in 1968, and her daughter, Zoia, in 1976. Besides a close friendship with Prince George and Princess Marina, Agnes de Stoeckl had also been close to Princess Victoria, and through her already knew Coppins well.

Baroness de Stoeckl was born in Paris as Agnes Barron in 1874, and raised in the world of salons. She married the Russian diplomat Alexander de Stoeckl in 1892. They lived in Paris and London, their world filled with Russian Grand Dukes and society figures. They were frequently in Russia and on the French Riviera. As she grew older, she was known as 'Auntie Ag' in the courts of Europe. She was a particular friend of Grand Duchess George of Russia (1876–1940), who had been born as Princess Marie of Greece and Denmark and was a sister of Princess Marina's father, Prince Nicholas. (Her husband Grand Duke George was one of several

members of the Russian Imperial family to be shot, later than the Tsar, in 1919.)

Shortly after the death of Edward VII, the Grand Duchess took a house in Harrogate as her daughter was weak and this was a fashionable spa. With them came Princess Victoria, in deep mourning, she being a first cousin of the Grand Duchess on the maternal side (Queen Alexandra). Thus began a close friendship between Agnes and Princess Victoria.

Agnes de Stoeckl tried to leave a more positive portrait of Princess Victoria than most have done: 'Princess Victoria was very generous and kind and her purse was forever opened for the needy.'[12] Her stories do not support this. Princess Victoria was by no means tactful. In Harrogate, she insisted on visiting the infirmary and distributing largesse. The party entered a ward with ten old ladies, all washed and dressed for the royal visit. They looked happy enough, but Princess Victoria insisted they were miserable and must be missing their homes. 'You think you are happy, but you are not,' the Princess told each in turn. By the time she left everybody was 'howling and sobbing', and she was delighted that they knew she cared for them. Later in the day the surgeon rang: 'For God's sake, don't let the Princess come near this place again. The matron has rung up that she can't calm the old women. They all say they used to be so happy and now they are miserable.'[13]

There was a time when Agnes de Stoeckl hoped that Princess Victoria would have the Grand Duchess to stay at Coppins. She put it to the Princess but received no response. Then she telephoned the Princess and said the Grand Duchess was 'in low spirits and depressed'. This produced an invitation to lunch at Coppins. Auntie Ag made up the Grand Duchess's face to look pale and ill, with faint lines under her eyes and no lipstick, so that Princess Victoria would take pity

on her. This ruse did not succeed. Princess Victoria was all set to take her in, but was alarmed at the sight of her, and thought she was so ill that she herself might become infected.[14]

The de Stoeckls had one daughter, Zoia, born in 1896, who married Alik Poklewski-Koziell. Their first boy, Romek, died young, and they had two other sons, Alexander and Vincent. Agnes was widowed in 1926, after which she frequently stayed with the Poklewskis in Poland between 1933 and 1938. Prince George and Princess Marina visited them there in August 1937, at which point the Poles very much took them to their hearts. Zoia had known Princess Marina in Paris before she married.

Just before the war came, Zoia and her children left Poland. In August 1939 Prince George invited them to Coppins for a weekend and in November they moved into one of the cottages on the estate. Agnes joined them. She described how, in the early years of the war,

> We used to go over at about a quarter to nine, the Duchess looking a dream of beauty in an evening gown – always punctual. He would come in a little late, looking so sleek, so soigné, so good-looking. We would have a cocktail, and walk into the dining room, the only light from four long candles on the table. The food on the sideboard was kept hot by electric heaters. He was so graceful, so tall, fair and slim. He usually served me, then the others would help themselves, he always last. Everything was perfect. He used to give orders every night for such-and-such a centrepiece to be put on the table. I used to forget half the time to remark on the beauty of it, but the Duchess would make me a sign and I would be loud in my admiration. He would be so pleased. We used to sit at the table until a quarter to

eleven o'clock. I would long to get up, but that was his special hour of relaxation. He would talk and discuss and drink several cups of coffee. When many guests were present, the servants served. After dinner we used to walk towards the Music Room. After a few minutes he would seat himself before one of the pianos and play endlessly.

In the summer, when he was at home, his delight was chopping trees and weeding, the two children running around and the Duchess helping him.[15]

There were two surviving Poklewski sons, Vincent, the younger of the two, becoming a lifelong friend of the Duke, and producing in later life a racy book of memoirs. Agnes de Stoeckl had been a key figure in encouraging Prince George and Princess Marina to visit Poland. There was even some vague talk about Prince George becoming King of Poland.

Duke: I was constantly over at Coppins Cottage as a child. Zoia had two sons. There was Vincent, and Alexander* was his older brother, who had a sad life and became an alcoholic. He'd been up at Cambridge, and while he was there he contracted polio and was quite ill. He was then always fairly delicate. He died quite young. He was very amusing, not as much of a character as his younger brother but still very good company.

There was never a real possibility that my father would become king. Newspapers liked to take soundings in the early days of the war after Poland had been occupied. There must have been a question along the lines of 'When Poland recovers from all of this, whom would you like to have as the king?' And

* Alexander Poklewski-Koziell (1924–66). His wife, Barbara (1932–72), also died young.

the vote was for my father. A record was found in the file. I have some film of that too. My parents went to the Potocki Palace and arrived in a horse-drawn carriage.

It was at Coppins that the Duke developed his love of cars.

Duke: I have always had an interest in cars. It must go back quite a long way. I enjoyed the dodgems in Olympia, after the war.

There was a big garage at Coppins that would hold four or five cars. That was overseen by Frederick Field, the chauffeur, who'd been with the Prince of Wales, before he came to my father. We called him Freddy. I always got on very well with him, but others found him tremendously self-important because he couldn't stop telling them what the Prince of Wales had said to him, or how he'd done this or that. I liked him, though, and he became a very good friend.

For security, a policeman came in the evenings and stayed the night in a garage, which must have been uncomfortable. He would leave in the morning. It wasn't very serious or very good security – nothing like nowadays. They were local police. I don't believe there was such a thing as special protection in those days.

We used to go to the village church quite regularly and into the village to go shopping and things. We had friends in the village, including the doctor and his family. My sister and I went to a little school in the village aged about five.

My sister had a pony called Kitty at an early age. I wasn't interested at all in horses. We used to go off, the two of us, to a famous riding school at Holyport, near Bray, on the river. The man who ran it was rather severe – as were his wife and daughter who ran it a few years after him – Horace Smith. He was a proper riding instructor of the old school, always wore highly polished boots, quite fierce with his pupils. His daughter, Sybil

Smith, was a doughty figure. I was never keen at that age – I didn't take much interest in it.

Horace Smith, the distinguished horseman, put his memories down on paper: 'I taught Princess Alexandra from the time she was five years old. Even at that early age, she showed the qualities that have not only made her the very good horse-woman that she is, but also that charm and sweetness of character that are becoming ever more evident as she grows to womanhood . . .' He also taught the Duke and Prince Michael: 'The young Duke had a very highly developed sense of humour, and on one occasion he reached over and tapped the horse I was riding behind the saddle with his stick, so that had I not had my wits about me I might well have been taken for a ride on my own! I pretended to be very stern, and the practical joke was not repeated!'[16]

Prince Edward on a pony at Bray

Then there were the animals at Coppins, as the Duke and Princess Alexandra recalled.

Duke: There were always dogs around. We had one or two smallish ones. My mother had one though she was never really a doggy person.

Princess Alexandra: The first dog our parents had, an Alsatian, was Dushka – the only Russian word I know. They had a Chow called Moof, but he was rather naughty and used to bite ladies in the village. He wasn't very popular. Much later my mother had Chin. It was very unlike her to have a Peke but she was very fond of him.

Duke: She had a dog called Chin or Chinny, that she was very fond of. A little shaggy sort of thing. She was photographed taking it for a walk here in Millionaire's Row.

We loved Bertram Mills Circus and, of course, it was a big annual event. One of the Mills brothers was particularly kind [Cyril Mills] and I discovered later that he had quite a war record.

A retired schoolmaster, a charming man called Wilfred Edwards, lived in Iver village. He used to come in and give me Latin lessons and we became good friends. He would always send me the *National Geographic* magazine, the American one. For years he sent me that magazine – I had piles of them! He was delightful and very kind. He had quite a large house on the edge of Iver village and often used to ask us for tea parties. Other than that there was the little local school that I went to during the war before I went to my prep school. It was quite a small group from Iver village, I suppose a dozen of us. They all became good friends.

My sister went to a similar school, a continuation of it, after I had left, before she went off to boarding school – to Heathfield.

Princess Alexandra was due to be confirmed at Heathfield, and Queen Mary had a plan to come down to take part. A recipe came for a chocolate cake that was to be made. It began with the extravagant instruction: 'Take 36 eggs . . .'

Princess Alexandra: In the end I wasn't confirmed at school – German measles. The King let me be confirmed at the chapel at Royal Lodge. I've got a little book by my bed to this day that the Bishop of Oxford gave me. I wasn't destined to be confirmed at school.

War was declared in 1939. The Duke and his sister remembered moving to Windsor.

Duke: Coppins was very close to London. A few bombs did fall quite near – it was thought just a pilot shedding his load on the way back. They killed one or two cows. We went to Windsor at the height of the Blitz for the first winter of the war and the first part of 1940 to keep us in relative safety. We weren't refugees. I don't think the idea ever arose.

Princess Alexandra: It was very kind of the King to have us at Windsor. Where were we? On the first floor? I still remember putting down a dust sheet, and then the bath water could only be a few inches deep.

Duke: A line round the bath. And you can remember that? You were only four at the time. There were guns out in the park. You could see them. Windsor must have been quite a target but it

was never bombed. There was lots of barbed wire. We were able to get out into the park. There was an exhibition in which we saw German aircraft that had been shot down. It might well have been in the quadrangle. When we weren't there, we were at Coppins, not in London.

Prince George and Princess Marina in wartime

The family was completed by the arrival of Prince Michael on 4 July 1942. Soon after his birth, tragedy struck with the death of Prince George in an aeroplane accident in Scotland. Agnes de Stoeckl witnessed the last days he spent with his family. She recorded that 4 July was a difficult day that ended well, the Duke 'radiant' at the arrival of his younger son. Every evening, he would leave dinner at 10 p.m., and carry the infant to his cot, where he spent ages watching over him: 'Nannie told me that each night as he lays his son in his cot, she discreetly leaves the room, but she can hear the Duke talking softly to him. Perhaps he is unconsciously preparing him for the future.'[17]

Prince Michael was christened by the Archbishop of Canterbury and the Dean of Windsor in the private chapel at Windsor Castle on 4 August. Crowds watched as the family set off. The only guests were the Royal Family, a few personal friends and the staff from Coppins. Queen Mary came over from Badminton, where she was living during the war, and King George II of Greece was present. Since, for some reason, the godparents remained silent, it fell to the Duke to confirm that the child had not been baptised before. Champagne was served. Agnes de Stoeckl saw the Duke of Kent on 22 August: 'I looked through the window into the Duke's study. The Duchess was sitting at the desk choosing photographs for the press; he was standing looking over her shoulder, their heads close together. I stood unseen for some time; I did not want to disturb that lovely picture. She looked so beautiful and he like a young god. His hair was golden from the sun's rays.'[18]

The Duke left for Scotland on 24 August, the Duchess making a sign of the cross as he drove away. The following day his plane crashed and he was killed. His funeral took place in St George's Chapel, his coffin descending into the Royal Vault. There it remained and there Princess Marina was able to visit it. Her first visit was soon after the funeral, when she was accompanied by Baroness de Stoeckl and her daughter, Zoia. Agnes de Stoeckl left an account:

The Duke of Kent's coffin, covered by his standard, lay alone surrounded by deep purple draperies. A cross made of woven gold seemed to watch over him. A light shone on all. We placed flowers around him; we were so far down no noise could penetrate. I pushed past one of the purple curtains and found myself in a long gallery, at the end an altar, a gilt cross and two candlesticks lighted by

THIS IS A PLACEHOLDER

small electric light bulbs – the only light in that gallery. All along either side deep shelves protected by a trellis of gilt wire. On these shelves lay many coffins of all sizes. I read the names of Kings and Queens of England, royal children and babies. The history of Great Britain lay hidden there, deep down below the surface of the earth. I said a De Profundis and returned to the others . . . The custodian told us nobody ever came there. The Duchess was the only one who ever descended those stone steps . . . The flowers are constantly renewed and often prayers are murmured near him.*[19]

The Duke was six years old when his father died.

Duke: The sad thing is I can only remember isolated moments – he was away so much because of the war. He went up to Scotland to do a naval job, although he'd left the navy quite some time before. I think he was in Naval Intelligence. I remember him coming back in RAF uniform because he became their director of welfare. So, I can remember him appearing but only for very brief moments. I can't remember conversations with him, but I remember him driving me in his Bentley somewhere.

We were up at Appleton, near Sandringham, with a governess, when he was killed. It must have been several days later that my mother came up to break the news. Ruth Fermoy lived in one of the Sandringham houses. I remember we met her daughters, one of whom married Johnny Althorp† – they were our sort of age.

* The Duke of Kent's coffin was moved to Frogmore the night before Princess Marina's funeral in August 1968.

† Viscount Althorp, later 8th Earl Spencer (1924–92), father of Diana, Princess of Wales. He was the equerry on the Queen's Commonwealth tour of 1953–4.

Appleton was a rather ugly, but very comfortable house. It had been Queen Maud of Norway's. It was offered to my mother as somewhere to go for summer holidays. We were there in 1941 or 1942. We loved it up there, helping with the harvest, and went to the sea.

We came back to Coppins at the end of September.

It was difficult for my mother bringing us up on her own. She really didn't have many friends in England; she had only lived here for five or six years. Most of her friends here were foreigners like her. She must have been terribly lost and lonely after my father died.

Princess Alexandra didn't really remember her father either.

Princess Alexandra: He used to have his breakfast in his bedroom. Once I upset the breakfast table and he was rather cross. I was very young. I was about four, but it's not very vivid. I fear it's all photographs.

One of those who comforted Princess Marina at this time was a Georgian cousin on her mother's side, Princess Natasha Bagration, later the wife of the diplomat, poet and translator Sir Charles Johnston. Her mother was Abbess Tamara, daughter of Grand Duke Constantine of Russia (grandson of Tsar Nicholas I). Princess Nicholas's father, Grand Duke Vladimir, was a son of Tsar Alexander II, so Natasha and Princess Marina were third cousins. They became close because Natasha was living in London in the early 1940s.

Years later Sir Charles Johnston recalled the friendship in his diary.

Sir Charles Johnston: Princess Marina loved Natasha because she was 'family' and intelligent. Outside the family her gift of friendship didn't operate to the same effect. Those close to her

were either protégés – émigré Russians and Poles whom she
befriended with that wonderful unshakeable loyalty and gener-
osity – or celebrities of a certain brassiness or brashness. It was
as if a kind of piercing quality was needed to get through to her
past the mist of vagueness, which separated her from those who
were not relations. Like Queen Alexandra, the three sisters had
the Greek-Russian family 'thing' to an extreme degree: genocen-
tricity would perhaps be the word.

She was six years older than Natasha and like an elder sister
to her. They had known each other in Yugoslavia before the
war, when the Kents, just married, were staying with Prince
and Princess Paul. A year or two later, when Natasha came to
London penniless, the Kents befriended her and entertained
her at Belgrave Square and at Coppins. Natasha's friendship
helped sustain Princess Marina during the tragic time after her
husband was killed in an air crash on war service. Two years
later, when Natasha and I came home on leave from Egypt, and
got engaged, the first thing N. did was to take me down to
Coppins for the night. 'C'est trés réussi,' said Princess Marina.
'Comme un gâteau,'* commented N. in telling me afterwards . . .
Ma'am's relationship with N. was full of jokes and *fou rire*. As
soon as they met, they became again the two young princesses,
brilliant, mocking, with the world in front of them.[20]

Duke: Natasha clearly loved my mother very dearly. The
Pembrokes† also played a big part in my mother's life. Sidney
Herbert, later Pembroke, became my mother's private secretary

* 'It's very well made . . . like a cake'.
† Sidney, 16th Earl of Pembroke (1906–69), and his wife, Lady Mary Hope
(1903–95). He was private secretary to Princess Marina 1942–48, and she was
lady-in-waiting. Later they lived at Wilton House, near Salisbury.

Princess Marina and Natasha Johnston at Coppins Cottage

in the war. The Pembrokes lived in a house that belonged to
Coppins, literally a hundred yards away across a field. It was
called Lower Delaford. Mary Herbert was the lady-in-waiting
and a very great friend too. Their son Henry was a little younger
than me. Although we were at school together we never were
particular friends, but we used to see each other on holidays,
and his sister Diana was a particular friend of my sister's.
Although Henry was never a close friend, he was my page at the
Coronation. We went to Wilton quite a few times in the late
forties, and early fifties.

3

The Fabergé Aunts

Princesses Olga, Elisabeth and Marina at Coppins

Princess Marina's two older sisters were important to her, especially in the isolation of her widowhood. I wanted to find out more about them and was able to consult three of the Duke's cousins.

The sisters were Princess Olga (1903–97), and Princess Elisabeth (1904–55). The King arranged for Princess Olga to come to comfort Princess Marina after her husband's death, which was quite a complicated decision: at that time Prince Paul, her husband, was considered to have let Yugoslavia down and was living in exile with his family in Kenya. Questions were even asked in the House of Commons about Princess Olga's presence in Britain.

Princess Olga had married Prince Paul of Yugoslavia in 1923. He became a reluctant regent of his country following the assassination of King Alexander in Marseille in 1934. During the war, he was pushed into an impossible situation and finally signed a pact with Hitler in a desperate attempt to save his country. He was exiled to Kenya and South Africa. After the war the family settled in Paris. Prince Paul died in 1976.

They had three children – Alexander (1924–2016), Nicholas (1928–54), and Elizabeth (born 1936). I knew Prince Alexander, who had been an RAF pilot and later a business-man, and lived with his second wife, Princess Barbara of Liechtenstein, in Paris. I knew Princess Elizabeth well, having first met her properly in New York with Sam Green, a mysterious and mercurial character who appealed to both of us. He somehow knew everybody – Cecil Beaton, John Lennon and even Greta Garbo. Princess Elizabeth had enjoyed a life far removed from the strictures of the British Royal Family. Several times married, the mother of the *Dynasty* star Catherine Oxenberg, she had nearly married the actor Richard Burton at one point. In later life, she returned to Belgrade where she worked tirelessly and successfully to reconstitute the reputation of her unfairly maligned father, long deemed by history to have let his country down, even arranging for him, Princess Olga and Prince Nicky to be buried in Serbia, a ceremony to which she invited me.

During the war Princess Marina was not so closely in touch with her other sister Princess Elisabeth, Countess Toerring (nicknamed 'Woolly') as she was living quietly in Germany, and thus communication was difficult, but she would appear in Britain later. She was married to Count Carl Theodor 'Toto' Toerring-Jettenbach and they lived at Schloss Winhöring,

near Munich in Bavaria. She died young in 1955, and her husband in 1967. They had two children, Hans Veit Toerring (born in 1935), and Helen (born in 1937), who grew up in Bavaria. He is a great expert on the royal families of Europe, and a fine photographer in his own right. I first met him at the ceremony in Serbia, when Prince Paul, Princess Olga and Prince Nicholas were reburied at Oplenac in Serbia in 2012.

His sister Helen has a home in Austria and a house in London, where I went to see her. I first met her in the 1980s, with Paul Louis Weiller. Older readers who remember Princess Alexandra's wedding in 1963 may recall the beautiful blonde bridesmaid in Westminster Abbey – Helen's daughter Elisabeth (1957–83). The family spent the war years in Bavaria, where the Schloss was fortunately not bombed, despite being close to Munich. Only after the war were they able to travel again. Helen married Archduke Ferdinand of Austria (1918–2004) in 1956. After that they divided their lives between Munich, Salzburg and London.

Both aunts were important in the life of the young Kents, as were their cousins, who remain close to this day. First I spoke by Zoom to Princess Elizabeth, daughter of Prince Paul and Princess Olga. She now lives in Belgrade.

Princess Elizabeth of Yugoslavia: My Aunt Marina was much gentler than my mother. And so humorous and elegant – she had everything. And I think she was pretty lonely after her husband died and I don't think the rest of the British Royal Family really gave her enough support. I know that she felt a little bit alienated by them.

The three sisters didn't want anybody to understand what they were talking about and so they would speak Greek. One day they were sitting at a big dinner party and one of them said

to another, 'Look at that man across the table. He looks like a fat frog!' and of course the man was Greek. I have never forgotten that story and ever since then I have always been very cautious not to say things like that in another language, in public. You never know. And I taught myself a bit of Greek because I got annoyed with them always talking about us in front of us. So I would learn phrases like 'That's not so' or 'That's wrong' and 'I don't agree'. They were really concerned that I understood more than I did, but it was really more an act on my part than anything else.

My grandmother liked me very much and my mother was petrified of her. If she was five minutes late to say good morning to her she would be very cross. But I could do whatever I wanted. I was sitting on her footstool one day and my mother said, 'Get up! That is your grandmother's footstool,' and she said, 'Leave the child alone.' So that didn't help my relations with my mother much. The letters my mother wrote to my grandmother were overflowing with admiration and love and devotion. So I got on with my grandmother very well. But I knew she was a little dictatorial and she was not very nice to my father when we got to Athens in 1941 after the coup. She wanted my mother to leave him, but she refused.

My Aunt Elisabeth was adorable. He was very difficult, her husband – Toerring. I didn't care for him at all, but she was kind and loving and very warm. Beautiful amber-coloured eyes, I remember. She was beautiful. The three sisters were incredible. I have a wonderful photograph of the three of them.

Then I went to see Helen Habsburg, daughter of Countess Toerring, on one of her visits to London. First she spoke about her parents' life in the war.

Helen Habsburg: Our house in Munich was bombed quite soon, as early as 1942. So my mother spent the war in the country at Winhöring, which is a big castle, with a farm. And we went to the local school. I am sure it was very difficult for my mother as she was not German and was very cut off from her own family. She did not speak German well and you weren't allowed to speak foreign languages. She was considered to be not only a foreigner but a dangerous foreigner, having a sister in England, and another one in Africa, who had been in Serbia. But she loved to go to the village to talk to the villagers, always dressed as simply as possible, and she wore no make-up. She was cut off from her sisters, hardly ever getting any letters, though correspondence came through Queen Louise of Sweden, as Sweden was neutral. She was the conduit.

Duke: I think life for them would have been quite difficult. I have often asked my cousin Hans Veit Toerring, who inherited the castle, about that time and he has said: 'Oh yes, they did live in one floor of that house.' There were no staff. It was just a matter of survival. It must have been pretty difficult for my mother because one sister was married to a German, whom she couldn't see, and another exiled in South Africa, and her mother locked up in Athens. We were too young to be aware of that but what those people must have gone through, divided families and so on. It must have been terribly difficult.

Helen Habsburg: My aunt, Princess Olga, was much more severe. She knew Russia and Serbia and Paris, having lived in all those places. I think that's why she was so insecure. She had such a difficult life.

I also talked on the telephone to Helen's brother, Hans Veit Toerring. He spoke first about his aunt.

Princess Alexandra, Helen Habsburg and Hans Veit
Toerring on the beach in Norfolk after the war

Hans Veit Toerring: Olga was a bit strict, but had a fantastic sense of
humour. I think my mother was the nicest sister. She had the best
heart. Marina used to come often to Germany after the war. Once she
and my mother came to see me at school, and I hated this visit. I
didn't want my friends to see these two very elegant women arriving.

The two aunts used to make terrible remarks, thinking no one
could speak English except them. Aunt Marina came to Munich
once, after my mother died, and my father gave a cocktail party
for people she'd known before the war, and the British consul
was there. My father introduced him. His name was Mr Somers
Cocks.* 'It's not possible,' said my aunt.

* John Somers Cocks, CVO, CBE (1907–64), consul general to Munich
1954–9.

Uncle Paul was a highly cultured man. He took me to Paris, to museums, and would show me two or three rooms and explain it to me. He was never boring. I developed my interest in art from him and from my father.

Then in Greece when my grandmother [Princess Nicholas of Greece] died and Philip Hay* and I were at her house, Psychico. Olga and Marina were in the front row and I was sitting in the second row with Philip Hay, when the old Greek lawyer, a friend of the family, was reading the will. He was rather a frail man, a little afraid of the situation, and he got muddled and turned two pages at once. 'Poor little tired brain!' exclaimed Olga. Philip and I had to leave the room, doubled up with laughter.

Princess Nicholas of Greece and her three daughters in Greece

* Sir Philip Hay (1918–86), private secretary to Princess Marina, 1948–68.

Duke: I was very fond of both my aunts but, of course, the younger one, Elisabeth, died young sadly, and I really didn't get to know her, but I saw Olga a lot.

HV: I thought Princess Olga was very beautiful, slightly austere, very disapproving but also, perhaps, a little insecure.

Duke: You're right. I certainly found her quite austere, wonderful to look at. She and my mother were very close, but she was not an easy person. One always felt she was watching for mishaps, which were all too inclined to occur. She was possibly quite shy. She must have missed so much. They were away in Kenya and South Africa for five years, then suddenly found themselves in Paris.

Uncle Paul, her husband was a very good friend and I got along with him particularly. But they had a terrible time with the ghastly occupation of Serbia – and then they were expelled. He didn't have a very good reputation, poor man, but he was placed in an impossible position. He had a pistol to his head from the Germans. They demanded all sorts of things from him that he couldn't provide. He was an immensely cultured man and knew a lot about art. That was much more his world than trying to run a country.

They had to depart into exile. They were regarded, I think, by the British government as enemies. It was impossible for the King and Queen to be in touch with them during the war. What they did manage – well, the King principally with Churchill – was to get my aunt here after my father died, somehow avoiding the rules and restrictions. In 1942 my mother was in a very low state so Olga came over and stayed for at least two or three months at Coppins.

Princess Olga staying with Princess Marina and the young
Duke after Prince George's death in October 1942

They were tremendously close and everybody was very fond of Uncle Paul. I think there was a lot of sympathy for him in this country, but some people felt he had betrayed the cause. There was no doubt that spiritually England was his home. He had been at Oxford in the early years of the century. He felt totally comfortable here. The war must have been a horrible shock for him. He was very depressed when he was in Kenya, and then they moved to South Africa.

They came back to live in Paris, where I visited them in 1950. It was the first time we had seen my uncle since before the war. They had just moved into a flat or a house. Then they bought a house where they lived for the rest of his life – rue Scheffer. Lilia Ralli lived opposite. She was a childhood friend of my mother and her sisters. We used to see a good deal of her.

Prince Paul was always rather bemused by the three sisters. He used to say that even after years of marriage he could never work out what they were all laughing about.

Princess Alexandra: The one we warmed to particularly was Elisabeth, Helen's mother, known as Auntie Woolly. We liked Auntie Olga – known as Pigga. Auntie Woolly was attractive, but not as good-looking as Auntie Olga.

After the war Princess Marina would visit Prince Paul and Princess Olga at Pratolino, their house in Fiesole, north of Florence. Cecil Beaton wrote: 'The three sisters in their heightened sense of excitement had again become like young girls from a Russian novel, and the month in the country spent quietly with Princess Olga and dozens of relations, at Pratolino, in Tuscany, was pure Turgenev.'[21]

Duke: I went to Pratolino for two or three summers. It is just up the hills from Florence. He inherited it in the mid-1950s from an aunt, a Russian, a Demidoff. It was a large estate but it was in considerable disrepair. It was stuffed full of furniture and objects Demidoff had left there, which were of no use to Paul and Olga so it was stuck away in some of the disused rooms. It was a huge house with a very large estate and a lovely lake. At the edge of the lake there was a famous Giovanni Bologna statue of the Colossus of the Apennines, made in 1579, a very well-known architectural landmark, a mythological figure. It was about ten times life-size.

Helen Habsburg: It was magic. The park was so pretty, left rather wild, and overgrown. The house itself was not pretty but Paul had lovely pictures and furniture. I remember a lovely

larege inlaid commode, with drawers, all ebony wood and silver. Princess Marina went to see them every summer. I remember seeing the aunts there, and then, of course, the cousins, Queen Helen of Romania, was there on the hill, and her sister Irene, Duchess of Aosta. Pratolino was lovely.

Prince Michael: Princess Olga was very funny, very good-looking when she was young. We always giggled a lot. At Pratolino they built a tennis court, and the only person who played tennis was Princess Elizabeth. We were farmed out to swim with the Duchess of Aosta. Years later I took my wife to visit her sister Queen Helen at La Sparta, which was a lovely house with a beautiful garden. I said, 'Can you remind me of the terrible time when you were kicked out of Romania?' She'd told me the story some time before. The young man who was sent to tell her to leave was called Bagerof. I was sitting having a dainty tea party with my wife. 'I remember so well you telling me that you were kicked out by a man called Bagerof.'

'I never said any such thing!'

I couldn't argue with that. She was a queen, after all.

They had a wonderful old Buick in Pratolino, a vast car, which Queen Helen had smuggled out of her country on a train hidden under covers. It still had a red R on the back for Romania. It entered Italy illegally so they kept it on the property. We could drive it around, which I did a lot, and then Prince Alexander, my cousin, because he couldn't see to back it when he was turning it round, took the hood off. But it was a splendid old car. It had completely bald tyres. Once I got stuck with it, trying to turn it round on a loose surface on a very steep hill. Every time I put my foot on the brake, I could stop it moving, but I couldn't get out. I had to stay there with my foot on the brake and I remember screaming, '*Aiuto!*' meaning 'Help,' and

eventually, after twenty minutes, a very old man with a shovel came along and pushed the shovel under a wheel. But it was a dodgy moment.

Latterly my mother and Princess Olga used to spend their summers in Pratolino. It was rather sad. They were only around sixty, and they spent their time sitting indoors, chain-smoking, never went out, never did anything, and that was their summer. And I remember Princess Elizabeth and my sister used to say, 'You've got to get out and do something.' They were very static.

4

Schooldays

In 1944 Prince Edward, who had succeeded as 2nd Duke of Kent at the age of six, entered Ludgrove School. To be a royal duke at that age, not to mention fourth in line to the throne, was to place a heavy burden on his young shoulders. That was an age when school contemporaries were unforgiving and cruel when they should have been compassionate and kind.

Ludgrove was and still is a preparatory school, near Wokingham, originally founded in 1892. The historian Sir Alistair Horne wrote of the 'rampant, unchecked bullying', which was a feature of his time there in the 1930s. A number of members of the Royal Family had been there, including Queen Mary's Teck nephews, the Duke's cousins, the Earl of Harewood, the Duke of Fife and Prince Alexander of Yugoslavia, and well-known figures such as Sir Alec Douglas-Home and Sir Osbert Sitwell. In later life, Sitwell described Ludgrove as if he had been in a Hell painted by Hieronymus Bosch. In Sitwell's day, the school was close to the celebrated lunatic asylum, Colney Hatch. Inevitably, the boys liked to speculate that the masters had recently escaped from it.

Duke: I was at Ludgrove for four years. I can remember lying in our dormitory just before D-Day and hearing all the aeroplanes going over on the way to Normandy at the beginning of June. I

can't say my time at Ludgrove was happy. I was very much
bullied. I had no father, which didn't help, and I was no good at
cricket or football, which were the two principal things that
mattered there.

Those schools were Victorian and barbaric in some ways.
There was a lot of beating, which was tolerated unfortunately.
My headmaster was quoted in the newspapers saying of me:
'He will be kicked about as much as any boy.' It is interesting
that the headmaster should make that comment. It was
certainly very true. It wasn't only the boys who kicked you
about either.

Today attitudes have changed so much. Now people are
horrified by bullying. It was rife in the 1940s. If you reported
bullying you would be called a sneak then taken down to the
gents and given a thorough beating. Bullying was almost encour-
aged by teachers as a way of keeping discipline. It was a normal
part of teaching methods unfortunately.

Later I got to know the boys who had been pretty thuggish
and they turned out to be perfectly nice people. They had been
corrupted by the school's ethos.

Perhaps significantly, Princess Marina did not send Prince
Michael to Ludgrove. He went to Sunningdale.

Prince Michael: At Sunningdale they couldn't have been more
agreeable people. The boys were chums and the teaching staff
were very good, except Matron, who was terrifying. She shopped
me to the headmaster who beat me. She was persona non grata.
There was a headmaster called Mr Dawson, whose father had
been running the Rootes group in the forties. I went to
Sunningdale in 1951. All my friends liked it very much.

The Duke entered Eton College in the Michaelmas term of 1948 and stayed until the summer of 1951. The college had been founded in 1440 by Henry VI as 'The King's College of our Lady of Eton beside Windsor'. When he arrived, the Provost* was Sir Henry Marten, knighted for tutoring Princess Elizabeth in the constitution. The headmaster was Claude Aurelius Elliott, and the lower master (headmaster for the younger boys) Julian Lambart. His housemaster was Geoffrey Nickson, who taught classics. Many of the masters were now legendary Eton figures, and some impinged on the national consciousness: Wilfrid Blunt (brother of Anthony Blunt) was the drawing master; (Sir) Neville Marriner, later a Companion of Honour, who would rise to be one of the greatest English conductors, was there teaching the violin. The precentor was Sydney Watson, later organist at Christ Church, Oxford, and conductor of the Bach Choir. Among the assistant masters, Giles St Aubyn, later a well-known biographer, taught history.

In those days, the annual fee was £278 to cover board, tuition and the school fund. It also included the river fund subscription, army class fee, specialist fee, laboratory fee and gymnasium fee, and certain specialised items such as stays in the school sanatorium. There was an additional all-inclusive games fee of £5 a year.

There was again a precedent for members of the Royal Family going to Eton, including the Duke's uncle, Prince Henry, Duke of Gloucester, and the Duke's cousins, the Earl of Harewood and his brother Gerald Lascelles.

* The Provost is the chairman of the school's governing body, chosen by the Crown.

The Duke on his way to Eton in 1948

Duke: I already knew Giles St Aubyn. He had been my holiday tutor before Eton and he came with us for the summer when we went up to Scotland, probably in 1947. He was pretty much a non-sporting man, so he wasn't particularly keen on things like stalking or fishing. He was good company and my mother liked him very much. It was an advantage knowing one of the beaks [masters] at Eton before I arrived. I used to see a good deal of him while I was a boy there and have tea with him.

Giles was already a good friend of the Duke and Duchess of Richmond at Goodwood and particularly of Nicky Gordon-Lennox.* He first took me there and that was how I got to know their family. I went for many years in a row and became good friends. Giles was very keen on cars. He had a Jaguar

* Lord Nicholas Gordon-Lennox (1931–2004), later ambassador to Spain 1984–9.

sports car when he was a beak at Eton, much to the envy of other beaks – I remember being taken out in it – and, of course, he was a notable historian and a great lover of opera and music.

Eton was better than Ludgrove, probably because we had our own rooms, which made a big difference. They were wonderfully old-fashioned with a coal fire every other night. The boys' maid cleaned the rooms, made the beds and lit the fire – something unimaginable now. These were much happier years for me. I made some good friends there.

My housemaster was called Geoffrey Nickson. He was a classicist. He was known at Eton because when he corrected our work, he wrote all over it in red ink and drew rather amusing pictures. I kept some as souvenirs for a while. 'Nicograms', we called them.

I was good at Latin. I found it congenial and took to it quite easily. But I was never really much of a classicist. I did Greek as well, which in some ways was more interesting. I can still read it, and that's the important thing.

I was also reasonably good at French because I'd had a French governess. My mother spoke fluently to her friends in French with people like Zoia. It was annoying for us when she spoke Greek, as we felt excluded. I couldn't speak any German – that came much later. It didn't really feature in one's life at that age. No Russian either.

I hardly knew Paul Channon* at school, though we were later great friends. We certainly didn't realise we were twins – born on the same day. We met occasionally for things like PT, but neither of us were games players.

* Paul Channon (Lord Kelvedon) (1935–2007), son of the diarist, Chips. Later an MP in Margaret Thatcher's government.

I did not have to play the Wall Game, but we did have to play the Field Game, which had complicated rules. I wasn't very good at it. They put me in goal occasionally, to keep me out of the way. I was also a wet bob [the Eton name for rowers as opposed to cricketers]. I rather enjoyed the relative freedom it gave everybody, up the river and down towards Maidenhead.

I would regularly make use of the School of Mechanics, which I remember very well. I went down there although you weren't supposed to go into it until you were an upper boy, which I wasn't at the time. I learned how to make things – I made a model car. That was tremendous fun and spurred my interests in mechanical engineering.

I remember a famous character called Hope-Jones, an eccentric maths teacher. He was a bit dotty. He used to throw chalk about and make us sing.

Another was Charlie Rowlett, who I think had been wounded in the First World War. He was wildly eccentric and came up with strange remarks. I also remember 'Bloody Bill',* who was quite fearsome. He had a reputation for being rather sadistic. He rode about on his enormous bicycle, which was twice the size of anyone else's, a long lanky sinister figure. We kept out of his way.

The headmaster was Claude Aurelius Elliott when I first went there, then [Robert] Birley. I went to breakfast with the Provost in the first half [term]. He was Henry Marten who tutored the Queen.

Kenneth Rose taught for one or two halves. But I didn't know him then. My mother also knew Kenneth quite well but that was

* H.K. 'Bloody Bill' Marsden (1888–1967), a famous Eton master, who lingered at the school into old age. He used to attend morning service in College Chapel and memorise the faces and names of all the boys. The weary figure in an old raincoat would be forever on the prowl, and would head into the school office next morning to report miscreants he had spotted out in the streets after 'lock-up'.

a bit later. He came into my life entirely through Giles St Aubyn in the early 1950s.

Luckily Coppins was just within the radius from the school that meant you could go out for the day at weekends, and I used to visit the housekeeper, Mrs Bruce, at Windsor Castle. She became a friend and would produce toffees out of her cupboard and provide tea as well. She was an old Scots lady, an old-fashioned housekeeper.

I developed an interest in literature a little later. I don't think it was much encouraged at school. I enjoyed all the usual things teenagers liked, such as Sherlock Holmes, but nothing much more serious than that. My love of P. G. Wodehouse developed at Eton, very early on, and I became a devoted fan of his and have been ever since. I have read a wide variety of novels, quite a lot of nineteenth-century novels by people like George Eliot, Thomas Hardy. And then I started reading a lot of history, largely modern history, which I still do and I enjoy very much, nineteenth and twentieth century, focusing on military history. I have a large number of books in that category, and current affairs, world affairs. I cannot bear getting rid of books. I know I ought to because I have far too many but I would regret it.

I produced an old school list with names of the Duke's contemporaries at school. This reminded him of many old friends. Several had been at Ludgrove with him.

Duke: Robert Benson, son of Sir Rex, was in Nickson's house. I had lunch with him a couple of weeks ago. He was an exact contemporary. There were two Butlers – one brother, Richard, was a very large chap! He had a younger brother, Adam, both of them sons of R.A.B. Adam was a minister at one time. I knew Ian Cameron, father of the former Prime Minister, particularly

well. He was a year or two older than me. Charlie Hambro was captain of the House, part of the banking family, and David Landale worked for the Duchy of Cornwall for a long time. Christopher Norman-Butler was related to Thackeray and later discovered lots of important Thackeray documents.

I was at Ludgrove with John Smiley, who became a Grenadier. Tyrone Waterford was quite a character, and I knew Philip Wroughton quite well. He became Lord Lieutenant of Berkshire. John Dawnay was keen on fast cars. Many of them died a long time ago.

Sydney Watson was the precentor and went on to conduct the Bach Choir. He was running the music at Eton at that time. I had piano lessons from him, but I'm afraid I gave up piano in about my second or third year because I was making so little progress – there was always some great thug who was chasing me out to play football so it was hard to find time to practise the piano when other people were trying to make me go running or play some idiotic game! I'm really sad that I didn't go on with my piano. I would have loved to be able to play.

We all had to sing in the Eton College Musical Society (ECMS) and we were given a trial for the choir. I never went near the violin. That would have been much too difficult.

I was taught art by Wilfrid Blunt. I was keen on pottery, taught by a man called Menzies-Jones, always known as 'Moans'. I became an enthusiastic potter and made lots of things, which I distributed to my family. It was something entirely new, more fun than drawing, which was more popular. I made mostly bowls because they were easy. Occasionally I would try to make weird animal shapes. But largely it was bowls, vases and things like that. They were straightforward. You put them in a kiln and cooked them.

Eton offered a huge range of sports and activities. There were so many societies. I remember vaguely having something to do with stamp collecting. I did a bit of beagling – because it was more fun than going for a run down to the locks. I used to hate that. You had to fill in a form or tick your name on a list to show you'd done what was called 'times'. Theoretically at least you were a member of the lower-boy football team, and they were very keen for you to keep terribly fit. I hated football and the idea that I had to go for runs or get fit was completely foreign to me. I would get out of it whenever I could. Of course you were severely punished if you were caught cheating or trying to evade the exercise. Many people considered Eton to be barbaric compared to today's schools. But we survived.

I wasn't at Eton long enough to enjoy the years of being a senior boy. I just made it to the upper school and then had to move on. I had hay fever and sinus infections and it was considered that the Thames Valley wasn't the ideal place for me so I went off to Switzerland.

The Duke was sent to Switzerland in 1951. Le Rosey is a world-renowned school, founded by Paul-Émile Carnal in 1880. The academic year is divided, as it has always been, between two campuses – the main one in twenty-eight hectares of land on the site of the renovated Château du Rosey at Rolle, Vaud, close to Lake Geneva, and the winter campus, a village of chalets in the ski resort of Gstaad. It has always been popular with the jet set, and attracted pupils such as the Shah of Persia, Prince Rainier of Monaco, the Crown Prince of Yugoslavia, and Kings Baudouin and Albert of the Belgians. While the Duke was there, the future Aga Khan, Prince Amyn Khan and Prince Vittorio Emanuele of Italy were among the international pupils. While today it costs over $133,000 a year

to attend, in his day it was considered expensive charging £250 a term (some reports said £600 a year).

It is particularly focused on developing bilingual talents, and there is a rigorous extracurricular programme of sport, technology, the arts, service learning and other cultural activities.

Duke: I went to Eton for three years and then to Le Rosey, which was so different. The interesting thing about it was the multinational aspect (this was quite soon after the war). The pupils came from all over the place. Some of their parents had been doing quite disreputable things during the war. There were some dodgy characters or, at least, the children of dodgy characters. After the war they had been skulking in all sorts of places. I made a few good friends but, of course, I was missing my friends at Eton so it wasn't easy to settle down at a new school. It was very different – no fagging, none of that – and there was probably less pressure but nothing like the range of activities. The school probably took only about a hundred people, maybe a hundred and fifty. It was all on a much more limited scale.

I was there at the same time as Prince Vittorio. I seem to remember he was rather bumptious. I don't think many people were aware at that time that he was the son of the King of Italy. The Aga Khan, Karim, was there and so was his brother, Amyn. I got on with Karim rather well, and came to know him better after school. Others? I've largely forgotten now, I'm afraid, but there were quite a few Americans. I don't remember any Russians.

The main school was at Rolle, a small town on the edge of Lake Geneva. I suppose we had good teachers. There was a joint headmastership between Dr Johannot and a Welshman, Hughes – he smoked a very smelly pipe. The most appealing

thing about Le Rosey was that in the winter term, we went to Gstaad. We lived in big chalets and skied every day so long as there was snow – there usually was. That was my first experience of skiing at the age of fourteen or fifteen, which I loved. Sadly I've stopped doing that now, but I don't forget. I had two winters there. We only skied during the January term. My standard of skiing then wouldn't have been enough to let me take part in a competition. It was assumed that all boys who went to Le Rosey could ski and if you couldn't you just picked it up. They didn't make any attempt to instruct you. I was taught by a geography master who couldn't really ski at all. Of course this was the early fifties, so all the equipment was very old-fashioned, all pre-war. There were no quick-release bindings or anything like that. But surprisingly there were few accidents. Very occasionally someone would hurt themselves, but not often.

The Duke skiing in Klosters

I used to lunch with Queen Ena of Spain. She lived in the Villa Fontaine in Lausanne so I would take a train along the side of the lake. She was very kind to me. She was living in exile there – what an extraordinary life she had had. Most of her early days had been spent with Queen Victoria at places like Osborne and Balmoral. Then she married King Alfonso and was almost blown up by an anarchist on her wedding day. Her life in Spain was not easy and she was a carrier of haemophilia, like the Tsarina of Russia. She lived apart from King Alfonso after they left Spain in 1931.

I was frequently taken out of school, for the funeral of my uncle, the King, and my grandmother, Queen Mary. Then there was the Coronation. The Far Eastern tour was by far the longest absence. That was about six weeks.

At the end, I took the General Certificate examination in Geneva with two other boys and passed well. This replaced the old School Certificate. I became bilingual in French and did well in algebra.

5

THE ROYAL FAMILY

After the war life at Coppins continued. In those days the main Royal Family comprised King George VI and Queen Elizabeth, the two princesses, Queen Mary, the Duke and Duchess of Gloucester and their two sons, William and Richard, and the Princess Royal, whose husband, Lord Harewood, had died in 1947. She had two sons, George, Viscount Lascelles (later Earl of Harewood), and Gerald Lascelles.

They were together at times such as Christmas. The King and Queen moved between Buckingham Palace, Windsor Castle, Sandringham and Balmoral. Queen Mary lived at Marlborough House; the Gloucesters had a large apartment, York House, at St James's Palace and a country home, Barnwell Manor, in Northamptonshire. The Princess Royal also had an apartment at St James's Palace and spent much of her time at Harewood House, near Leeds. Other members of the Royal Family, such as the Earl and Countess of Athlone and Prince Philip's grandmother, Victoria, Dowager Marchioness of Milford Haven, had apartments at Kensington Palace. Until 1944, although not during the war, Princess Beatrice, the last daughter of Queen Victoria, also lived there, though the Duke did not recall ever meeting her.

Duke: Queen Mary came to Coppins from time to time. More often we went to her, either at Marlborough House or Badminton.

I can certainly remember going to see her once at Badminton, maybe a couple of times, but my sister stayed there for at least a couple of weeks, perhaps longer. Later I went several times for the horse trials, and the Beauforts* were very kind. But I was never a very horsy person – horse trials are not the sort of thing I greatly enjoy.

I found Queen Mary, my grandmother, quite intimidating, but maybe that was because she was shy and I was too. I don't think she found it very easy with young children, and I was on my best behaviour – 'We're going to see Granny, so don't do this, don't do that,' which immediately terrorised me.

Princess Alexandra: She was wonderful. I went to stay with her at Badminton and she started me off doing tapestry, and I've got a map I made in 1944. She was very kind to me, loved our father particularly of our family – he loved art like she did. We were brought up to be very respectful of her, curtsy to her.

And then there was my mother's mother,† who lived in Athens, and that was a different sort of relationship.

Duke: I didn't see my mother's mother till years after the war because she lived in Athens. I had a much less clear picture of her but I think she was very kind.

The King, George VI, started wonderful family Christmases at Sandringham and also at Balmoral. They very kindly let us use Birkhall, which the Prince of Wales now has as a holiday

* The 10th Duke of Beaufort (1900–84) and his wife, Lady Mary Cambridge (1897–1987). He was Master of the Horse, and she was a niece of Queen Mary, who spent the war at Badminton as their guest.

† HI and RH Grand Duchess Helen of Russia (1882–1957), wife of Prince Nicholas of Greece.

house, because no one else was going there. So we went every summer for about five years around the end of the war and afterwards. My mother had never been to Scotland before, so for us children it was a completely exciting new adventure, discovering how to fish for trout or shoot a rabbit. As time went on, I started going to Balmoral and quite often went on my own, without any of my family. Queen Elizabeth [the Queen Mother] was always so kind to me. I had several happy years going to Balmoral.

The King used to ask me to stand in his grouse butt at Balmoral. There was a lot of grouse in those days and I remember getting into trouble for saying something like 'Oh, you missed that one,' and he replied, 'You could have been more polite.' That was all great fun. There are some lovely photographs of Balmoral with some great characters – David Bowes-Lyon, Lord Salisbury, who was a considerable old friend of the King: I didn't really know him but I did know his wife. Then there was Jack Eldon – he was always very funny, teasing people – and Arthur Penn.* I was only about twelve, much the youngest out of the whole house party.

I don't suppose I had good conversations with the King. I don't know how good any conversations are at the age of twelve or fourteen. I was still pretty shy, but he was quite a shy man. I don't think conversation with young children was his cup of tea really. The fact that he allowed me to stand by him when he was shooting was quite an honour.

* Hon Sir David Bowes-Lyon (1902–61), brother of the Queen Mother; 'Bobbety', 5th Marquess of Salisbury (1897–1972); 4th Earl of Eldon (1899– 1976), a lord-in-waiting; and Sir Arthur Penn (1886–1960), Treasurer to the Queen Mother.

Queen Mary, the Kents, the Gloucesters and Princess Margaret of Hesse

Queen Mary, Patrick Plunket,* the Duke and Duchess of
Gloucester and their two sons were regulars at Sandringham
Christmases, but not the Princess Royal. Her sons came into my
life much later, especially the younger one Gerald, as we shared
a love of motor-racing and jazz. He wrote books on jazz. I used
to see a good deal of him, and I came to know his older brother,
George [Lord Harewood], later, mainly through our shared love
of music. My grandfather used to say [of his love of classical
music]: 'What's wrong with my grandson George? His parents
were quite normal.'

We all went to Sandringham for Christmas. That was the great
thing. Presents were distributed the night before. They still do

* Patrick, 7th Lord Plunket (1923–75), equerry to the Queen, and Deputy Master
of the Household. His parents were killed in an air accident in 1938, and he was
partly brought up with the princesses.

that. You arrived probably the day before Christmas Eve, and on Christmas Eve there would quite often be a shoot. Then you would come in and have tea. Then the table was laid out in the ballroom with the presents. The same continued at Windsor when Christmas moved there: tables beautifully laid out with white cloths on them and then a red ribbon with your name on it. At some point in the afternoon you took presents you were giving and put them in the right places, without looking at your own bit of table because you mustn't see what you were getting.

On Christmas Day there was Communion in the chapel, before breakfast. And then church on Christmas morning.

The only aunt I really knew was Princess Alice Athlone,* and I remember going for lunch with her once. She was a delightful lady, but completely deaf so you could have some quite amusing conversations. She was great fun, very sharp, a tremendous enthusiast. She didn't play a big part in my life. She had a large apartment here in Kensington. Everybody loved her. She used to travel around London on the bus. And she was also quite a snappy dresser. My brother Michael knew her well because he stayed in her house for some time.

Prince Michael: When I had to take my dreaded promotion exam in the army in the early seventies and I didn't do well, it was my brother who said to give it another go. I said, 'I'm not going to do that again, waste a year of my life, being able to wax lyrical about how you provide socks to the front line,' but he said, 'Oh, come on!' so I did. By then I had met my wife-to-be who was very patient – this was 1975. I knew I had to be

* HRH Princess Alice, Countess of Athlone (1883–1981), the last surviving granddaughter of Queen Victoria. She lived at Clock House, Kensington Palace. Not to be confused with Prince Philip's mother, another Princess Alice.

Princess Alice, Countess of Athlone

somewhere away from what you might call earthly distractions so
I got in touch with my aunt, Princess Alic Athlone. 'Look, I've
got to be completely shuttered away for the next three months to
take these hideous exams.' She said, 'Well, you must come and
stay with me,' so I did and Princess Alice was frightfully good
company. She was as deaf as a post. She'd tell me the most fasci-
nating things: 'Do you remember the Duke of Cumberland*'?

And out would come a complete non-sequitur: 'Oh, yes,
sometimes, but be careful of the bottom one.'

Then she'd get it right: 'Yes, I remember the Duke of
Cumberland. Horrid man. Oh, he was so dirty, he would never
clean his collar, black mark all around his neck, horrid man.'

'Do you remember the Diamond Jubilee, 1897?'

* HRH Prince Ernest Augustus, 3rd Duke of Cumberland (1845–1923), son of
the blind King George V of Hanover.

86

'Oh, yes, and I also remember the Golden Jubilee, 1887. I lived at Claremont, which is in Surrey, and I was picked up by my nurse in a carriage and driven to London, to Buckingham Palace. There was quite a hill near Claremont, which we had to go up. In a car you don't notice it but for a couple of horses it was quite an effort. At the top of the hill, the horses stopped and were watered. The coachman went in and came out with two steins of beer, one for the nurse, and one for himself. But his waistcoat was all undone. I was only four years old but I knew it wasn't right!'

She was fascinating, with a remarkable memory. I'd been to Barnwell to stay with Princess Alice [Duchess of Gloucester], and Prince Richard and Birgitte were there with their children and I told her, 'I went to Barnwell and the two children were playing in the dog baskets after lunch.'

And she said: 'Unsavoury!'

The remarks she came up with were so funny.

Duke: Then there was Princess Marie Louise, whose face I can still remember but I have no idea where she fitted in.* She lived in Fitzmaurice Place where the Lansdowne Club is now. She knew a lot of people and was a great traveller. She went out to the Gold Coast and Ghana, and wrote a rather nice book about her life.

There were constant visitors, Continental ones, Greek ones and so on – it was very international. After the war, all our European cousins started coming over, though of course the Germans were excluded for years. They came later and I got to know my German cousins then. I got to know the Yugoslavs, as

* HH Princess Marie Louise (1872–1956), daughter of Princess Helena and Prince Christian, therefore a granddaughter of Queen Victoria.

they were called, after the war but I didn't see them before that. Alexander was in the RAF and Nicholas was at school somewhere like Downside.

Prince Michael: Prince Nicholas was killed in Datchet in 1954. He was on his way back from some do, and he was driving his XK120 Jaguar. The car turned over. And the irony was that he was untouched but drowned in a ditch. It happened in the early morning because we were all woken and told about it. I remember how shocked everyone was. He was very much the darling of the family. He was artistically inclined so he would have been the favourite. After that, if you went driving with Prince Paul, and you went above 30 m.p.h., which I did quite often, in Pratolino for example, he would be very nervous.

Duke: Nicky's sister Elizabeth became a great friend, whom I still see quite a bit. All these cousins would turn up. We wouldn't know where they'd come from. I would get hopelessly confused with who was who, whether they were Greek or Russian or Serbian. Grand Duchess Xenia, the Tsar's sister, had a house at Craigowan, which is next to Balmoral, during the war. That was where I met her.

I knew Peg Hesse*well. She'd had a very difficult time, too, because, of course, the Hesses were bound up with the Nazis. They had a lovely house, Wolfsgarten, south of Frankfurt, where I used to go to stay with Peg. And she was delightful, gracious. She was a friend of Benjamin Britten. They buried a lot of things in the garden during the war. Later she was very good at getting people together.

* HRH Princess Margaret of Hesse (1913–97), born the Hon. Margaret Geddes; married Prince Louis of Hesse in 1937.

My mother had many friends and she liked entertaining, so we had lots of people for lunch or dinner at Coppins. Charlie Johnston's wife, Natasha, was a very close friend. And there was another called Turia Campbell, who was half Russian at least – she worked for the BBC and ended up living in a Russian house full of mosaics, Debenham House in Addison Road, west London.

Sir Charles Johnston and his wife Natasha at Coppins

I wouldn't describe Cecil Beaton as a friend, but we got on perfectly well. He did some photographs of my wife and me. He was a friend of my mother and took pictures of her. I think she was one of his most glamorous subjects.

I can remember Winston Churchill coming to Coppins. I think my mother must have asked him to lunch, towards the end of the war. I must have been about nine, and I remember him saying, 'And who is this?' of me. It was quite something to have actually met him.

We called George Galitzine 'Porge'. He could be very funny with his imitations. I knew him for at least forty years, and I particularly remember him at Coppins, where he was a great favourite of my mother. She loved to invite him at every opportunity. Although he was quite a lot older than me, his boyish charm meant that he got on with all ages. He possessed a gay and buoyant spirit.

Prince Michael: George Galitzine was a great friend, with whom I used to speak a bit of Russian. Tragically he died in Eaton Square. He and his wife came out of the church and were on their way back to their flat and he dropped dead. George was a fascinating source of information when I started learning Russian in the sixties.

Duke: I knew Ali Forbes* a bit, never very well. My mother quite liked him. He was a useful spare man for dinner parties and that sort of thing.

Malcolm Sargent became a good friend, I suppose from the end of the war. We went to one or two of his concerts, and I remember him coming down to Coppins.

'Chips' Channon was quite a friend. He knew everybody. I think most people regarded him as an incorrigible snob, and perhaps not entirely trustworthy. He may well have been a bit of a gossip too. I think that was probably my mother's view. She liked him, and he was a friend, but she would only trust him so far, had to be a bit careful. He was a great friend of Prince Paul – they'd been at Oxford together. Uncle Paul was a little older.

* Alastair Forbes (1918–2005), cosmopolitan journalist with extensive international connections, Known for his wit and his enthusiastic enjoyment of his own jokes. Coincidentally, the uncle of US Secretary of State, John Kerry.

My cousin Philip was a regular visitor to Coppins. He and my mother were cousins and she saw a lot of him in the early days. She always had great admiration for him and affection. His name can be found in the Visitors' Book a great number of times in 1944, and my mother was among those who were keen that he should marry Princess Elizabeth.

After the war, in June 1948, my mother gave a costume party that I was not allowed to come to, and I was looking out of my bedroom window, seeing people arriving, some in fancy dress. It was the first big post-war party. Cecil Beaton was one of the guests. He had quite forgotten that he was meant to come and turned up at 3 a.m. with Christian Bérard,* having got lost in a deep ground mist. But the band was still playing and there were lots of gallops and polkas.

Cecil Beaton was the subject of one of my mother's portraits. She loved painting, mainly portraits, and she was a very good portraitist. Unfortunately she didn't do many and she tended to give them to the sitters. She did one of my cousin, Princess Margaret, a rather good one, I seem to remember. Otherwise it was chiefly friends or family – Natasha Johnston was one, and Garrett Drogheda† another. They were never commissions. She did them for her own amusement. There were never more than a dozen or so.

Of course, my grandfather, Prince Nicholas, was a good artist. He made a living from his pictures. To my great regret I only have one from when they were living in Paris. I would have loved to have owned more or seen more because he was a very fine painter.

* Christian (Bébé) Bérard (1902–49), French artist, stage designer and illustrator.
† Garrett, 11th Earl of Drogheda (1910–89), managing director of the *Financial Times* and chairman of the Royal Opera House, Covent Garden.

Prince Michael: There were dancing classes at York House [St James's Palace] with Queen Mary and she always had a stick, and she used to hold her stick between her legs. In those days the Gloucesters lived at York House and the house tended to be a bit of a base.

Duke: After the war we could travel again. We went to Jersey for the holidays and that was the first time I ever flew, but we didn't go overseas till a bit later. My sister spent time in Paris with a French family the Parises,* and I remember going over then, but this would have been the early fifties.

These years were not easy for my mother because she was never given a war widow's pension. Tommy Lascelles, the King's private secretary, maybe felt it would look bad for a member of the Royal Family. Luckily Queen Mary helped her considerably. Even so, she had had to sell a lot of my father's collection at Christie's in 1947 – nearly four hundred lots, including Chinese enamelled porcelain, English and Continental porcelain, some particularly fine Dresden and Sèvres, needlework and embroideries, English furniture, including a great deal of Chippendale, French furniture, silver and glass. That was one sale. In another there were sixty-seven pictures and drawings, three Claude Lorrains, a Boldini, which Cecil Beaton bought, Dutch paintings, a Van Dyck, and a Christopher Wood.

The first sale raised £55,642 in two days. The financial issue did not go away. A while later, in July 1952, there was a discussion about the Civil List requirements of the Queen and the

* Henri, Count of Paris (1908–99), and his wife, Isabelle (1911–2003). He was pretender to the throne of France.

Royal Family. The point was made by William Astor, MP for Wycombe (son of Nancy Astor), that when Prince George, Duke of Kent, died, the provision of £35,000 from the Civil List had ceased. Thus Princess Marina and her family had 'had to depend not on what they had up to then received by right from Parliament but on what they received ex gratia from the King and other members of the Royal Family'. He pointed out that, even as a widow, she had worked hard for the WRNS during the war and for many charitable institutions, that there were at that time very few members of the Royal Family and it was necessary 'for all of them to take part in public work'. He proposed she should receive two-thirds of the former provision, a suggestion greeted in the House of Commons with 'ministerial cheers'. However, R. A. Butler, the Chancellor, pointed out there was a reserve fund of £25,000, which could help the Duchess. 'They were all aware,' he said, 'of the very great services rendered by the Duchess of Kent before and since her tragic bereavement. [Cheers] They were aware of the circumstances in which she had unfortunately been placed.'[22]

* * * * *

I talked to the Duke's cousins about their memories of Coppins, as they visited Princess Marina during these years. Princess Elizabeth of Yugoslavia had first remembered meeting her cousins at Coppins around 1939, recalling 'the sandbags in the garden and I vaguely remember my uncle George but just fleetingly'.

Princess Elizabeth: I think it is lucky for Prince Eddie that he wasn't number two of the family because he could shine on his own without that pressure – I think to be number two in any

Princess Elizabeth of Yugoslavia at Pratolino in the 1960s

family that is rather successful is a very huge pressure, whether you are a woman or a man. It must be torture.

Well, I can tell you who saw Eddie more often than I did – Helen [Habsburg]. So she told me he was rather rough, rather grumpy and rather difficult. I know from the letters I sent him, copies of what my mother wrote, saying that he was a very difficult child. He would have many tantrums and used to be very difficult. These days you would never guess that.

We all went to Birkhall for a weekend, invited by the Queen Mother. I made tremendously good friends with Alexandra – we were like twins. And, as a result, we were so naughty, we were not allowed to go to the same school. She went to Heathfield and I went to Tudor Hall, which I think was pretty cruel because we would have had a much happier time together. We used to play hide and seek in the garden and chase each other through the bushes. Michael was too small to join in because he was only

seven. I remember meeting Prince Charles in a pram. I guess he must have been not even a year old. He was born in November and this was next summer so he must have been eight or ten months old. I remember him very clearly.

I remember the Braemar Games and tossing of the caber and eating baps in Scotland. We all had a wonderful time. I always think Eddie and I and Alexandra were very close. But I was especially close to her.

Princess Elizabeth agreed that Princess Marina did a good job of bringing up her children single-handedly:

I think so. I absolutely adored my aunt. She was one of the most wonderful people I have ever met, not only beautiful and charming, but she was funny and she was artistic and she entertained beautifully. She had interesting friends and through her I met Danny Kaye,* who was a star. There were so many funny things that happened with Alexandra, which amused him so much that he made comments about it in a radio programme.

My Aunt Marina was longing for Alexandra to learn French and Alexandra totally resisted learning it, so my aunt got her a French maid and the maid was called Regina. So Alexandra used to speak in English with a French accent, thinking it was French. And my aunt was listening to this conversation and she said, 'Regina, Regina, there is a "speeder" on the wall,' (meaning a spider), that was one thing. And the next thing that happened was she went bathing and the maid's bathing suit fell down, so she yelled across the beach: 'Regina, Regina, *votre bustie* sticky outie.' My aunt collapsed laughing. She told the story to Danny Kaye who used it in another radio programme. He had just had

* Danny Kaye (1911–87), popular American singer, dancer and comedian.

95

tea with some friends in the country and they served the most delicious jam called 'sticky outie jam' and we were all sitting there listening to this on the radio, absolutely dying with laughter. It was heaven. So Alexandra has always been very funny.

We used to play games in the evening, word games or card games, and lovely teas were served in a special room with sandwiches and cakes and a beautifully arranged table. Alexandra and I would sit in my uncle's office next to the living room and play jazz records – Fats Waller and Louis Armstrong . . . everything. We were jazz freaks.

Eddie and I and Alexandra all loved a book we grew up with called *1066 and All That*. Absolute classic, right? We used to die laughing over it. We loved the idea of the wave of 'Eg' kings that came from Denmark. Always Eg-something – like Egbert. And his nickname for the Queen Mother was 'Egg-whisk' and he calls me 'Egg' when he sees me. He always calls me 'Darling Egg'. So it has remained a sort of idiotic joke since we were teenagers.

And the other cartoonist we adored was Ronald Searle. Those pictures of cats. They still make me laugh. And St Trinian's – all that sort of thing. We used to laugh about a lot of silly things.

This inspired a conversation between the Duke and Princess Alexandra about the servants at Coppins.

Duke: Edith Arter was my mother's dresser, always called 'Arter'. She retired in 1957. And Bysouth was my mother's butler. There was a second driver/gardener called Arthur.

Princess Alexandra: There was an amazing housekeeper called Alice [Cross]. She was very fierce and I think I did something she didn't like very much . . . She took against Philip Hay: 'That booger Hay!'

Duke: I don't know what poor Philip was meant to have done.

Princess Alexandra: And there was another chauffeur –
Mr Nutbeam. And the gardener, Mr Beckingham. I think he got
quite cross with me because I took strawberries and I had shorts
on with buttons that got caught in the netting.

Duke: Yes and pulled the netting off. I do remember that.

Princess Elizabeth: We ran in and out of the bushes chasing
each other. Once Alexandra and I were stealing strawberries and
we heard the gardener coming, but the button on her shorts got
caught in the net and she couldn't escape. She tried to hide,
sitting down, and she ended up kneeling on the strawberries. I
laughed so much. I couldn't help her.

Prince Michael: In those days all the staff were known by their
surnames. There was a chauffeur called Field, who had been in
the navy and served in a battleship called *George V*, and who had
been with the Prince of Wales, whose name came up frequently
– 'When I was with the Prince of Wales . . .' He was quite a
character.

And our cook was called Mrs Keeble. She made chestnut purée
with whipped cream, for which she will be for ever remembered.

Our butler was called Bysouth. Just after the war Mrs
Roosevelt visited Britain and my mama entertained her to tea.
Eleanor Roosevelt and she were chatting away, and my mama
turned to her and said, 'Would you like some more tea, Mrs
Bysouth?' whereupon Princess Olga, who was also there,
dissolved into laughter.

I loved Coppins and I have an enormous number of memo-
ries of people coming and going, funny things, and people like

Douglas Fairbanks, and Danny Kaye. Danny Kaye was a great joy. Beverley Nichols* was another. I remember one day in the drawing room there was a fire in the grate and suddenly there was a huge bang. The plate behind the fire moved away from the back of the fireplace, and knocked the entire basket of blazing coals onto the carpet. Everyone rushed about, went for fire extinguishers and yelled and screamed, and there was Beverley Nichols on his knees shovelling the cinders off the carpet.

Beverley Nichols was impressed that if a guest wished to 'wash their hands' at Coppins, they asked to 'see the statue of King Edward', which faced the door of the lavatory in the hall.[23]

Prince Michael: We had a farm at the top of the property. Mr Griffin, the farmer, had a boat at Datchet, which he kept on the river. I remember milking the cows.

Coppins was the cosiest house possible. I used to drive cars up and down the drive, and any guest who came – for lunch, to play tennis or whatever – I, a frightfully precocious child, used to say, 'Very nice to see you and can I drive your car?' They were obviously amazed as it wasn't something they were asked very often and I used to drive the car up and down the drive. I was quite adept at it and never hit anything. I would say that before I took my test, I had driven about ninety cars, mostly up and down the drive. The drive is about three hundred yards.

Princess Elizabeth: We were invited to a ball [in about 1950]. I think we were both fourteen, Alexandra and I. She lent me a pink dress or a blue dress, I don't remember which. We were so

* Beverley Nichols (1898–1983), prolific English writer and playwright.

shy and we didn't know anybody in the room and all the dow-
agers were sitting, watching and gossiping. And the dance
started and we all had to take a mirror, look in the mirror and
choose a boy to dance with. I nearly died of embarrassment. So
the only boy Alexandra and I knew was Eddie, so guess who got
him? She did. So I fled and sat in the corner. It was terrifying. So
different from nowadays when people have a whole different
way of communicating. But that was torture.

In 1947, Princess Marina's sister, Elisabeth, Countess
Toerring, paid her first visit to Britain since the war, bringing
her children Hans Veit and Helen with her.

Helen Habsburg: We went to Coppins after the war, on a Pan
American flight. It was the first time we had been to England.
We landed in Northolt and went to this dream place. In Britain
my mother always spoke English to us and we always answered
in German so she didn't know if we could speak English at all.
We didn't say a word in English to her, but when we got there,
suddenly the cousins were there and we were all talking away in
English quite happily. She was very pleased about that. We were
told not to speak German if we went shopping near Coppins.

That was the first time I saw Marina. We felt immediately at
home with her because my mother had talked about her so
much. She was so much in our lives. We had seen photographs
of her wedding, back at home. We also felt completely at home
with our cousins. It was a lovely house, so lovely in the way it
was decorated, and easygoing, with a lovely butler and cook.

When we went first to Coppins, Queen Mary came to tea. I
remember that distinctly – her funny car. Of course we were
only interested in the car and the sofa, asking her, 'Can we sit on
it?' 'Yes, you can.' We knew that she was German but she

wouldn't talk German after the war. She brought us presents. She obviously thought I was the older one. I got a lovely box, an etui, with little bottles in it and pink enamel tops, very nice, and Hans Veit only got a football or something. He was very disappointed. But we sat with her and talked a bit but we didn't go and see her in London sadly.

Coppins had a very cosy, warm atmosphere. There was a lovely nanny whom we loved, but we took part in everything – lunches and dinners, we were always there, not separated. Lots of games, tennis, swimming and riding. I loved riding. Sidney Herbert and his daughter Diana came and we went riding with her in the meadows. Sidney was a great tennis player. The real intimate friends were the Poklewskis. They knew everything and everyone, and adored the Duke of Kent. Zoia and the mother used to come to lunch almost every day. Down the road one would see them coming and then we went up to have tea with them. They had a lovely Polish cook, who made the best jams and the best cakes, very good food.

Natasha Johnston I remember very well, and Turia Campbell, who was very sweet. As a very young girl, Turia had been a lady-in-waiting to my great-grandmother, Grand Duchess Maria Pavlovna, and left Russia with her. Turia was completely unpretentious, never pretending to be anything she wasn't. When she visited us, she always brought us presents, and my aunt always said it was particularly special from her because she would have had to take a bus to go out and buy things for us. My aunt was very much aware of things like that.

Elisabeth, Countess Toerring, died in Munich on 11 January 1955. Princess Marina, the Duke and Princess Alexandra attended her memorial service at the Greek Cathedral in Moscow Road on 26 January.

Hans Veit Toerring: My mother got flu every winter. In the winter of 1954/55 she got very bad flu and we had to take her to the hospital. She wrote a diary every day, and one evening towards the end, she was writing and her handwriting started off more or less normally but then tailed off. Then it was became all right again and then it floated away. A policeman came to us very early in the morning and woke my father, and we went to the hospital. But she had died all alone. She died of a brain tumour, as would my Aunt Marina later.

Princess Alexandra: Auntie Woolly died in 1955. It was terrible for my mother.

6

EXCURSIONS FROM LE ROSEY

King George VI and his daughters at Coppins,
with Turia Campbell behind them

The Duke had not long flown back to Le Rosey at the beginning of 1952 when, on 6 February, King George VI died at Sandringham at the age of fifty-six. He had gone to London Airport to bid farewell to Princess Elizabeth and the Duke of Edinburgh as they set off on a tour of the Commonwealth. They had got as far as Kenya when news of his death summoned them home.

Duke: I can remember it vividly. We were up in Gstaad and the call came early one morning to get home. I was flown back to

RAF Northolt and went straight to Coppins. It was my first major experience of royal ceremonial. The King's body was brought by train from Sandringham and taken in procession to Westminster Hall – the Great Hall, which had only just been repaired after all the damage to the roof by German incendiary bombs. The lying-in-state followed the traditional pattern, but this time the flags of the Dominions and Colonies were displayed against the south wall. Commonwealth ministers who were present in London joined the Royal Family for a short service. Yeomen of the Guard and Gentlemen-at-Arms stood vigil. Peers and members of the House of Commons were massed on the west and east walls.

There is a dramatic photo of the three queens waiting for the coffin to arrive at Westminster Hall, Queen Mary dressed in full Tudor mourning, which is rarely seen now. My cousin Philip and my uncle, Harry Gloucester, had followed the coffin through the streets of London. The rest of the family were waiting until it arrived at 4.10 p.m. I was there with my mother, and we followed the Queen and other members of the family in for a short service conducted by the Archbishop of York. My mother took my sister Alexandra and me to see the lying-in-state, and it was touching to watch the crowds, who had queued over Lambeth Bridge and on the South Bank of the Thames, filing slowly past the bier.

On the day of the funeral, I joined the Dukes of Edinburgh, Gloucester and Windsor for the funeral procession, walking in front of visiting kings (Denmark, Greece, Sweden and Iraq) and presidents (such as Tito of Yugoslavia, and Celâl Bayar of Turkey), and immediately behind the carriage containing the Queen, the Queen Mother, Princess Margaret and my aunt, the Princess Royal. It was a long walk to Paddington, past the Cenotaph, along the Mall, where Queen Mary watched the

procession pass from her balcony at Marlborough House, past what was left of 145 Piccadilly, the King's home before his accession, and up Park Lane to Paddington. The Duke of Edinburgh and the Duke of Windsor wore naval uniform, the Duke of Gloucester a military greatcoat, and I wore an overcoat and top hat. I was only sixteen.

Over the years, several articles criticised the jaunty angle of my hat, but the truth is that no one had told me how to wear it. We joined the train at Paddington and there was a shorter procession from Windsor station to Windsor Castle. During the funeral service in the Quire, which was slightly enlivened by an Easter hymn, the body of the King descended slowly into the Royal Vault.

This was the first time I had seen the Duke of Windsor, my uncle. My mother had talked about him a bit but never in polite terms. He'd been back to England before, but the family had never seen him. The funeral was the first time he appeared in public. He had no idea who I was. I remember him asking, 'Who is that boy?' Cousin Philip introduced me. We'd only ever met when I was a baby. He was my godfather, as well as my uncle.

A few days later I returned to Switzerland, flying out with my Aunt Mary, the Princess Royal. I was soon home again for Easter at the end of March, flying into Northolt. I was confirmed by Eric Hamilton, Dean of Windsor, in the Royal Chapel at Royal Lodge. The Queen, Prince Philip, the Queen Mother, Queen Mary and Princess Margaret joined my mother and Michael.

In March 1953, Queen Mary died at Marlborough House. The Duke had seen her at Sandringham at Christmas in 1952, though she seldom left her room in that last year. When she fell ill, the Duke was again brought home from school to accompany his mother on visits to her at Marlborough House, and after her death to attend the lying-in-state.

Once again the Duke walked with his uncles and Prince Philip in the funeral procession. In the Quire of St George's Chapel they were joined by Queen Mary's brother, the Earl of Athlone, to witness her descent into the Royal Vault.

Those were two sad family reasons for being taken out of school. In distinct contrast, in the autumn of 1952 he accompanied Princess Marina for several weeks on her Far Eastern tour. There had been no royal tours overseas during the war, but in the new reign, with the Commonwealth becoming a more relevant feature, they became important. Between 1953 and 1954, the Queen and Prince Philip would undertake an extensive tour of the Commonwealth, with long stays in New Zealand and Australia. Princess Marina's Far Eastern tour of 1952 was an important forerunner.

Duke: There weren't so many members of the Royal Family available in the early 1950s. In the first years of the Queen's reign, the Queen Mother undertook some trips, notably an important visit to America. She went quite often to Canada, and sometimes Australia, New Zealand and other Commonwealth countries. Princess Margaret made several visits to the West Indies and was at the Jamaica independence ceremony in 1962. My uncle Harry Gloucester had military commitments and visited many Commonwealth war cemeteries. He presided over Independence in Malaya in 1957. My Aunt Mary, the Princess Royal, visited Nigeria in 1957, made a four-month tour of the West Indies, and presided over Independence in Trinidad in 1962, and Lusaka, Northern Rhodesia, in 1964.

It had been announced in June that the Duke would accompany his mother on her six-week tour of Singapore, Malaya, Sarawak, Brunei, North Borneo and Hong Kong. The stated

purpose of the tour was for Princess Marina to visit the 1st Battalion, The Queen's Own Royal West Kent Regiment, of which she was Colonel. She was also invited to open an anti-tuberculosis hospital in Singapore. The Duke was approaching his seventeenth birthday and it meant missing a considerable chunk of his school term at Le Rosey.

Before that the family had a holiday at Birkhall, went to Crathie Church on Sundays, and the children joined the Queen and Prince Philip at the Braemar Games. Princess Marina took them to visit the memorial to Prince George on Eagle's Rock, Braemore on the tenth anniversary of his death – a white granite cross with the names of those who lost their lives in the accident. They went south in preparation for the tour. The day before they departed they called on Queen Mary at Marlborough House to say goodbye. Princess Olga came to the airport to see them off on 27 September.

A *Times* leader praised the Duchess of Kent for her commitment, her beauty, and her understanding of the importance of her charitable role. The trip was considered important, emphasising how much the work of the Royal Family was a family business: 'The Duchess of Kent takes to the Far East a sense of participation in the affairs of a united family circle, which is accepted as symbol and warranty of the British family of nations.' The tour, it was noted, would be 'strenuous and not wholly without danger'. One of its features, as it turned out, would be to see wartorn cities in Commonwealth countries gradually coming back to life.

With some percipience, *The Times* leader writer, possibly Dermot Morrah, commended the decision to take the young Duke: 'The inclusion of the Duke of Kent in the tour is a welcome indication that another royal generation is serving its apprenticeship to the family calling. In the fifteen years or

so before the Duke of Cornwall [Prince Charles] is of an age to take his part, the Queen will have need of all the help her kindred can give her as deputies in her great role as the representative personality of so many realms.'[24]

They stopped briefly in Cyprus, Bahrain and Karachi, Princess Marina writing to Natasha Johnston:

'*Nous voici à Ceylon depuis ce matin*. Terrific heat. Perfect flight. Very comfortable & delicious food. First night Cyprus, left there at 10 yesterday. Stopped at Bahrein at 5 for 2 hrs. Had supper with the Sheikh. Stopped at Karachi last night to re-fuel & got here at 10 to-day. Beautiful place & lovely flowers. Enormous house, very comfortable. Had baths, then lunch, then slept. Big dinner tonight. We leave to-morrow morning at 7. It's pouring & very hot & sticky.'

In Bahrain they were received by the ruler, Sheikh Sulman Bin Hamed Al-Khalifah, at the Royal Palace of Manama. They arrived in Colombo to stay with Lord Soulbury, the admirable Governor General, who had made a speech in Sinhalese within a month of taking up his appointment in 1949. A large crowd, mostly women and children, cheered their arrival. They arrived at Kallang Airport, Singapore, where the climate was humid, and stayed there between 1 and 13 October, after which they visited the Federation of Malaya between 5 and 9 October.

Singapore produced an uninspiring Governor called John Fearns Nicoll, and the more inspiring Malcolm Macdonald, the Commissioner General for South East Asia, at the airport. Government House was 'a palace'. Malay children wore *hari raya* costumes while the Chinese children were in white. The

visit was relatively soon after the war, and in a speech at City Hall, Princess Marina commended the restoration of the city, its now flourishing trade, and stressed: 'You are now engaged upon a project of far-reaching significance – casting into one mould elements derived from many different cultures, a plan which in itself testifies to the good will and good sense so characteristic of the people of this island.'

While Princess Marina undertook her engagements, the Duke was taken to RAF stations at Seletar and Tengah, climbed into the cockpit of a meteor-jet fighter and saw various activities of the Far East Air Force. He flew between the stations in a Valetta aircraft and saw a bandit cap, which had been presented to the operations-room staff by the 1st/2nd Gurkhas. The Duchess was praised for her stoicism in the heat, working twice as hard as most locals would in the debilitating climate. The Duke was commended for his interest in all things mechanical, for having taken the wheel of a naval motor launch and for being a 'natural shot'.

The Malayan visit took place at the time of the Malayan Emergency. An armoured car with gunners alert drove alongside the arriving air-force transport plane, there were police dogs with the waiting guards, and the Gurkha riflemen had fixed bayonets. Neighbouring houses had been searched. The time of arrival had been kept secret, resulting in few crowds, but many turned out later for a parade of voluntary workers from all the different communities.

Duke: I had done two terms at Le Rosey when I had a message from my mother that she was going to the Far East on a great tour and would like me to come with her. Of course, I hadn't a clue about any of it. I didn't know any of the countries or anything about them. The Malayan Emergency was in full swing. It was a

major trip and lasted six weeks. We started in Singapore. The pretext for going was opening a hospital. Then we went on to Kuala Lumpur because one of her Royal regiments was engaged there – and we stayed with Gerald Templer.* He was a great character. He had a reputation for toughness – 'The Tiger of Malaya' – an ideal person to be running an operation of that kind. He was pretty ruthless, I think. He became Colonel of the Blues, the Royal Horse Guards, later on at the end of his career. I'm not going to repeat his famous comment about Dickie Mountbatten . . .†

From there we went across to Borneo, some wild and undiscovered places. Then we went up to Hong Kong.

Johnny Althorp had been seconded to my mother from the Royal Household to be with me – he became a very good friend. We had a week or so together in Hong Kong, which was great fun. The whole journey lasted the best part of six weeks and, of course, long journeys in those days were quite an undertaking. We did fly but in short hops everywhere. On the way back we stopped in Athens, and that was the first time I recall meeting my grandmother [Princess Nicholas of Greece]. Between countries we mostly travelled by air with the RAF.

We set off on the Far Eastern tour in a BOAC Argonaut. I was entirely a spectator, because at this point, still being at school, I hadn't decided what I wanted to do. I think part of the object of taking me was to open my eyes to ideas and possibilities, as it proved to be. Rachel Davidson,‡ Bernard Norfolk's sister, was

* Field Marshal Sir Gerald Templer (1898–1979), High Commissioner in Malaya 1952–5, responsible for defeating the Malayan National Liberation Army during the Malayan Emergency.

† Admiral of the Fleet Earl Mountbatten of Burma (1900–79), a distant cousin of the Duke, and uncle of Prince Philip.

‡ Lady Rachel Davidson (later Pepys) (1905–92), sister of the 16th Duke of Norfolk. She was lady-in-waiting to Princess Marina, 1943–68.

with my mother as her lady-in-waiting. My mother's private secretary, Philip Hay, was also with us. We had a lot of laughs – I can only remember it being fun. Philip Hay had been a prisoner of war. His health was pretty delicate. He had very bad lungs and had to be careful. It was quite unusual to send a member of the Royal Family out there, so it was a very courageous thing for my mother to do. I don't think anyone else had done it since before the war. Normally if you went out, you stayed out. Of course, my Gloucester uncle was the Governor General of Australia, but otherwise nobody went abroad.

I went to a rubber plantation, and I had a go with an Owen gun, soldiers watching in the background. They found interesting things for me to do. It was necessary for a sixteen-year old – they had to do something other than letting me tag along behind my mother the whole time, which would have been a bit boring. While she undertook onerous duties, I swam in the Malacca Strait. I did go with her to the jungle fringe to inspect her regiment, which had seen heavy casualties in an ambush a year earlier. There was torrential rain.

I don't remember ever being aware of a dangerous situation. I knew, of course, of a previous High Commissioner, Henry Gurney,* that he had been murdered not far away, but beyond

* Sir Henry Gurney was killed in an ambush on 7 October 1951. He had implemented various plans to settle the 'Emergency'. He was a brave man who refused to allow what he called 'a bunch of rebels' to dictate the actions of the High Commissioner. He travelled in his official car with a Union Jack flying and a minimal escort. Heading to Fraser's Hill, he came round a corner to be met by a fusillade of shots. All of the policemen were wounded, as was his driver. Lady Gurney and the private secretary dived to the floor. Sir Henry got out, closed the car door, and headed to the cover of the high bank at the side of the road. He was instantly shot dead.

that there wasn't much awareness of any danger. Certainly when we went on that jungle expedition we were very heavily guarded, armed cars and things. I think we expected to be ambushed or something to happen.

I met so-called 'retired' headhunters. And they showed me parangs still adorned with human hair. They were brilliant people, those chaps in the jungle.

A reporter recorded that the regiment had killed fifty-nine terrorists in the last year. It was also noted that the Suffolk patrols, under the command of Lieutenant Colonel P. A. Morcombe, had discovered two camps where up to fifty armed terrorists had been living, with observation posts and slit trenches along the winding road that Princess Marina would inevitably have taken. They had been occupied for three days and the terrorists had only just retreated before the Suffolks arrived. *The Times* correspondent wrote: 'The road over the pass is in fact an ideal terrorist ground. It is over-looked by a hundred and more good ambush positions, and men of the Suffolk Regiment are to be congratulated for their vigilance and jungle-craft.'[25]

Observing the Duke at this time was the pipe-smoking journalist Bernhard Wicksteed, who noted a similarity to his father, not only in looks but in the way he walked. Referring to him as 'a lucky blighter' to be on such a trip, he observed an innate shyness in him:

He is clearly fascinated by anything mechanical and his shyness leaves him when he talks to men who can tell him how anything works. Reporters have all noticed how he appears more at ease with craftsmen than governors, with sergeant armourers than colonels and high

commissioners. In this industrial age, when labour rela-
tions are more important than palace protocols, this trait
of his may prove invaluable . . .[26]

Duke: I was given a Malayan *kris*, of which it was said that, if
drawn, it could not be put back into its scabbard until blood was
shed. The Sheikh of Bahrain gave me a curved scimitar, normally
used to lop heads off, and the Iban trackers attached to the 1st
Battalion of the Queen's Own Royal West Kent Regiment gave
me a parang, which they had made. And there is a little story
that goes with that because it was my seventeenth birthday in
Singapore. We had just come back from the jungle expedition to
Government House, Singapore, and they gave me this huge
cake. The parang was presented, and I thought it would be a
good idea to use it to put out the candles. It was quite big and
sharp, of course. As I lowered it towards the candles, I heard a
tinkle behind me and, to my horror, I saw my mother holding
her hand up to her face. I had indeed slit her eyebrow with the
sword. Had she been standing half an inch closer, it would have
been terrible.

Thank God it was all right. But that was a bad moment . . . a
very bad moment.

In the 1960s Princess Marina gave the parang in question to a
military museum in Maidstone, telling them that her son had
'nearly beheaded' her with it.

The day after the Duke's birthday, Princess Marina wrote
to Natasha Johnston from her room at Government House,
overlooking an inner court:

Nous sommes rentrés hier matin de Kuala Lumpur. We spent
5 very interesting & enjoyable days with the Templers.

*Lui est absolument charmant & quelqu'un d'exceptionel.** *Beaucoup de charme.* We spoke a lot of you. He loves you. He is much thinner than when I met him with you. We had some good laughs too! I told him your hedgehog story & we laughed a lot! I found a letter from Olga here & she tells me of your outings. I'm so glad to feel this trip is a success. People are so kind here, & everything has gone & is going so beautifully. Eddie is having a wonderful time. He had a nice birthday yesterday & several presents. Enormous cake at dinner & film after (bad, alas!). We haven't seen any newsreel of ourselves yet as they were all flown to England! Have you seen any? . . .[27]

If all was more or less well in Government House, trouble was not far away. Seven terrorists in the Kuala Kubu murdered a Chinese rubber tapper and his son by cutting their throats with a parang. A Malay policeman died of wounds, and nine terrorist camps were discovered. The next day the Duke met schoolboys and schoolgirls of all races at the Raffles Institution, dancing with some of them.

On 14 October they travelled to Kuching, Sarawak, in a Sunderland flying boat, and became the first members of the Royal Family to visit Britain's youngest colony. The Duke went on a thirty-six-hour fishing trip to Turtle Islands, enlivened by the north-east monsoon. He fished for barracuda, known to be the most belligerent fish in those waters.

Duke: That was in Sarawak, up on the coast where Johnny Althorp and I went to spend three or four days with Sir Anthony

* 'We returned from Kuala Lumpur yesterday morning . . . He is charming, an exceptional person. Much charm.'

Abell.* Sarawak is a country on the north-west coast of Borneo. It has an indented coastline, lots of low-lying swamps leading up to hills covered with forests. There is a huge number of rivers, and it rains a lot of the time. There is hardly any game, though some rhinoceroses, some crocodiles and a great number of snakes and lizards.

We had dinner with Tom Harrisson. A well-known figure in those parts, he was famous for having done a wartime survey, citizen's ideas, an investigation into public opinion around the country. He took us out on the beach to watch turtles laying their eggs, 126 eggs. He knew all about turtles. There are two species, and they breed in large numbers on the turtle islands between Santubong and Tanjong Datu. The green turtle eggs are soft-shelled and look a bit like ping pong balls. It was special to be allowed to visit the Turtle Islands as the government did not let tourists go there so as to protect the turtle egg industry.

Tom Harrisson was a maverick character. He had studied birds at Harrow, lived among cannibals for a year, and was the first European to be dropped into Borneo to organise guerrillas in Sarawak and North Borneo before the Allied landings. To give you an idea of the kind of man he was, he activated the head-hunting tribes of North Borneo against the invading Japanese.

Then he ran the Sarawak Museum between 1947 and 1966. He won a DSO in 1946 and later an OBE. He took on responsibility for the Turtle Islands in 1947. He lived in a little bungalow on the island, the house made of wood and thatched with palm leaves. When he had guests he organised a picnic

* Sir Anthony Abell (1906–94), Governor of Sarawak 1949–59, and High Commissioner to Brunei.

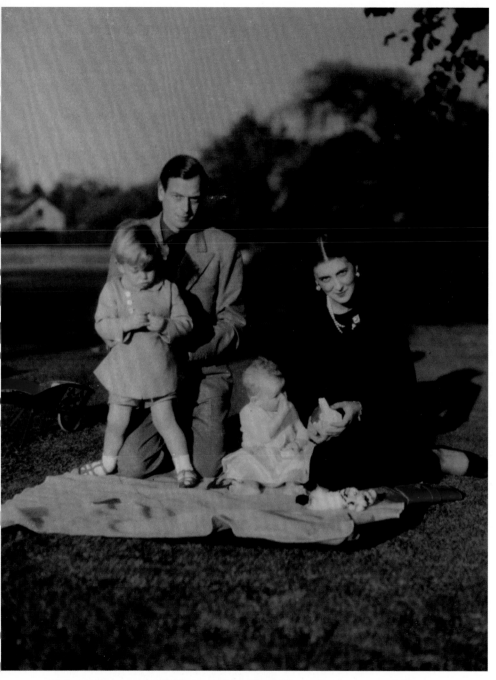

Prince George and Princess Marina with their first two children,
Prince Edward and Princess Alexandra

Princess Marina with Princess Alexandra and Queen Mary at Coppins

Princess Marina, her mother Princess Nicholas, and her sister Princess Olga

Prince Edward with his uncle King George VI at Frogmore

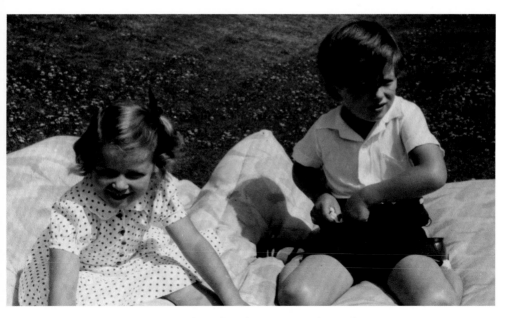

Prince Edward and Princess Alexandra

Prince Edward in the
arms of his father

Prince George with his
two elder children

Visitors to Coppins

Princess Marina with Danny Kaye

Princess Marina with
Winston Churchill

Princess Marina with Prince Philip

Princess Elizabeth and
Princess Margaret

The funeral procession of Queen Mary, 1953.
Left to right: The Duke of Edinburgh, The Duke of Windsor,
The Duke of Gloucester, and The Duke of Kent. Behind them:
Prince George of Denmark and the Earl of Harewood

Princess Marina and the Duke in Sarawak with Temengong Tama Weng Ajeng
of Long Akar, paramount chief of the Kenyan tribe of Sarawak

Coronation group, 1953. Left to right: Hon Henry Herbert (page to the Duke), Lady Rachel Davidson (train bearer to Princess Marina), the Duke, Prince Michael, Princess Marina, Princess Alexandra, Hon Katharine Smith (train bearer to Princess Alexandra), and Philip Hay (private secretary to Princess Marina, carrying her coronet)

Wedding at York Minster, 1961 – the bride curtseying to the Queen. Left to right, front row: Antony Armstrong-Jones, Princess Margaret, Prince and Princess Paul of Yugoslavia, Prince Michael, Princess Alexandra (hidden), Princess Marina, Queen Ena of Spain, The Queen Mother, Prince Charles, The Duke of Edinburgh and the Queen. Foreign royalty behind

The Duke saluting at the Independence Ceremony
in Sierra Leone, 1961

Prince Charles and
The Duchess of Kent
at Balmoral

The Queen in Scotland

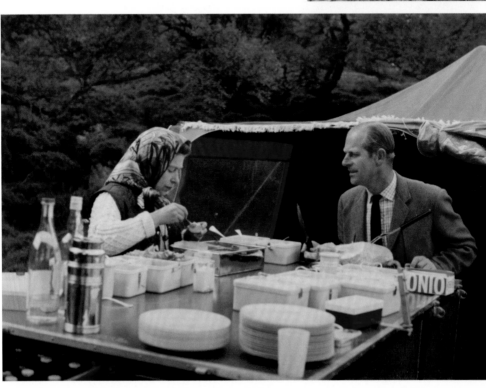

The Queen and The Duke of Edinburgh at lunch, Balmoral

using china from the dinner service of Rajah Vyner Brooke, the last white rajah of Sarawak, which Tom Abell had given him for the Sarawak Museum. Sadly he and his third wife were killed in a bus accident in Thailand in 1976 when the bus drove into a parked truck in the dark after sunset, with a teak log jutting out at the back. It impaled the passengers in the first two rows of the bus.

The Times correspondent summed up the Duke's trip:

> All this has happened against an exotic background that still captivates Englishmen who have been part of it for a lifetime. He has heard the gongs of the Chinese and the xylophone-like kromong of Borneo, and has passed little ships which sail to faraway islands scarcely changed since Conrad's days. The Duke has enjoyed the last 18 days, but he is still interested most in machines. Aircraft, ships, cars, weapons and motors of all kinds have attracted his knowledgeable attention, and on the last day in Singapore he was found riding a Malay policeman's motor-cycle in the grounds of Government House.[28]

Duke: There was a very kind policeman who said, 'Yes. Take my motorbike and ride it.' He just put it at my disposal. 'There you are.' I had never ridden a motorbike in my life and I rode it about all over quite large grounds at Government House, even on the golf course, which mustn't have been popular.

They flew on to Jesselton, North Borneo, on 17 October, hunted wild pigs, and the Duke took possession of a civet cat. On 21 October they were welcomed by the Sultan of Brunei. The visit included two nights at Bukit Serene with Malcolm

Macdonald, and a visit to Hong Kong, during which the Duke visited the services in the New Territories, driving along steep tracks hewn from the mountain face by the Royal Engineers. The Duke and Lord Althorp stayed on alone for some days. A tank regiment was there and the Duke had his first drive in a tank. Altogether the Duke and his mother travelled 21,000 miles, Princess Marina undertaking about sixty formal ceremonies, and as many informal ones.

Duke: We stopped to see my grandmother [Princess Nicholas] in Athens. That is the first time I actually remember meeting her. I think we spent a couple of nights there. And then it was back to school. It had been extraordinary. I was very lucky at that age to be taken on a trip of that kind.

Princess Marina wrote to Natasha Johnston: 'Eddie went back to Geneva yesterday & I miss him terribly. He is so sweet! & loved being here & everybody was so kind. He has had a marvellous time.' On her return to London in December, she was met at the airport by members of her family, as was traditional in those days. She was given lunch at London's Guildhall and had to make a speech.

Duke: She had to make a speech? She would have hated that. It always rather alarmed her – it was said she found it difficult because of her pronounced Greek accent.

Princess Marina said: 'Not one of the countries I went to escaped the terrible consequences of wartime occupation, and it was most heartening to see with what courage and determination men and women of every class and creed are joining together – often in the face of very great danger – to

build anew on firm and broad foundations. We, who are accustomed to live in peaceful and ordered surroundings, owe to these countless people an immense debt of gratitude. I should like, too, to say something of the gratitude and admiration which I feel – and which I am sure is shared by all of you – towards the men and women of many races who in these far countries are giving their utmost – and in some cases their lives – to repair the havoc brought on them by the war, and to rebuild the fabric of just and ordered government so tragically shattered by an alien and ruthless determination.'[29]

The conclusion on the tour was that mother and son had been indefatigable, that they had made every effort to see as much of the peoples and countries as possible. Asians had been entertained alongside Britons at every opportunity. The anti-cessionist movement in Sarawak was found to be dead. The loyalty of the old-established Chinese families in Singapore, Penang and Malacca was strong. Independence was the ultimate ambition of most thinking people, yet there had been intense excitement and a warm welcome given by the millions of Chinese, Malay, Indian and Dyak subjects as well as many races and tribes, all living under British protection.

Duke: My mother's 1952 tour led to her travelling more widely, sometimes with my sister, Alexandra, who was soon fully integrated into royal duties, even though she was in her early twenties. They went to Canada and the USA together in 1954. My mother presided at the independence ceremony for Ghana in 1957. It was the first African colony to be granted independence, so that was a wonderful historic event. There is a lovely photograph of her dancing with Kwame

Nkrumah.* Philip Hay, her private secretary, specified that her speech had to be printed on parchment. That sounds demanding but it was only so it wouldn't slip – she would be wearing white gloves. Then she and my sister had quite a trip to South America in 1959.

She became a very international representative of the Royal Family. When she went to South America, it was the first official royal visit there for thirty years. And one of the reasons given for sending her was that her sense of fashion would appeal to the sophisticated South American ladies.

Quite soon my sister was travelling on her own. She went to Australia in 1959 and to Nigeria for the independence ceremony. The Australian visit also included Thailand, Cambodia, India, Iran and Turkey – she was only twenty-two – and Queensland's centenary celebrations.

When she went to Japan, she was instrumental in reinstating relations with the Japanese.

Princess Alexandra: I went to Australia in 1959. They were terribly kind, the Australians. I don't think they particularly wanted me to visit them but they were very generous. My mother took me to South America – that was an adventure – Mexico, Peru, Chile and Brazil. I was very lucky to do that, because I was so young.

I went to Nigeria in 1960. That was rather an alarming responsibility, giving the country its independence. Then there was Japan in 1961. I got odd letters from people asking, 'Why did you go there?' because their families had suffered. The Emperor collected 'bottom scrapers'. They were intended for use on the bottom of the sea but the name was unfortunate. The Japanese

* Kwame Nkrumah (1909–72), first Prime Minister and President of Ghana.

were very friendly. We went to Kyoto. Philip Hay came with me: he had been a prisoner of the Japanese, and used to get malaria.

Duke: Princess Chichibu, Emperor Hirohito's sister-in-law, was a great help. She became a very good friend. We loved her, and she did a lot for Anglo-Japanese relations. She paved the way for Emperor Hirohito to come on a state visit in 1971. I remember *Private Eye* magazine had that famous cover.* My wife and I met Hirohito on our visit to Japan in 1973 to open the British Export Marketing Centre. He was a friendly, rather cuddly figure by that time in his life. He spoke no English at all but he was most hospitable. He gave me a book on marine biology – crustaceans.

*The Duke and Duchess with Emperor Hirohito
and Empress Nagako of Japan in 1973*

* The caption on the front cover of *Private Eye* (8 October 1971) showed the Emperor in London and read: 'NASTY NIP IN THE AIR'.

At this point, 1952, I hadn't decided on a future career. There was much discussion as to what I might do, but I'd seen the army in the field in Malaya, which made pretty clear to me where I was going. I'd hoped for the air force but I don't think I would ever have got through their exams. You couldn't have thrown somebody of my age straight into royal duties. It would have looked very odd. But my sister started very early, at eighteen.

Prince Philip took an interest in the Duke, aware that he was a young man without a father.

Duke: At Easter 1952, Prince Philip took me to inspect the aero-engine works of D. Napier and Son in Acton. That was fun. I've always enjoyed anything to do with engines or manufacturing. About a year later we flew from London Airport to Exeter in a turbine-airscrew Viscount with Prince Philip at the controls. That certainly pushed my interest along. Also in 1953 I joined him on visits to Vickers-Armstrong at Chilbolton, where he flew the latest turbine-airscrew Viscount for forty-five minutes, to Hursley Park and South Marston. He was at the controls for most of the flight back and I was on the flight deck. He was a very keen pilot, and must have fulfilled an impressive number of flying hours.

I wouldn't say that Prince Philip was a mentor, but he was helpful, certainly. He would have spoken to my mother about my prospects, or lack of them, as they were close friends as well as cousins. He was always kind and helpful, but not greatly involved, although he took me to the Olympic Games in Helsinki in July 1952. We based ourselves on board a rather nice boat – I think it belonged to Trinity House – and it made a very useful hotel. We were in Helsinki for several days, and I remember watching the swimming.

We watched the decathlon two days running, and went to a service in the Vanho Kirkko in which Prince Philip read the lesson. On the last day of the Olympics Colonel Harry Llewellyn helped secure Great Britain a gold on his famous horse, Foxhunter.* From there we went on to Norway for King Haakon's eightieth-birthday dinner in the medieval castle of Akershus. It was altogether an exciting visit.

* The rally proved to be Foxhunter's greatest moment. There had been a disastrous round in the morning, but in the afternoon Llewellyn and Foxhunter jumped a calm, faultless round, just brushing one of the fences without disturbing it. The British team won the Grand Prix des Nations. Lieutenant Colonel Sir Mike Ansell described it as 'the most brilliant and faultless round of the 1952 Olympiad'.

7

THE CORONATION

The royal Dukes in front of the peers. Left to right: The Duke of Edinburgh, The Duke of Gloucester and The Duke of Kent. Non-royal Dukes and Knights of the Garter are immediately behind them

Soon afterwards, on 2 June 1953, the Duke took his place in a chair in front of the peers in Westminster Abbey for the Queen's Coronation. There were three royal dukes in a row, the Duke of Edinburgh, the Duke of Gloucester, and then the young Duke. Behind him were the peers of the realm, in their red velvet and ermine Coronation robes, and nearby a clutch of officers-of-arms in tabards, Gentlemen-at-Arms and other officials.

On the way to the Abbey, Prince Philip accompanied the Queen in the Gold State Coach.

Duke: In March 1953 I was informed that I would be playing a prominent role at the Queen's Coronation. Although I was only seventeen and therefore technically a minor, I would be seated in front of the peers alongside my cousin Philip and my uncle, Harry Gloucester, as one of the three royal dukes who would do homage to the Queen after the Archbishop of Canterbury. Unlike the Duke of Gloucester, who was a personal ADC to the Queen, I was not asked to ride on horseback in the Coronation procession. I would accompany my mother, sister and brother in the second carriage – in the procession of the Princes and Princesses of the Blood Royal – leaving Buckingham Palace at 9.40 a.m. and arriving at 10.14. I felt very nervous. It was the first thing I'd ever done like that in public.

It is extraordinary to think that the Coronation took place nearly seventy years ago. Most people will only know it through films or television. It was arranged to take place more than a year after the Queen's accession. It is an important rite of passage in affirming a new monarch in their role. The accession is, of course, immediate: the moment the King died, my cousin became Queen, even though she did not know it for some hours, being at that time in Kenya. Following the accession, the cabinet met to note 'the grievous news' that George VI had died and to discuss the proclamation. There is normally only one accession council, but because the Queen was abroad, this time there were two. At the first, the draft declaration was read, and at the second, the Queen, now returned to Britain, made the Accession Declaration and took an oath to preserve the Church of Scotland, as required by the Act of Union of 1707. She was then proclaimed Queen at a number of important places, such as the balcony at Friary Court, St James's Palace and the steps of the Royal Exchange in the City of London.

Next, in order to comply with the 1689 Bill of Rights, she had to make the Declaration of Faith. She did so at the first State Opening of Parliament in the presence of the peers and the Members of Parliament in the chamber of the House of Lords.

Meanwhile the extensive plans for the Coronation got under way: guests were invited from all corners of the globe, troops mustered, Westminster Abbey prepared, and discussions took place on the intricacies of the ceremonial and the service. A fascinating booklet, with more than eighty-eight maps, detailed every move to be made by those with specific roles in the ceremonial. Garter King of Arms wrote: 'These very rough notes and plans are not intended to show how exactly the ceremonies are to be performed, but to provide a handbook to show how they can be performed . . . What is planned on paper often turns out differently in practice.' Because there was so much going on, some people were moving forward to perform their task while others were retreating. Otherwise it would have gone on all day. Sometimes it became complicated. The Anointing alone needed thirteen maps, and at one point Garter wrote: 'There should be no collision if all move at the same pace: the Great Chamberlain, for example, is behind everyone else and so, although he crosses their paths, he has a clear way: as does the Sword.'

I was brought home from Switzerland once more and my mother took me to a rehearsal at the Abbey at which a thousand people were present. The next day there was another Coronation rehearsal, and then a garden party for seven thousand on a perfect summer day, with lots of overseas guests, who had come for the Coronation, many wearing colourful national dress. We all went to a ball at Hampton Court, and the next day I had to go with my uncle Gloucester to London Airport to meet yet more distinguished overseas guests.

At dinner the night before the Coronation, there was exciting news: climbers Edmund Hillary and Sherpa Tenzing had reached the summit of Mount Everest.

On 2 June 1953, we duly arrived at the Abbey at 10.14 a.m. and processed to our places, my mother, sister and brother to the Royal Box, and I to my chair at the front. The Abbey was already very full, some of the guests having been there for many hours. I had to wait on my own for quite a long time in front of all the peers until my cousin and uncle joined me – they were in the Queen's procession. I was in a state of some trepidation about the part I had to play.

The ceremony was almost overpowering. A number of bishops and some of the great war leaders, like Field Marshal Lord Montgomery, were playing important roles. I saw it all, but I didn't know who most of the people were. Since then, of course, I have seen the pictures and watched the film and I recognise them – Alanbrooke, Alexander of Tunis, Portal of Hungerford* and so on. It was even more alarming to know that it would be televised in front of the whole world.

The ceremony played out – the Anointing being the holiest part. The cameras were diverted, while four Knights of the Garter held a canopy over the Queen. None of us had to do anything except follow the service until the moment the Archbishop crowned the Queen. At that point two heralds turned to face the peers and peeresses. They raised their batons. This was a sign for us to put on our coronets.

By now we had reached map 68a. My part did not come until maps 76 to 77. After the crowning, the Queen was 'lifted' into

* Three Field Marshals – Viscount Montgomery of Alamein (1887–1970); Viscount Alanbrooke (1883–1963), and Earl Alexander of Tunis (1891–1969); and Marshal of the Royal Air Force Viscount Portal of Hungerford (1893–1971).

her throne. Now my page, Henry Herbert, came forward to hold my train. Another page stood near the Queen: Duncan Davidson, son of my mother's lady-in-waiting and nephew of Bernard Norfolk, the Earl Marshal, was there to hold the coronets. I followed my uncle Gloucester, summoned by Garter.

My chief anxiety was that I would forget my lines. I had been given the impression that I had to remember them so I had learned them by heart. Of course, when the time came, the Bishop of Durham – Michael Ramsey, who would later preside at our wedding in York Minster – held up a card with the words on it so I had not needed to worry. I knelt down and read aloud: 'I, Edward, Duke of Kent, do become your liege man of life and limb, and of earthly worship; and faith and truth I will bear unto you, to live and die against all manner of folks. So help me God.'

It was quite daunting.

The whole service was pretty long and it was certainly very impressive. It got to the point where people were eating sandwiches out of their coronets. After my turn, I remember an elderly peer's robes, which would have probably been owned by his grandfather, virtually disintegrated when he got up to do his homage. That was Lord Mowbray, the senior baron, and Lord Hastings promptly fell over when he knelt down.

In the days that followed my mother took my sister and me to the Thanksgiving Service at St Paul's Cathedral. There was also a lunch at the Guildhall, we went to the Royal Tournament – and I became godfather to Henry Lascelles, son of my cousin, Gerald Lascelles.

Princess Marina had invited the children of her sisters to the Coronation and they sat in the Royal Gallery immediately above the Royal Box. Princess Alexandra and Prince Michael were in the Royal Box. I asked them for their recollections of the day.

The Duke doing homage to The Queen

Princess Alexandra: I don't remember it at all, which is rather odd, for something so stupendous. I remember my cousin Elizabeth had a very pretty pink dress from Dior, and mine was white with sequins, from Norman Hartnell. The Duchess of Norfolk played the part of the Queen at the rehearsal.

Prince Michael: I remember it vividly. I was at Sunningdale. The 'Coronaggers', everyone was calling it. And they would say, 'For prep next Wednesday we're going to be doing . . .' and I would say 'I'm sorry, I'll be at the Coronaggers rehearsal.'

I had been following the events to do with the climbing of Everest, and suddenly the door burst open and someone shouted, 'They've conquered Everest!' They'd actually done it a few days before and kept it back to make the announcement on the day before the Coronation.

127

I remember all the wonderful clothes we wore – shoes with buckles, kilts, not to mention the dark green velvet jacket – frightfully smart. Everyone else's clothes had been meticulously looked after and ended up in the London Museum, but all of mine disappeared. Nobody could find them.

I also remember the spectacle, and how glamorous the Queen was. I was only eleven, but she was stunning, and the whole thing was overwhelming. There was an element of magic, certainly for me.

We had these endless rehearsals. We had to walk down the aisle, but that was enough to prise me out of school. The joke was on me a few weeks later when we were all trooped down to a local cinema. I must have been a rather dim child, because halfway there I realised I was going to see myself, and so were all my mates, wearing fancy dress.

Helen Habsburg: My mother came to the Coronation, with my brother and me. I was still at school near Munich then and my brother went to Ettal Abbey. So we came over. We sat up in the gallery and could look down. We had a marvellous view from there. It was magic. Of course, being young, we didn't take in so much. I was amazed that a Queen could be so young – she looked so fragile. It was quite unbelievable. But we didn't recognise anybody, except the Queen of Tonga.

Princess Olga didn't come to the Coronation. Elizabeth came, and unlike our clothes, she had a lovely pink ball dress. Puppa Hessen* was there and they all came to lunch at Coppins. We started the day at Coppins. We couldn't all have stayed in London so we went to the Abbey very early. Princess Alexandra

* Puppa – Princess Dorothea of Hesse (b. 1934), daughter of Prince Christopher of Hesse-Cassel and Princess Sophia of Greece, therefore a niece of Prince Philip.

had a white dress with sequins on it, which I also admired. Later in the day we ran round the streets in the crowds and had a lot of fun.

Princess Elizabeth: It was a very long day, very cold and wet. We weren't really a part of it. And it was quite hard to see from so high up in the gallery.

Hans Veit Toerring: I was at a Benedictine school in Bavaria at that time, Ettal Abbey, rather like Ampleforth. On the day, we were at Coppins and the footman put out a morning coat. But it had to be white tie, so after a little bit of a fight, that was put out too. After a very early breakfast we left in two cars, my aunt with Mr Field, the chauffeur, a bit of a tyrant, in the Rolls-Royce and we in the second car, a Humber. On the main road, one of the plugs blew out, there was no one to help, and we could have spent the whole of the Coronation on the roadside, but our driver managed to put the plug back in again and slowly we got to London. We sat in the gallery above the Royal Box and had a fantastic view, looking down on it. Later there was a reception at the Palace and three yards away we saw Winston Churchill. I was introduced to him and shook hands with him. That was a great honour. Crown Prince Akihito of Japan was there and we had a long conversation. He made friends with Kraft zu Hohenlohe* and later went to stay with him at Langenburg.

When I was invited to this great event, my father had to write to Father Stefan at Ettal to ask if I could leave for a week. He gave as the reason: 'Coronation of a relative'.

* Prince Kraft zu Hohenlohe-Langenburg (1935–2004), son of Prince Gottfried and Princess Margarita of Greece, therefore a nephew of Prince Philip.

8

THE ARMY

In September 1953, the Duke enrolled for officer-cadet training at Sandhurst, in preparation for life as an army officer. In October he sat the Civil Service Commissioner's examination to enter the Royal Military Academy. He had already set his heart on joining the Royal Scots Greys. News of his chosen career provoked a leader in *The Times*:

> His decision to become a regular soldier has been until now a well-guarded secret . . . The Duke of Kent will carry with him to Sandhurst in September the nation's best wishes for his new career. During his visit to Malaya last year he showed a more than ordinary interest in armoured cars, motor-cycles, and machine guns . . . The Army will take the Duke of Kent as it finds him, and offer him – as it offers every young officer in the making – the opportunity of a man's life, friendship and service.[30]

The author and former soldier Allan Mallinson told me that in 1999, when he was chairing the selection boards for entry to Sandhurst, the Duke visited to mark the fiftieth anniversary of their move to Wiltshire after the war. The board kept an index card for every candidate who had ever attended, noting his, and later her, performance. Mallinson asked to see the Duke's from the 1950s. He was somewhat taken aback to

discover that in the psychometric tests, designed to assess a candidate's innate intelligence rather than educational attainment, and which were always conducted 'blind' – that is, without the marker knowing the candidate's identity – the Duke had scored exceptionally highly.

The Duke arrived at Sandhurst on 10 September, shortly before his eighteenth birthday. He passed the written exam and entered the Academy on 10 March 1954. The *Daily Mirror* announced: *'Royal Duke to join up as a private'*.

Duke: The Regular Commission Board tested one's ability to be an officer so I can only assume that the *Mirror*'s article was written before I'd done that so it wasn't certain that I was going to Sandhurst. I went straight to Sandhurst that September and it was the loneliest place on the planet, but in due course great fun.

The *Daily Mirror* told its readers that to the NCOs the Duke would be treated like any other soldier in respect of his quarters and his food. They suspected that after a month at Sandhurst, he would be 'more in awe of the sergeant major than of any general' and have 'a wholesome respect for him'. [31]

Duke: That is quite certain. Sergeant Major Lord* was the Academy sergeant major, which means he was the senior RSM, a very important figure in Sandhurst life. And this one was

* Sergeant Major John Lord (1908–68); a Grenadier Guard, and former policeman, he was later in the Parachute Regiment. He was captured at Arnhem in 1944 and sent to Stalag XIB at Fallingbostel. He served as RSM Sandhurst 1948–63. In the media, he was sometimes known as 'The Voice'. He also trained King Hussein of Jordan, who appeared on his *This Is Your Life* programme in 1959.

very influential. He was the first Academy sergeant major after the war. He'd been a prisoner of war, where he had taken control of all the prisoners and kept them going. He was a most impressive man. Certainly I felt I owed him a considerable debt because he gave me a lot of help as a young cadet, totally innocent and naïve, not knowing anything. He was most sympathetic and kind to me, although he could also be very tough.

John Lord was a legendary figure. He liked to quote the Duke of Wellington: 'The first duty of an officer is, and always has been, to train the men under his command that they without question beat any force opposed to them in the field.' He also quoted Napoleon, who said that the two levers for motivating men were interest and fear. He thought a bit of fear didn't do any harm, but the ultimate goal was self-discipline. He maintained that flexibility and cheerfulness were good qualities in a soldier. He quoted General Eisenhower too: 'The art of leadership is getting someone else to do something you want done because he wants to do it.'

I finished Le Rosey in the summer of '53 and started Sandhurst about six weeks later. That was quite a shock. I'd never had any military discipline before that. I was there for not quite two years. At the late school stage I was much more interested in flying, but I had never been any good at basic arithmetic. In order to qualify as a pilot in those days you needed a reasonable grasp of scientific subjects. I went to talk to Prince Philip about it, and he suggested the army.

At Sandhurst I won the Sir James Moncrieff Grierson Foreign Language Prize and passed the examination for French interpretership. I never had to use it and I wouldn't be a very good interpreter. I certainly wouldn't be able to do it now.

I was promoted to junior under officer on 5 February 1955.

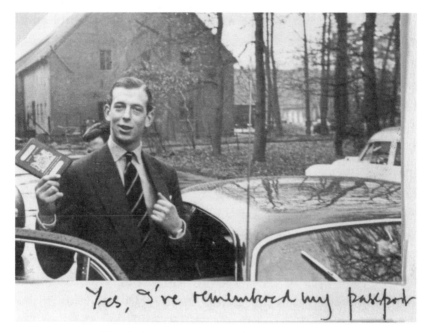

Yes, I've remembered my passport

The Duke on his way to go skiing in Munster.
On a previous trip he had forgotten his passport

It was reported that the Duke was keen to join the Greys, described as 'once high among the crack cavalry regiments and now fully mechanised'. Another cutting found him dancing to Edmundo Ros in a London nightclub, leaving at 4.15 a.m. and being on parade at seven. On 1 June a great number of the Royal Family, including the Duke, attended the marriage of Viscount Althorp to the Hon. Frances Roche in Westminster Abbey.

Charles Graves,* journalist brother of the poet Robert Graves, a man noted for his extensive coverage of society

* Charles Graves (1899–1971), brother of Robert Graves, dismissed by the poet's biographer as 'a journalist infamous for his vulgarity', Martin Seymour-Smith, *Robert Graves* (Hutchinson, 1982), p. 9, though better remembered in his obituaries.

antics, gave a sensible assessment of him at twenty-one, noting: 'The Duke dislikes publicity, but accepts it with a good deal of patience.' It sounds as though press intervention was already a feature of royal life, even in the 1950s. One newspaper had printed a photograph of him smiling at a debutante and looking with delight at a ring on her finger. The ring had been superimposed. It was suggested he might marry Princess Beatrix of the Netherlands, whom he had never even met. Graves recorded the Duke's admiration of the bands of Tommy Kinsman and his enjoyment of the revival of Fats Waller hits. Finally, the journalist Robert Pitman,* a household name in his day, was concerned by the vulgarity of the tabloid attacks, writing, 'It is the question of what position the young Duke really occupies in the State. Soon he comes of age. What future is planned for him? What public career is being prepared for this lively young man?'

Pitman examined the role of royal dukes over the past century. He dismissed the possibility of a royal duke being appointed commander-in-chief of the Army, like the be-whiskered old Duke of Cambridge, a grandson of George III. With some prescience, Pitman suggested a plan: 'Up and down the Empire, in industry and commerce, a thousand exciting opportunities are open to the Duke of Kent. Is there any reason why he should not seize them?'

Pitman quoted the 1952 Select Committee on royal income: 'There are several members of the Royal Family who, by virtue of their position near the Throne, are excluded from ordinary commercial activities and must, of necessity, devote their lives to public duties . . .' He felt that the Duke could

* Robert Pitman (1924–69), star columnist of the *Daily Express*.

pursue an independent career without tarnishing his name and, like Princess Marina, could be supported out of the £95,000 Supplementary Grant.[32]

One of the articles suggested he might become a mechanical engineer.

Duke: I certainly had the idea of studying engineering more closely. I think the army rather eclipsed that. It's an interest that's remained with me all my life.

Another suggested he might have been appointed Governor of Cyprus.

Duke: I was only about twenty-one. What a ridiculous idea!

On 3 August 1955 the Duke was appointed to the Royal Scots Greys by the War Office Commission Board. It formed part of the Royal Armoured Corps and had been abroad for seventeen years.

He joined the young officers' course at the Royal Armoured Corps, Bovington, and was there on an eleven-week course between 28 August and 12 November. At Bovington, mathematics were deemed as important as soldiering. He drove and maintained the very newest type of tank under the watchful eye of Troop Sergeant Major Mackenzie, Royal Scots Greys.

Duke: I then joined my regiment at Crookham, near Aldershot. We were placed in very scruffy old barracks, which had been built before the First World War and were most uncomfortable, then to Catterick in a rather similar camp. But we all rather enjoyed Catterick because it's such a lovely part of the world and

Marchpast at Catterick

a jolly society up there. I got to know my future wife there and many friends. For younger officers it was one big party – we hunted and shot. There wasn't a great deal of military life, even though we were training young national servicemen.

In June 1956 the Queen came to Edinburgh to present the regiment with a new guidon. My mother and sister were there too.

I had to preside over a court martial in December 1957. I had my green Aston Martin and arrived at the court in dress uniform. The case in question involved a twenty-five-year-old trooper, accused of being absent without leave from May to November. He had been living with a Dutch woman who was waiting for her divorce. She threatened to gas herself if he left. Eventually he took his chance and returned to his unit. The court decided he should be detained for six months. Court martials were a regular duty for army officers.

Then we moved about, to Germany and Hong Kong. I went to some interesting places but I didn't see action of any kind. I was in a tank regiment, so we went to more static places, like Hong Kong and later Cyprus, but mostly Germany.

9

RECREATION

The Duke's approach to life has always been dutiful, but as his daughter, Helen, pointed out he was also able to enjoy his early life, especially when he was a junior officer.

Lady Helen Taylor: He had those early years when he could have fun, with his fast cars, and when he was in the army, so he was able to indulge in some youthful wildness. Apparently he was known as 'Fast Eddie'. It's just his greatest joy, peering under the bonnet of a car, and inhaling the fumes. He has remained a devoted petrol head to this day.

This was supported by other members of the family.

Earl of St Andrews: He's always loved going to Silverstone and Goodwood – a big part of his life.

Prince Michael: My brother always liked motor-cars – we shared that. We used to go down to Goodwood on Easter Monday – a big motor-race there with Freddy Richmond, who was the present Duke of Richmond's grandfather. He was a dear man, who was quite into motor-racing, and used to drive MGs at Brooklands before the war.

In the 1950s the Duke attracted a lot of press attention on account of his car crashes. Most of these took place while he

was at Sandhurst. It must have been especially worrying for Princess Marina, considering that her nephew, Prince Nicky of Yugoslavia, son of Princess Olga, had died in a car accident.

In July 1954 the journalist Geoffrey Wakeford (later a biographer of Princess Marina) suggested that the nineteen-year-old Duke might not be allowed to drive except when accompanied by an experienced driver. The second crash was kept secret at first, but was exposed in the *Daily Mail*. It was said that the Duke of Edinburgh had ticked him off about the first. This time apparently the Queen asked for an explanation. He was returning from a party in a large garden in Pelham Street given for Elizabeth Gage, and had been driving normally at 5 a.m. The next thing he was picking himself out of the wreckage of his Sunbeam.

Vincent Mulchrone, a former RAF pilot, then with the *Daily Mail* from 1950, left an exaggerated report – the Duke was swathed in bandages, the accident happened at Pinetree Hill, the blue saloon Sunbeam took four feet of bark off a tree, then plunged into a roadside ditch, eight feet deep, mounted the other side, struck some concrete and the Duke emerged with his face bleeding. A workman said he was lucky to escape with his life. On 21 July a leader addressed the issue: 'It is really for the young man to ask whether his exploits at the wheel are not inflicting needless worry on his mother, on the other members of the Royal Family, and on the public.'

The *Sunday Express* said: 'Would it be better if this young man paid more attention to his studies and gave less time to nightclubs and dances? He appears to have far more leave than his brother cadets.' This was contradicted by Kenneth Rose, who checked and found that cadets were free from 12.15 Saturday till 10 p.m. on Sunday, though expected at

church parade one Sunday a month. Special leave could be granted till 7.20 a.m. parade twice a week.

The outpourings of the press passed the Duke by, but not all the attention was from the tabloids, even if it was speculative. Marshall Pugh pointed out inaccuracies in a raft of accounts, what he called 'a wilderness of waffle'. As the Suez crisis loomed, it had been suggested that the Duke had been partying in Dublin, when in fact he was in Catterick, that he had become an arbiter of fashion by wearing Glen Urquhart check trousers with his morning coat at the wedding of the Marquess of Hertford (following his father's example), and that the accounts of the car accident were likewise exaggerated. He concluded that the Duke 'may be accident prone. He is certainly publicity-prone.'

The Duke's first accident occurred a few weeks later on 20 June. He had taken possession of his first car, a Hillman shooting brake, which collided with another vehicle at Sunningdale, when he was driving towards London at ten forty-five. He lost consciousness and sustained head injuries. He had been flung half out of his vehicle, his legs remaining in the car while his head and shoulders were under one side of the other vehicle. He was taken to hospital in Chertsey, then transferred to the National Hospital for Nervous Diseases in Bloomsbury.

He was discharged from hospital on 30 June, and convalesced for some days. He was back on parade at Sandhurst when Field Marshal Lord Montgomery took the salute. His mother and sister were there for the occasion.

In October he was present when Emperor Haile Selassie of Ethiopia took the salute at a ceremonial parade at Sandhurst as part of his state visit to Britain. In November the Duke of Gloucester unveiled the west window in honour of King

George VI, in Sandhurst's Memorial Chapel, and the Duke of Kent read the lesson.

He had a second car accident on 26 November 1954 when he hit a tree trunk that had blown down across the road, suffering no injury and being on parade the next day. All the Kents were at Sandringham for Christmas that year, the Duke shooting with Prince Philip and the Duke of Gloucester.

There was a third accident on 15 July 1955 in which he suffered superficial abrasions near Camberley early in the morning. He was not seriously hurt. While he was in hospital at Sandhurst, he took a French test and came out top.

The accidents provoked a lot of press coverage.

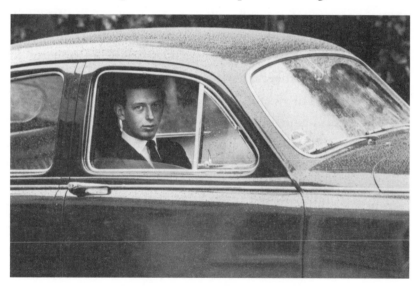

The Duke at the wheel of his Jaguar

Duke: At least two if not three happened when I was at Sandhurst. I don't remember the first accident, but I do remember waking up in Chertsey Hospital. That was probably the worst one. I think I hit my head rather hard, went to a hospital in London and spent ten days there.

Later I had a new Sunbeam Talbot, which in those days was made by the Rootes Group. It was a very nice medium-sized saloon. By today's standards it was not very fast but it was all right. I was about to leave Sandhurst, and it was a week or two before Sovereign's Parade, the big day when you finish. I probably fell asleep because I was at a party in London the night before, which I probably wasn't meant to be at, but people did go to parties. I put my car into a ditch. I wasn't hurt, just cut by broken glass. I thought I had to be patched up for Sovereign's Parade so that I would be presentable. It was all right. I survived.

Prince Michael: My brother had a number of hideous car accidents. After one of them, I remember being collected by our third chauffeur, whose name was Mr Rawlings, in a family van. 'There's been a terrible crash on the level crossing you know.' He suddenly pulled in and said, 'Good God,' and called the police. My brother had fallen asleep and wound up with his head six inches from the wheels of another car. My mama didn't really know the details, though she knew there had been an accident and that he was all right.

The Duke left hospital on Saturday, 23 July, was back on parade on the Monday, and one of six hundred cadets at the passing-out parade, where the salute was taken by the Duke of Edinburgh the following Thursday. Princess Marina was on the platform and Princess Alexandra and Prince Michael were watching. Prince Philip spoke: 'Your most important and most difficult job when you leave here will be to lead men. Your next job will be to understand and to learn how to use your technical equipment. This may not be so rewarding as the leadership of men, but unless you can thoroughly master

the machines as well as thoroughly understand the men, you will never be properly equipped to exercise executive military command in any sphere . . . As you grow older, try not to be afraid of new ideas. New or original ideas can be bad as well as good; but whereas an intelligent man with an open mind can demolish a bad idea by reasoned argument, those who allow their brains to atrophy resort to meaningless catch-phrases, derision and anger in the face of anything new.'

The sword (the top award for the year) went to Senior Under Officer S. T. G. Morgan, and the Queen's Medal to C. W. Beckett. The adjutant, Major A. B. Mainwaring-Burton, rode behind as the senior division marched up the steps of the grand entrance. On the morning of the passing-out parade, David Wynne-Morgan (who went on to a more respected career in public relations) extracted what he described as an 'exclusive' interview, in which the Duke explained he would not be driving for three or four or months as he no longer had a car.

Duke: My father had a succession of Rolls-Royces and my mother was left one after he died. A deal was done and Rolls produced a splendid car for my mother, which continued in service till long after she died. We used it for years. We must have finally sold it around 1990. Heaven knows where it finished up. We just used it for big formal occasions. We didn't go shopping in it.

I've always been a car enthusiast. I had a succession of Jaguars and I still have one.

During the mid-1950s the press and gossip columns also focused on parties, of which there were a great number. A typical article of the time appeared in November 1955, Peter

Dacre writing: 'The Duke will find romance lurking at every discreetly shaded nightclub table and every theatre twosome. It is bound to happen to any young man in his position. It is even more certain with the Duke, who has already shown himself to have all the normal interests of a good-looking young man.'

Duke: There weren't that many other young people in the family to write about, so I was picked on. Now unfortunately there are many more.

There was a considerable social life and I went to a good many of gatherings. There was a famous one at Wilton given for Diana Herbert, the house floodlit and dancing in the Double Cube Room. I went from Sandhurst. Actually people were very kind. We did manage to escape to London a few times.

The Duke and Princess Alexandra with members of
European royal families, at a party in Sweden, given
by the King for his granddaughters in 1960

The society pages recorded numerous parties in June 1955, notably one given by the Glenconners for Emma Tennant,

and by Lady Dawson of Penn for her granddaughter, Polly Eccles, and for Charlotte Bowater.

The Duke went to Northern Ireland for the coming of age of James, Marquess of Hamilton (now Duke of Abercorn). He spent two weeks in Nice, and at the Villa Bienvenghue on Cap Camarat near St Tropez, owned by a Belgian industrialist. In the party were Fionn O'Neill, Tatiana Orloff, niece of Lord Howard de Walden, and Theresa Crossley.

The Duke stayed at Balmoral in September 1956 and a month later celebrated his twenty-first birthday with a dance for 140 at Coppins, including the Queen and Prince Philip, the Gloucesters, Princess Olga and her daughter Elizabeth. For this the Duke was given a week's leave. His birthday provoked a lot of discussion in the press, including the report that some journalists succeeded in infiltrating the party and had to be turned out.

As the gossip columnists kept singling out girls, most of whom married soon afterwards, other journalists and commentators considered his future. With his majority he had acquired the right to take his seat in the House of Lords, and become the owner of Coppins. There were numerous accounts of the birthday party. True or false, the journalists maintained that he took to the dance floor with the Duchess of Kent, although she had sprained her ankle playing tennis (another account has her in a wheelchair), then with the Queen, and his aunt, the Duchess of Gloucester. Apparently, in advance of the party, 'he was laughing all day' while Princess Alexandra and their cousin Princess Elizabeth of Yugoslavia turned cartwheels on the lawn.'

In 1956 Princess Marina took over a new apartment at Kensington Palace, which was to be her home for the next twelve years. Her mother, Princess Nicholas, died on

14 March 1957 and Princess Marina took her three children to Athens for the funeral. The Duke and Crown Prince Constantine stood guard over the coffin, which was covered with the Royal Standard of Greece and the Imperial Eagle of Russia.

In 1956 and again in 1957 the Duke was named as one of the six Counsellors of State during the Queen's absence abroad, first in Denmark and then in Canada. He did not have to act as such, there being six appointed, but only a tandem of two undertaking the duties. In July the Queen and Prince Philip visited his regiment at Catterick and he was on hand to escort them. The Duke of Buccleuch gave a hunt ball at Bowhill; Princess Alexandra had her twenty-first birthday party at Kensington Palace; the Duke was given the Freedom of the Clothworkers Company, and attended a performance of *My Fair Lady* with Princess Marina and Princess Alexandra.

In 1958 he opened a race meeting in Berwickshire, driving a D-Type Jaguar at 100 m.p.h. round the circuit at Charterhall.

Duke: Charterhall belonged to a regimental colleague called Alex Trotter and he used to allow racing there several times in the year. I went there for a race meeting and met this character who had a Jaguar D-Type. The car was driven by Jim Clark, who later became a very famous British driver, some would say the finest of all, alongside Stirling Moss. He won more Grand Prix races, some twenty-five, than any other driver at that time. Sadly he was killed, aged thirty-two, taking part in a Formula Two race in Germany in 1968.

I remember driving that D-Type. The idea of being allowed to drive it unsupervised, unaccompanied, is simply inconceivable now. Luckily I managed to get it home without crashing it.

In May the Duke watched the Dutch Grand Prix in the Netherlands. He acquired a 3.8-litre Jaguar on his return from Düsseldorf.

Skiing vied with driving in those years. In January 1959 he came seventh in the downhill championships in the German Alps. In 1960 he came fifth in the skiing slalom in Austria in February, and on 1 April was promoted to temporary captain. In January 1961 the Duke took part in more skiing competitions, this time in St Moritz.

Duke: I was a keen skier. When we were based in Germany we used to try to get as many people to come and ski as possible. We had wonderful parties. St Moritz was a lovely place but I have not been there for many years. And the race meeting, we can call it that, was a big event for us.

My mother and sister came out to see me. I don't think our team ever achieved any distinguished results but it was a lot of fun. I did break a bone in my foot, which was all too easy to do with the equipment of those days. We had what were called 'safety bindings', but they weren't very reliable. Even with them you could injure yourself. I think many people did – there were a lot of damaged knees. That was quite a common occurrence, especially if we were racing. Then the skis were heavy and long. Nowadays they're much shorter and easier to move on.

I never did the bobsleigh professionally. I once travelled, with a passenger, down one of the bobsleigh runs in St Moritz but it wasn't racing. I did it just to see what it was like. I was quite determined never to race. I left that to my brother. He was quite an expert – he was in the team that competed in the World Bobsleigh Championships in Italy in 1971. He had quite a bad accident. He was at the controls and crashed at 65 m.p.h. He had a badly fractured jaw and bruised his left elbow. He was

practising for an international competition in Japan. Next year he was official non-travelling reserve in the 1972 Winter Olympics out there. He was very keen on his bobbing – even more so than skiing. They used to have terrific accidents: there were four of them sitting in this very small space, going very fast down a solid ice track. If you went off the track, goodness knows what happened.

I did the Cresta once or twice. I never did it from the top because a novice was made to start halfway down from what was called 'Junction'. It was only when you had done Junction a couple of times at a reasonable speed that you were considered safe to go from the top. It would have been great fun, I think. It was very difficult to combine skiing and Cresta because the Cresta took up a lot of time. One sat and waited around for one's turn, which I thought could be better spent skiing. I'm glad I tried it, though.

In January 1962, the Duke took part in the Commonwealth Winter Games in St Moritz, having practised hard at Ehrwald, in Austria. He was scratched from the men's slalom ski event, because the course was badly cut up. Then in 1964 the Duke was on crutches after a ski fall in St Moritz, though no bones were broken. He had sprained his left ankle and torn two ligaments.

Although the press continued to link his name with many young ladies, he had by now met Katharine Worsley, bringing her to stay at Coppins for the first time in May 1957.

When I was working on this book, I went to see the Duchess of Kent at their home, Wren House, Kensington Palace. She said to me: 'I just wondered if there was anything I could particularly remind you of that you wouldn't have known I'd gone to with him, or something like that. I slightly barged in.

I didn't mean to.' On the contrary, it was good to have her take on a number of subjects. The Duchess told me: 'I remember going to dinner the first time ever, and there were such interesting people – comics. Princess Marina loved funny people. Danny Kaye was there, and I remember being astounded. What have I walked into? She did a lot of entertaining.'

Katharine Worsley began to appear in press photos with the Duke, notably at Silverstone in 1958.

Duke: We actually met at Blenheim Palace, of all places, at the Heythrop Hunt Ball. I had keen hunting brother officers in the Greys, several of whom lived in that part of the world, around Blenheim, hunting with the Heythrop. I wasn't a hunting person at all. Anyway, I went to the ball, which was a great stroke of luck for me. It's quite a place to have a party.

The Duchess of Kent: I was a guest of Robin Fleming* at the ball. At home in Yorkshire I certainly did go hunting.

Duke: We could meet in Yorkshire, but Catterick Camp wasn't that close to Hovingham, Katharine's family home. It was forty-odd miles away, over Sutton Bank, which is quite a ridge. I did pay a few visits.

* Robin Fleming (1932–2020), merchant banker with Robert Fleming & Co. He then lived at Barton Abbey, Oxfordshire, and was serving in the Royal Scots Greys.

10

EARLY ROYAL DUTIES

Royal duties impinged on the Duke's life with increasing regularity. He was again appointed a Counsellor of State but excused from any service as he was abroad. On 9 December 1959 he took his seat in the House of Lords. His service in Germany was interrupted when he came home for Princess Margaret's wedding to Antony Armstrong-Jones at Westminster Abbey on 6 May 1960, returning to Düsseldorf three days later.

Duke: My cousin Margaret married Tony Armstrong-Jones in Westminster Abbey. The marriage was conducted by Geoffrey Fisher, who was still archbishop until the following year. It was the last occasion when the royal ladies wore long dresses to the floor, with hats. We all wore morning dress, except Dickie Mountbatten, who appeared as an admiral in full dress uniform. He could never resist dressing up. I sat just behind the Queen between my mother and sister. Lots of Commonwealth prime ministers were present as it coincided with a Commonwealth Conference. Margaret and Tony left rather dramatically in the royal barge from Tower Pier and sailed away on their honeymoon in HMY *Britannia*.

Sometimes he was needed in his own right, in particular for two state visits in 1960. It is traditional that the Queen should receive a state visit from a European monarch, usually in London, then pay a return visit. If there is a change in

monarch, the process is repeated. Sometimes there is a political reason for a second such visit. Presidents also make state visits, but usually for a defined purpose, and certainly not whenever there is a new one. The format is invariably designed to a formula: the arrival, when the visitor is met by a member of the Royal Family at an airport or port, then escorted to London to meet the Queen and other members of the Royal Family. There are two state banquets, one given by the Queen and a return banquet given by the state visitor. A wreath is laid on the tomb of the unknown warrior in Westminster Abbey and very often the state visitor goes to some part of Britain that especially interests them.

Duke: State visits in those days were rather more complicated. Now the visiting heads of state just arrive and disappear to their embassy. They arrive for the official greeting on Horse Guards. But at that time it all started at one of the airports, then Victoria station. There was a lot of hand-shaking, then the Palace, state banquet, and everything else. It was quite a drawn-out and elaborate business.

There were several state visits to Britain each year and each one lasted for several days. The Royal Family attend both the banquets.

I had been with my regiment in Germany for nearly two years when I was suddenly called back. 'You have to come home immediately.' It was to do with the state visit of King Bhumibol of Thailand: my uncle, the Duke of Gloucester, had had to pull out. He had slipped a disc at Barnwell and been ordered to rest so he cancelled all of his engagements. I was on exercise: one minute I was in a tank, then at home.

My sister went to the airport to greet King Bhumibol, as she had met him in Thailand earlier in the year. I waited at Victoria

station with the Queen and Prince Philip, the Duchess of
Gloucester, the Princess Royal and my mother to meet the King
and Queen of Thailand there. In those days the arrival was
filmed live on television. The police also used cameras for the
first time to monitor crowds and traffic during the entire visit. I
went to the state banquet that evening, and the next evening we
went to the King's dinner at the Royal Thai Embassy. As I was in
England I also went to a Palace garden party before flying back
to Germany.

The King of Thailand was a charming man and a keen musi-
cian. He was a jazz saxophone player and a composer. He played
with people like Benny Goodman. My mother loved that and
after the formal state visit was over, she threw a party for him – a
dinner and dance – to which the Queen and Prince Philip came.

In October I was called back again for the state visit of King
Mahendra of Nepal. He and his late father had been prisoners of
the antique Rana oligarchy until 1950, when the old regime had
been overthrown. He had been King since 1955 and had
achieved a lot in bringing to Nepal some enlightened and pros-
perous order. It was said that he wanted to make Nepal the
Switzerland of Asia, neutral and on good terms with its neigh-
bouring countries. To the British, Nepal meant Gurkhas and
Sherpas, and there was a strong Gurkha element in the state
visit. Lord Slim,* a heroic figure, and one of the outstanding
military figures from the Second World War, was present at the
airport, and later in the visit there was a Gurkha review in the
gardens of Buckingham Palace. In her speech at the state
banquet the Queen referred to the eve of her Coronation and the

* Field Marshal Viscount Slim (1891–1970). He led the 14th Army to victory in
the Burma campaign in the Second World War, and was later President of the
Burma Star Association.

thrill of hearing how it had been a Nepalese and one of her
Commonwealth citizens who had reached the summit of Everest
together – Sherpa Tenzing and Edmund Hillary.

The King had shown great independence of spirit growing up
and, among much else, had rejected the custom of having two
wives – it was said to give the succession a double chance. He
had elected to be monogamous. During his five years on the
throne, he had travelled more widely through his country than
any of his predecessors. It was an interesting balance. He was a
progressive-conservative monarch, quite prepared for his powers
to be eroded as representative government was established.

That was the man I was sent to meet at the airport. It was
extraordinary to think that there was no one else to do it. The
first time, it was daunting, but little by little that kind of engage-
ment began to build up. The Crown Prince, who was studying
in Britain, came with me. There was a bad fog and all the planes
were stacked up, unable to land. When the King and Queen
arrived, I had to present to them the suite who would be with
them for the visit. I then accompanied them to Victoria station,
fog delaying the train by forty-five minutes. The whole Royal
Family were there, including the Duke and Duchess of
Gloucester, my mother and sister. I was then in the carriage
procession with the Duke of Beaufort to the Palace. There was a
state banquet and the next day I went with the King to the
Guildhall. There, he told the assembled dignitaries that the
Queen and Prince Philip were coming on a state visit the follow-
ing year. Charmingly he said, 'You may come along too, as many
of you as possible, whenever you can, and see our land for your-
selves. We will try to make you feel as much at home as you
have made my wife and myself feel over here.' He gave me the
Order of Tri Shakti Patta, first class with chain. The visit also
included a performance at the Royal Opera House.

King Mahendra of Nepal with the Queen at Covent Garden during his 1960 state visit. The Duke and Princess Marina are in the second row

A few days later a Heron of the Queen's Flight took me back to my regiment in Germany, while the King and Queen of Nepal stayed on for a fortnight to visit places like Oxford and the Highlands. They clearly enjoyed their visit enormously.

Their later history was sad. King Mahendra died of a massive heart attack in 1972 at the age of fifty-one. Crown Prince Birendra took over but died tragically in 2001 when his son shot him and eight other members of the Nepalese Royal Family, including Princess Shanti whom I had met on the state visit. It was a horrific massacre. Queen Ratna survives in her nineties.

The Duke came home for Christmas. He and Princess Alexandra were both given the Grand Cross of the Royal Victorian Order on Christmas Day. Queen Victoria founded the order in 1896 to recognise personal service to the Sovereign. Princess Alexandra had already undertaken several royal tours, and it was given to the Duke partly so that he could wear it when he undertook the important role of representing the Queen at independence ceremonies.

In those days the Grand Cross was usually given to members of the Royal Family. More recently, the Queen started her sons, Prince Andrew and Prince Edward, as CVOs; they rose gradually to KCVO, and finally to GCVO. Prince Michael of Kent was made KCVO in 1992 and GCVO in 2003. The Duchess of Kent was appointed GCVO at the time of the Silver Jubilee in 1977.

The Duke and Princess Alexandra are now the senior GCVOs in order of appointment.

In 1958 the Duke had undergone a strenuous six-week riding course at Aldershot, and then, on 14 October, he left with his regiment to be stationed in Germany, travelling out by car. After that, the Duke returned to Britain where he took up a desk job at the War Office.

Duke: I took up a new post on 13 February 1961, as GSO 3 Chief of the Imperial General staff. On my first day I was met at the War Office by Lieutenant Colonel J. M. Brockbank. My boss was Sir Francis Festing, a great character. He was the CIGS as he was called in those days – 'Imperial' was still there. I worked in his office as a very junior staff officer for about a year, or just over. I went a couple of times on visits, but mostly I sat in his office reading correspondence. Voluminous papers came in.

Although there were already two highly qualified staff officers sitting there, occasionally they'd pass bits to me, and say, 'Would you like to look at this and work out an answer?' It was a completely new experience. I started there in 1961, so it was only a month or two before the independence ceremony in Sierra Leone, and I think Dickie Mountbatten, needless to say, had had something to do with it. 'I suppose you ought to do a staff job, old boy!' and I said I thought that might be rather fun so he fixed it up. I think he may have rung up Frankie Festing himself and said, 'Take the boy on.'

He was a great schemer, Lord Mountbatten. I didn't really know him until after I'd married. And then he used to invite us down to Broadlands. He was very kind to us both. There was no scheming where we were concerned. We had passed that stage.

Francis Festing was a tremendous sword man and from time to time he would discover, on his way to the War Office, that there was a sale on. We would get a message: 'The chief will be in a bit late today. He's popping into Sotheby's to look at some swords.' He had a very distinguished war record and there were three sons. Matthew, who died recently, became head of the Order of Malta. Andrew was a very good portrait painter. He painted a group picture for Buck's Club in which I appear, and then he did my portrait, more than once in fact. He painted the Queen once too.

Not long after starting this post, I was off to Sierra Leone with the Instruments of Independence. This was a relatively new phenomenon. In the 1950s, there was a great appetite for independence, with Harold Macmillan talking about 'the wind of change . . . blowing through' the African continent in 1960. A number of countries had been granted independence from the Crown over the years, mostly notably when Dickie Mountbatten

handed over India in 1947. It was more than understandable that countries wanted to govern themselves.

It became a tradition that the Queen would send a member of her family to the country in question to preside over the transfer.

As early as August 1960 the question of who should go to Sierra Leone was being discussed at the Colonial Office. It was the Queen's choice as to who should represent her, but recommendations could be made. Having observed Nigeria, Sir Maurice Dorman, the Governor, apparently thought Sierra Leone would like Princess Alexandra, but the Queen decided to send me. As the plans were put in place, the political situation declined in Sierra Leone, and there was some question as to whether or not I should go. A message from the Queen was devised before the visit, but it was held over for the time being:

I have it in command from The Queen to read to you the following message from Her Majesty to Her people of Sierra Leone:

'I have entrusted to my cousin the duty of acting as my representative at the celebrations of the independence of your country.

My husband and I are looking forward with pleasure to our own visit to you later this year but today our thoughts are with you. It is with special pleasure that I welcome you to our Commonwealth family of Nations.

You step forward into the councils of the World at a time of rapid change but I know that Sierra Leone, grounded firmly in her own traditions, will play a worthy part there.

I send you my own good wishes and pray that God may bless and guide you throughout the coming years.'

This was my first visit to Africa. What an experience it would be. I had just got engaged to Katharine Worsley in March 1961, and Sierra Leone was in April, so I had to leave her to do that. Luckily Philip Hay came with me. Before I left I had a meeting with Iain Macleod, while Duncan Sandys and Lord Perth* came on the trip.

I was flown the three thousand miles in a Heron of the Queen's Flight, stopping in Bordeaux, spending a night in Gibraltar and one in Dakar. There had been some political trouble before I arrived in Freetown on 24 April. Eighteen leaders of the All Peoples' Party, then the opposition, were arrested for trying to call a general strike. They wanted a parliamentary general election before independence. They were accused of trying to obtain explosives and of sabotaging the lighting at key places where the ceremonies were to take place. On 21 April there were explosions at two power stations in Freetown.

The great thing about this independence was that it had come about by what the Mayor of Freetown called 'the British trad-ition of evolutionary constitutional development' and not as a result of bloodshed or revolution. I thanked him for his welcome and, in particular, for including Katharine's name in his address and for presenting me with a golden key. In my speech I pointed out: 'As a small settlement, Freetown was given its name nearly 170 years ago; this week that name acquires fresh signifi-cance, as the capital of a newly independent and sovereign country.' They were pleased that I said I would tell the Queen all about it when I got home.

* Iain Macleod (1913–70), then Secretary of State for the Colonies; Duncan Sandys (1908–87), then Secretary of State for Commonwealth Affairs; and the Earl of Perth (1907–2002), then Minister of State for Colonial Affairs.

Everything was based on British practice. At the Sierra Leone parliament there was a ceremonial handing over of the state papers and a Sierra Leonian was dressed in the Speaker's role.

I was a junior captain in the Scots Greys, and it was very hot and sticky, but I had to wear a uniform, which included a sword and spurs, for most of the ceremonial events – hardly ideal in that climate. The contrast between all of that formality and the reality of Sierra Leone was considerable. It was a very poor and deprived country. There were no hostilities going on at that time but the chief means of survival was diamonds, which were in the hands of about one big corporation. When you walked down the main streets, some of the people were naked because they had no clothes at all.

But they were lovely people and the Governor was a very nice man called Maurice Dorman. He and his family couldn't have been kinder to me. They had a very large and grand Government House. They had taken on many locals as gardeners and odd job men to create local employment. I felt lucky enough to be asked to officiate at the independence ceremony, presumably because nobody else was available.

On Independence Day I was finally able to deliver the Queen's message, and to welcome Sierra Leone into the Commonwealth.

On the day of the Duke's arrival, Sir Maurice Dorman, the Governor, reported home:

His Royal Highness received a very warm welcome in Freetown today. There were cheering crowds lining the whole route and he obviously made a most happy impression upon all the people. His visit could not possibly have got off to a better start. At the civic welcome he spoke very well and the crowds outside the pavilion listened

attentively and appreciatively ... We had two more
bangs on Saturday night: small charges of gelignite were
dropped into drainpipes on a bridge. They did no damage
of any kind at all ... The incompetence and foolishness
of these men is to be seen to be believed ...[33]

Two days later Sir Maurice again reported: 'His Royal
Highness has continued to create good impressions and to
meet and make friends with many Sierra Leoneans. He is
particularly good on a public platform, and his speeches have
gone down well. He was very good at State Banquet.'[34]

On that day, the Duke was swimming in the pool at
Government House when a group of APC supporters gath-
ered on Queen Elizabeth Playing Fields near Government
House and announced that independence would not happen
unless the Duke addressed them. The rumour spread that the
Duke would speak to them, and crowds gathered, many
people drunk, and police reinforcements were brought in.
The Deputy Commissioner of Police finally told them that
the Duke was not involved with politics, that independence
would go ahead regardless, and that their meeting was illegal.
He said he would turn a blind eye if they dispersed, which
they did.

Another feature of the visit was the presence of the
Archbishop of York. He was there in connection with Fourah
Bay College, the first Western-style university in West Africa,
which had long been affiliated to the University of Durham in
Britain. The Duke was made an honorary Doctor of Civil
Law at the college.

Duke: Archbishop Ramsey was a wonderful figure, with big
peaking eyebrows. He came along. He was to marry Katharine

and me in York, about six weeks later. People were fascinated that he was the same age as the film star Cary Grant. They belonged to such different worlds.

The Duke invited the Dormans to his wedding in June and they came over specially, as did Sir Milton Margai, the Prime Minister of Sierra Leone.

Duke: On my return there was a City of London lunch welcoming me as a citizen and member of the Clothworkers' Livery Company, but really to mark my visit to Sierra Leone, and my engagement. The Lord Mayor, Sir Bernard Waley-Cohen, made a big thing about it, stressing that I was a new recruit as a 'deputy Sovereign'. I found it terrifying and I had to make a speech – I think it was largely written for me.

He also greeted my fiancée, referring to her as my 'fair lady'. He added a further light Shakespearian touch: 'Our thoughts will be with you on 8 June, when all that may be left of a winter's discontent is made glorious summer by this daughter of York.'

11

THE WEDDING

Cecil Beaton's snapped portrait of the bride

The Duke's engagement to Katharine Worsley had been announced on 8 March 1961, shortly before he went out to Sierra Leone, and the wedding set for 8 June. This had to be approved by the Queen, to comply with the Royal Marriages Act of 1772, instituted by King George III to ensure that none of his immediate family married people of whom he disapproved. All of the Commonwealth prime ministers were informed of the forthcoming wedding.

Duke: I wonder if they would be now.

162

Needless to say, the press went into overdrive, detailing the progress of the romance, and coming up with recondite facts, such as that the bride descended from Oliver Cromwell. Genealogists could only trace relationship between bride and groom by mutual descent from Edward I, the Duke descending in over twenty generations from the King's marriage to Eleanor of Castile and Katharine Worsley from the King's marriage to Margaret of France (through Earls of Kent, Fairfaxes and others). Oliver Cromwell's daughter, Frances, married Sir John Russell. Their daughter Elizabeth married Sir Thomas Frankland and their daughter, Mary, married Thomas Worsley, of Hovingham. The bride's maternal grandfather, John Brunner, was a partner of Ludwig Mond, who together founded Brunner Mond, the chemical firm that became ICI. Sir William Worsley, the bride's father, was a keen cricketer and Lord Lieutenant of the North Riding of Yorkshire. He had been county captain for Yorkshire for two years in the 1920s and was later president of the MCC.

It was the first time there had been a royal wedding in York Minster for 633 years. The previous one was in 1328 when Edward III married Philippa, daughter of the Count of Hainault. It was said from Bishopthorpe Palace, the Archbishop's residence in York, that the decision to solemnise the marriage in York Minster was 'not altogether a surprise' but 'magnificent news'. It was suggested that the service would be from the 1928 prayer book, which did not oblige the bride to promise to obey.

Duke: Three days later the Queen and Prince Philip gave a dinner party for us at Windsor Castle. My mother and Alexandra were there. Michael came over from Sandhurst. Also there were

King Paul and Queen Frederika of the Hellenes, and their daughters, Sophie and Irene.

During the next days I attended a dinner for Commonwealth prime ministers, and went up to Hovingham for a weekend.

The press announced that John Cavanagh would design Katharine's wedding dress, with Bellville Sassoon doing the bridesmaids' dresses. Schoolchildren in the North Riding would be given a holiday on the wedding day.

Crowds gathered in the small hours of the night and could be seen cooking sausages on rudimentary devices for breakfast and playing cards to while away the hours.

On the day, the royal train arrived at 1.45 p.m. to be greeted by Lord Scarbrough in his role as Lord Lieutenant of the City of York. The royal guests left the train in stages, first the members of the Royal Family, then foreign royal guests. The Queen Mother arrived at York Minster at 2.15 p.m. with Queen Victoria Eugenie of Spain, who had entertained the Duke so often during his Le Rosey days. Finally, to deafening cheers, the Queen, Prince Philip (in uniform) and Prince Charles arrived at 2.25 p.m. The Duke and Prince Michael came from Nawton Tower, one of the homes of the Earl of Feversham, where they had been staying, as had Princess Marina. Princess Anne was the chief bridesmaid. The wedding began at 2.30.

The bride entered to 'O Praise Ye the Lord . . .' and they left the Minster with their famous organist, Francis Jackson, playing Widor's Wedding March, which became popular at many weddings, the Grand Choeur Dialogue by Eugène Gigout, and Bach's Prelude and Fugue in E Flat.

Duke: Archbishop Ramsey was already on the way out as Archbishop of York. He'd been appointed to Canterbury, and our wedding was almost the last thing he did before leaving York. We loved him and he gave a rather splendid address. Of course, the decision to get married in the Minster caused, as you can imagine, quite an upheaval, and the Lord Chamberlain's Office was not best pleased. It was a big affair – the Minster was filled to capacity, which I suppose was fifteen hundred people. Then quite a few were invited to Katharine's home at Hovingham, which meant travelling across Yorkshire, twenty miles to the reception. It was a lovely day, which I still remember vividly.

The ceremony was televised. This had greatly disturbed the dean, Dr Eric Milner-White, but he was put firmly in his place by the Archbishop. On the day, there were twenty cameras in operation, six within the Minster. The BBC were televising the arrivals, the ceremony, and even the going away from Hovingham, so much of the day was given to coverage of the wedding.

The BBC and a division of Rank Precision Industries in Leicester had developed a new zoom lens that could bring an object twenty times nearer the viewer. It was all very advanced for the time. An optical lens was positioned inside the camera side by side with the image orthicon pick-up tube and associated electronic equipment, and mirrors were used to fold the path of light from behind the lens. Richard Dimbleby did the commentary. By now he was most proficient, much better than he had been at the Coronation. The event was even shown live in France, Holland and Belgium.

I wore full dress uniform, which no one wore at that date but the regiment had some in store. I had to borrow one. Michael was my best man. He was then an officer cadet at

Sandhurst. King Juan Carlos and Sophie* met at that wedding.

I asked the Duchess if the wedding had been a daunting experience.

The Duchess of Kent: I loved my father very much indeed. We went together obviously. I don't remember fear. Archbishop Ramsey was a wonderful figure in every sense. I knew him well.

Duke: It was a large affair. It was incredibly exciting to have it there.

Prince Michael: I remember when my brother and Katharine came away from the altar and bowed to the Queen. As I was at Sandhurst in those days, it was quite a thing to be part of.

Duke: Twelve Gentlemen-at-Arms were on duty in the Minster. They had come to York on a special train. Everything had had to be meticulously planned. There was a lovely man at the Lord Chamberlain's Office called Norman Gwatkin, an ex-brigadier in the Coldstream, and he was in charge of the planning, with Eric Penn, another former guardsman. They didn't have very long to get it all ready. We announced our engagement in March and this was in early June so there wasn't much time. The Royal Family all came up on the train. From what I heard afterwards they all had rather a good party. They had lunch with people like Tino of Greece [later King Constantine], who was a great tease.

* The same year the future King Juan Carlos of Spain (born 1938) married Princess Sophie of Greece (born 1938), daughter of King Paul and Queen Frederika.

He and my sister and my younger cousins all had quite a jolly time.

Prince Michael: A lot of us went up on the Royal Train to York, and for some reason Princess Mary, who, of course, lived at Harewood, was with us. At one point King Constantine disappeared and dressed himself up in British Rail waiter's attire and no one thought he was anything other than a waiter. He came up to the Princess Royal, who, dear lady, was never affected with hysterical laughter, and said, 'Your whisky.' 'No thank you.' A few minutes later: 'Your whisky.' 'No, I don't want whisky.' After about four times, he revealed himself as who he was, and it didn't go down frightfully well.

Noël Coward was delighted with his seat in the choir and noted, 'Prince Eddie looked exactly like his father.' Kenneth Rose was quick to point out that they put the wrong coronet on the service sheet. Douglas Fairbanks was there, and Cecil Beaton took the wedding photographs at Hovingham Hall. The press secretary, Commander Richard Colville, insisted on being there and, Beaton wrote, 'proceeded to make things pretty difficult for me'.

The guests on the special train returned to London from Malton at 7 p.m., dining on smoked river trout, roast turkey and chipolatas, followed by strawberries with liqueur and cheese.

Cecil Beaton's account has never been published in full before:

The [wedding] day was certainly full of excitements and surprise, & some of it was extremely touching & pleasant. The dignity of the ceremony in the towering

167

Minster was quite overpowering, & the fanfares blaring in competition with the organ sent cold shivers down one's spine. The various processions of royalty were amusing & fraught with pictorial or fashion drama . . . But on her own merits the bride herself, like an Italian or German primitive with her neat blonde head, the tilted nose & forward tilted tiara & long swan neck, was a real star. She moved with a ballet dancer's ease & grace.

The twenty-mile drive, in police escort, from York to Hovingham was terrifying, going at 60 miles an hour through country lanes that were lined with cheering, Union Jack-waving yokels was the last stage of our anxiety progression. The sight of Geoff [Sawyer], my assistant, in the ballroom, surrounded by cameras, was the greatest boon & relief of the day. The photographic session that followed was frustrating to a degree. The four press photographers used up all the Duke's patience . . . I was taking the only good picture of the day, one of the bride alone, when Colville* shouted to me to do what I was told & to take groups. When the entire Royal Family were arranged like dummies in a row, & I had taken my surfeit of pot shots at them, the D. & his new wife had to leave. I had to shout to take one or two pictures of them together. The old Duchess of Kent looked angry & panic-stricken that I was taking so long & soon the entire room was again empty except for Colville with the four press photographers looking down

* Commander Sir Richard Colville (1907–75), the Queen's press secretary, a dour figure, thus nicknamed 'Sunshine' by Sir Martin Charteris, the Queen's private secretary.

at the floor at a sad little lump of off white; the bride's tired rose bouquet was being perpetuated.

Of the nightmare session I could remember only a few instances. As usual I made a fool of myself with the Queen, saying how kind it was of her to let me take this picture. It wasn't kind of her. She was only one of 20 in a group. She didn't even know I was taking it . . . Her complexion outstandingly pink & white as always & her pale mauve dress audaciously bright. Eileen [Hose] noticed two very definite frown marks on an otherwise flawless porcelain complexion & also that the Queen was trying to ease her heels out of her shoes. The shoes that were obviously killing her. Eileen noticed too that the Duchess of K. [Marina] & the D. both gave their cigarettes to Philip Hay, who became a mobile human ash tray.

The Queen Mother, as usual, was an adorable bundle of puff & charm. The D. of E. was particularly polite to me & perhaps after all he doesn't hate me as much as I think he does. Pss Marina & Alexandra wished to be congratulated on the success of their choice of garments. 'So you do approve, do you?' Not the moment to say that the only startlingly successful appearances were the Dior Princess Olga (blazing with diamonds) & the Albrecht Dürer hat of Maria Camella Hambleden . . .

Now for the garden party. The crowds in the marquee were too dense for comfort & I found Prince Paul more of a refreshment then the lobster patties supplied by a York caterer. He complained of the abominable New York dress of his daughter . . .

The train journey home was a bit of a nightmare . . . Midnight had struck at King's Cross before we arrived &

by the time we had seen the hazy impressions of that wild nightmare 15 minutes in the ballroom turn to reality in the form of black and white photographs at Camera Press, it was two o'clock . . . but the black & white results we had seen had justified most of the bother, the anxiety, the rudeness from Colville . . . etc., etc., for under impossible conditions & in spite of Colville, one beautiful picture had been taken. A very nice girl, with an unusual strength of character, had become a Cinderella Princess . . . Today's success must have meant a lot to her. It is a triumph that is soon over & forgotten, but it must be a great thrill to know that you are the hitherto unknown person that has suddenly become the heroine of these cheering exciting crowds & to other unknown millions.[35]

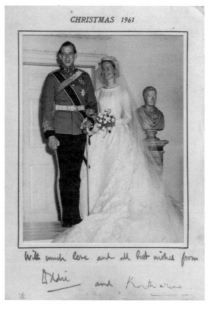

The Duke and Duchess's Christmas card in 1961

Duke: After the wedding, we went to Birkhall for a couple of weeks, and to Majorca where we'd been kindly lent Villa Camanda, a beautiful house right on the sea, at Formentor, by Whitney Straight, a friend of my mother. Because Whitney was a director of Rolls-Royce, they managed to provide an aeroplane as well, so we were very spoilt.

12

THE PRIVATE SECRETARY

Sir Richard Buckley and the Duke

Sir Richard Buckley

The private secretary is an important figure in all of the Royal Households, running the formal and official life of a member of the Royal Family. This involves dealing with all official correspondence, the organisations, patronages and presidencies, overseeing royal engagements at home and overseas. Reconnoitre visits have to be made, and the private secretary will seek to guide his boss on which official invitations to accept and so on.

Now that the Duke was married, he needed his own Household. Until this point, everything had been steered by Sir Philip Hay, his mother's private secretary, who remained with her until her death, and stayed on as treasurer to the Kents.

Now Lieutenant Commander Richard Buckley joined as the Duke's private secretary, serving until 1989. I was keen to catch up with him. I had met him in 1972 at his office in York House, St James's Palace, when I was working on *Burke's Guide to the Royal Family*. Today, of course, such information would be on websites, but in those days, there were meetings in offices. For that book I went to see all of the royal private secretaries.

I didn't see him again for many years, but in April 2015, I was invited to a dinner in Windsor, where Sir Simon Bland, who had been the Duke of Gloucester's private secretary, was staying the night before a Royal Victorian Order service. The Buckleys made up the party. Sir Richard lived at Coppins Cottage, and although I had been to Iver in the past, I had never identified where Coppins was so it was a great opportunity to go there. I was aware of the irony: usually people like me ask the private secretary if they can have a meeting with the member of the Royal Family. This time it was the other way round: I asked the Duke if I could see his private secretary.

Sir Richard was then ninety-three. He died on 31 January 2022, his 94th birthday. He had come to work for the Duke straight from the Royal Navy. How had this come about?

Sir Richard Buckley: In the run-up to going to sea, I had been teaching at Dartmouth, which was super. I got married, wanted to hang on with Tessa before I pushed off to the Far East, and I was invalided because of short sight. When it was all over, I was

in the classic position of having a wife, a baby, a dog, no home and no job. A long-standing friend got me interviews and finally Peter Orchard,* super guy, at De La Rue, made me an offer. We were discussing the terms, as I needed enough to buy a house, when the telephone rang. It was the Admiralty asking if I was sorted. 'Yes,' I said, 'thank you very much. Very kind of you to ring.' Had I actually signed up? No. Would I think of working for the Duke of Kent?

That threw me into a dilemma, particularly as a great friend of mine had been an equerry, and another was a naval equerry to Princess Marina. I rang them both and they said, 'Grab the job.' Was that good advice? I've no idea. I've had a lovely time. I enjoyed it.

The Duke was very generous. He paid my contributions into the Royal Household pension scheme back to the day I joined him. That made it all possible and I could send my children to school. Hurrah, hurrah. They were a lovely couple and as neighbours perfect.

I travelled with him a lot. He loves travelling and gave independence to several countries. He went to lots of places with the army, doing a proper soldier's job. In those days he would write to me from Germany if he wanted something done here, handwritten letters, quite clear. You can see, with hindsight, how he was coming away from being 98 per cent army and 2 per cent royal.

Duke: We certainly did a lot of travelling together.

HV: It gave Sir Richard a really interesting life. He thoroughly enjoyed every minute of it.

* Peter Orchard (1927–93), chairman of De La Rue, 1987–93.

Duke: So did I. It was quite a shock when he announced that he had to leave and I had to find a successor. That wasn't easy. Everything I did, I'd started with him, including the British Overseas Trade Board. If he thought something was a bad idea he would never hesitate to tell me so. But equally, if he thought something was a good idea, or might be a good idea, he would do his best to encourage me. He was always extremely helpful, but if he thought I was making a mistake, he didn't hesitate to say so, which is what a good private secretary should do!

I had discussed Princess Marina with Sir Richard.

HV: The Duke holds her in very high esteem, I think, don't you?

Sir Richard: Absolutely. Of course, she had lived at Coppins until the Duke married. Then he moved in, and she moved out to London. She was quite daunting as a lady, sweet and loved by people everywhere, but quite different with me.

HV to the Duke: He said he was intimidated by Princess Marina.

Duke: Oh, was he?

HV: Well, I suppose he was very young when he started and came out of the navy.

Duke: Yes, that's right. I never thought of her as being an intimidating figure. He might have, which is understandable, I think.

13

UGANDA, HONG KONG AND GERMANY

The Birth of George

Soon after her marriage, the Duchess of Kent began to undertake royal duties. The Duke recalled, 'It evolved gradually – it started off with local things at Iver and expanded.'

The Duchess of Kent: They were very kind to me. I think they gave me slow working time, not putting too much onto my shoulders at the beginning. It was gradual. I met such interesting people, and remained in contact with them. That's the exciting bit. Suddenly they're a friend and you're talking to them, learning, learning, learning.

Duke: I seem to remember the first thing came up when we had been married for about a month and went back to Coppins, and some figure in the village decided there should be a welcoming party. It was a very touching thought. The few people we knew in Iver got together and there were speeches.

The couple settled at Coppins, Princess Marina now moving permanently to the apartment at Kensington Palace that she had occupied since 1956. This phase of their lives can be seen in the Duke's cine-films. One afternoon, as this project drew to

a close, I showed the Duchess of Kent a cine-film of the Duke emerging from the house, followed by a posse of dogs. He had just exchanged a Jaguar saloon, with the number plate 3500 DU, for an E-Type, to which he transferred the number plate.

The Duchess of Kent: That's definitely my husband. The walk hasn't changed. The love of cars hasn't changed – or the love of dogs. We always had a Labrador and we had a poodle too. How lovely to see that.

The Duchess of Kent with her Labrador,
Columbus, and her poodle, Charlie

The Duchess gave birth to her first son, George, at Coppins at 3 p.m. on 26 June 1962, a few days earlier than expected. He was tenth in line to the throne, and weighed six and a quarter pounds. The Duke rushed from his office at the Ministry of Defence to join Princess Marina and Sir William and Lady Worsley, who were all at the house.

The baby was immediately entitled to the courtesy title of Earl of St Andrews. Kenneth Rose, who dwelt in the world of titles, was quick to point out that when George inherited the dukedom he would become a non-royal duke. He gave the example of Prince Alastair of Connaught, who was demoted as a prince in 1917. As the Duke of Connaught did not have subsidiary titles, he had one from his mother, the Duchess of Fife, and became Earl of Macduff.

The baby was christened George Philip Nicholas. A nanny called Mary McPherson was engaged to help look after him.

According to Anne Scott-James, the well-known newspaper columnist, he arrived at what she called 'a time when the Throne is going through one of its intermittent buffetings'. In particular Prince Philip and the Snowdons were being attacked in the media. She asked what quality the new baby most needed, and concluded: 'Respectability.' With or without accuracy, she praised the Queen Mother for flying to Canada in an ordinary passenger plane, Princess Marina and Princess Alexandra, who were 'kept disgracefully short of money, considering the work they do', for shopping 'off-the-peg', and Lord Harewood for being a first-class administrator in the arts.[36]

The Duke was called on once again to help with a state visit when the President of Liberia arrived at Dover on 10 July.

Duke: I went to Dover to greet President Tubman of Liberia and his wife, as they arrived on their state visit to Britain. We travelled by train together to London. The following day I went with them to a lunch at the Guildhall and in the evening there was a reception at Lancaster House. After that I had been invited to dine with the Bodyguard – the Gentlemen-at-Arms – at their

mess, nearby, in St James's Palace. One of the guests was the Prime Minister, Harold Macmillan, and I sat next to him. At a reasonably early hour he said: 'Well, I have to go as I've got a great many things to do.' This turned out to be the famous Night of the Long Knives – Selwyn Lloyd* was one of the victims.

An interest of the Duke's, which became more prominent in the summer of 1962, was flying. He learned to fly in a Havilland Chipmunk at White Waltham, instructed by Flight Lieutenant Derek St John Homer (1936–2006), who had trained at Cranwell, won the Philip Sassoon Memorial Prize and passed out as the second best all-round cadet. Prince Michael took flying lessons at the same time, and the brothers chalked up their first solo flights after ten hours of instruction.

Duke: Although my father had died in a flying accident, I was not put off. I did fly in an amateurish sort of way and achieved a pilot's licence. I used to love it. I flew a certain amount here, mostly from White Waltham. Flying instructors need to be strict so if you did something silly you were jolly well told off, as it could be dangerous, to put it mildly. If you lost concentration for a few seconds you might find yourself going off in the wrong direction. I flew purely for pleasure. Almost everyone learned to fly in a Chipmunk. The Queen's Flight had one for Prince Philip. I stopped after a couple of years and took it up again when I went to Cyprus, flying a Cessna. We were right on the airport there so I flew all the time.

* Selwyn Lloyd (1904–78), Conservative minister. He served as Chancellor of the Exchequer from 1960 until July 1962.

Soon afterwards, the Duke and Duchess undertook their first official overseas visit together.

In October 1962 the Duke represented the Queen at the independence celebrations for Uganda and the Duchess accompanied him. They went on to visit Kenya and Tanganyika. The invitation came in May, at a time when it was not certain that the necessary negotiations for independence would be completed by October. The Queen was asked to 'graciously consent to send a representative to the Uganda Independence celebrations . . . provided that the necessary discussions can be completed and arrangements made in time . . .' She, personally, chose the Duke of Kent.

This news was not received straightforwardly in Uganda. Prime Minister Milton Obote maintained that most Ugandans thought the Queen herself was coming, though she never undertook independence ceremonies. He then said that 'the Rulers' would only be pleased if the Duke of Edinburgh, the Queen Mother or Princess Margaret came. He felt that the Duke of Kent was 'a young man and totally unknown in Uganda'. Reginald Maudling, then Secretary of State for the Colonies, had to reassure Obote, via the Governor, Sir Walter Coutts, that the Duke was the right choice:

I might mention that the Duke of Kent is now 26 years old. He represented The Queen at the Sierra Leone Independence celebrations last year with conspicuous success. He and his young wife are well-known and popular figures here (their wedding last year was a major State occasion) and I am sure they will be very popular in Uganda. As The Queen's cousin and a

Independence celebrations in Uganda, 1962. Lady Coutts,
wife of the Governor is behind the Duke and Duchess

serving officer (he is now a Captain) he is in every way
a fitting Representative.[37]

Duke: We went together to Uganda, where there were wonder-
ful wildlife parks and much beautiful country. At that time
Milton Obote was Prime Minister and Uganda had a number of
kings, of whom I remember two: the Kings of Toro and Bunyoro.
Then there was the Kabaka of Buganda, King Freddie. His ances-
tors had been there long before Europeans set foot in the place.[*]

In the run-up to independence, the Governor, Sir Andrew
Cohen, had exiled the Kabaka but had to allow him to return in
1955, when he became something of a hero in Uganda. He was

[*] Mutesa II (1924–69), 35th Kabaka of the Kingdom of Buganda, an ancient
territory within Uganda. He was elected first President of Uganda in 1963.

British-educated and liked to think of himself as an English gentleman. He had a commission in the Grenadiers, of which he was very proud. He was charming and very friendly. When we went to call on him, he gave Katharine and me a pair of small garden tables, which were supposed to have initials carved on the top. One had the initials and the other didn't. When he handed them over, he said, 'I wanted to make you two tables the same, but the damned fellow,' meaning the carpenter, 'went and bogged it absolutely.' I never forgot that phrase.

Uganda had been a protectorate of the British Empire since 1894. When we arrived in October 1962, Obote and the Kabaka were on the runway at Entebbe to meet us, along with the Governor, Sir Walter Coutts, and his wife. We arrived in a Britannia aircraft, and there were thousands of children waving the new Ugandan flags. The capital was about to move to Kampala, but we stayed at Government House on top of a hill overlooking Lake Victoria. There was a canoe regatta in Entebbe harbour, canoes coming from Lake Victoria, with competing tribes. One of the features of independence was that the twenty-eight tribes that make up Uganda were all to come together.

The Kabaka gave a cocktail party at his palace, with a guard of honour of troops in tropical uniform, and outside, the people in the crowd gave their traditional salute – the fist closed with the forefinger raised, a sign of loyalty to the Kabaka. I wore tropical uniform, white jacket with the Royal Victorian Order ribbon, Katharine often in full evening dress and tiara in the sunshine. We had the band of the Scots Guards on parade for the big independence tattoo in Kololo Stadium. On the dot of midnight Sergeant Major Sydney Small lowered the Union Flag, which had flown in Uganda for seventy years, and in its place the new Ugandan flag was hoisted.

There was an impressive daytime celebration. I conferred the status of city on Kampala with a message from the Queen,

wishing them 'continued happiness and prosperity through the years to come'. It wasn't saying goodbye, as Uganda immediately became a full member of the Commonwealth. Obote was quite a fervent African nationalist, but he favoured the Commonwealth as an organisation in which people could talk informally and uphold certain common principles. Next morning I opened the new parliament in Parliament House. Obote handed me the speech and I read these words about the government's plans:

> It will aim to stimulate confidence in the future of Uganda as a united country, bound together in common nationhood. It will at the same time pay due heed to the traditional beliefs and customs of the diverse peoples of Uganda. It will respect the rights of the common man. It will, under the constitution, recognise the special status and dignity of the hereditary rulers of the kingdoms and of the constitutional heads of the districts.

Every time I used the phrase 'my government' as is traditional, Jomo Kenyatta, the Kenya nationalist leader, looked angry and flicked his fly whisk. After the ceremony he was heard to mutter: 'It's not her government. It's Uganda's government.'

I didn't actually meet Idi Amin on our visit, but I heard later that he had been on the guard of honour and greeted us on arrival. He had been at Sandhurst and in the King's African Rifles and would rise to prominence later.

We visited Murchison Falls national park and saw a huge crocodile on the side of the Nile, then herds of elephants and hippos bathing. Katharine opened the new Mulago Hospital in Kampala, her only solo engagement there, during which she toured several wards and met some small boys on crutches. The

hospital had been largely funded by the British government. The celebrations ended in the foothills of the Mountains of the Moon, where I exchanged greetings with three African kings, including the Omukama of Toro.

Uganda was certainly an enchanting place. I think, of all the places we went to, it stands out.

The Duchess of Kent: The Uganda visit was absolutely wonderful. Each visit was – in its own different way. And you learned so much from them, gained so much, I loved briefing myself really well. I went knowing the names of people so it was easy to walk out and not be too shy.

Duke: One of the best things about Uganda was that they were kind enough to stretch out our visit for a week or more. The actual ceremonial lasted a couple of days. After that we went off to look at the wildlife in the national parks. We saw all sorts of superb animals and birds and even spent a long weekend in the Queen Elizabeth Park. We went on from there to Tanganyika, as Tanzania was then, and to visit the Serengeti, a huge national park. It was absolutely *bursting* with wild animals. We saw large herds of antelopes, buffaloes, zebras, ostriches and more. It was a fabulous experience, and I took a lot of film.

The Duchess of Kent: We went on safari in Uganda and twice in Australia. There were a lot of bonuses on these trips – it wasn't all work. Wasn't I privileged to see these places?

Duke: Uganda's not much in the news but I think its later story is of interest – particularly for the contrast: the high hopes expressed at independence, then the awful disasters that came quite soon afterwards. It's worth reminding people about that.

The Duke, a keen photographer

Milton Obote became the first Prime Minister, having been selected by Sir Walter Coutts. When he left in 1963, Obote was still Prime Minister and the Kabaka became president. But any hopes for a democratic government in Uganda were soon dashed. In 1964 a series of mutinies brought a number of army officers to the fore, including Idi Amin Dada, who became deputy commander of the Ugandan armed forces. Soon after that Kenyans were banned from leading positions in government and in 1966 Obote suspended the constitution and declared himself president. Buganda tried to break away so Obote and Amin attacked the Kabaka's palace. He went into exile in Britain, and came to a sad end in a small flat somewhere in east London. Uganda became a republic, and a lot of people were terrorised and tortured. Obote's life was threatened in 1969 and after that he declared himself supreme leader. When he went to the Commonwealth Conference in

185

Singapore two years later, Idi Amin ousted him and became president.

For the next eight years Amin was president, and hundreds of thousands of Ugandans were tortured and killed. When I looked back at my 1962 visit on YouTube, everyone seemed so excited at being independent with a bright future ahead of them. It was tragic what happened to so many. Amin relished torture. Apparently he used to say, 'I like you very much, my friend,' turn to his henchman and say, 'Give him the VIP treatment,' after which death would come as a merciful release. It is said that three hundred thousand Ugandans died.

The basement of the Mulago Hospital, which Katharine had opened, was used as a morgue for many of the victims.

I remember how worried everyone was that Amin might turn up for the Commonwealth heads of government meeting, which coincided with the Silver Jubilee in 1977. Two years later, he was overthrown by Tanzanian forces and Ugandan exiles. Obote returned, more lives were lost, and he was overthrown in 1985.

I went back in 2012, for the fiftieth anniversary of independence. By then President Museveni had been in office since 1986. I could see very little change. The country didn't appear to have advanced significantly. I asked lots of questions and they kept telling me how much things had improved and how many more miles of road they had built, but I couldn't actually see much difference.

I asked the Duke if he thought the Ugandans were happier by then, politically.

Duke: I don't know. If people had thought about it they would have realised you couldn't just hand over a country to a regime

that had absolutely no experience of self-government, no under-standing of people's rights, no administration.

The whole thing happened in a tremendous rush and there was not nearly enough preparation. We had done our best to prepare them for something we would have considered in, say, ten years' time but not the next year. That was a tragedy.

The Duchess of Kent: Independence wasn't as good a dream as they'd hoped it might be. Few succeeded in what they wanted to do.

After Uganda, the Duke and Duchess went to Tanganyika and on their way home, stopped in Kenya to open Nairobi's new television centre. The Duke said how glad he was to be concerned with the introduction of 'this new and compelling medium. Its coming to Kenya at this time represents a great achievement and something of a challenge.'[38]

Back in the army, in November 1962 the Duke left for Hong Kong, where he was joined presently by the Duchess and George, who travelled there in a regular trooping plane – in those days a journey of more than twenty-seven hours, with a stop in Istanbul. Nanny McPherson came with them, and a Chinese amah was also employed.

The Royal Scots Greys had been stationed in Detmold, Germany, since 1958, but since July 1961, the Duke had been a staff officer to the Chief of the Imperial General Staff at the War Office. Now he was transferred to Hong Kong, purely as a military officer, second in command of a Centurion tank squadron, with the rank of captain. It was made clear that he would not be undertaking any royal duties there unless specif-ically invited to by the Queen.

The Duke with George in Hong Kong in 1962

The Duke and Duchess lived in a three-bedroom second-storey flat in Barbecue Gardens, on Castle Peak, on the Kowloon mainland. The Chinese media were interested in his arrival, and the Governor, Sir Robert Black, had to deter them from photographing the building. The Duke enjoyed go-kart racing and competed in a race between Hong Kong and Manila. He also took up polo. The Duchess was able to push her pram about almost unnoticed, though the rogue photographer, Reg Davis, took a snap of her doing just that. They tended to avoid smart Hong Kong dinners in favour of dinners in the mess. They enjoyed sailing and waterskiing. In June 1963, the Duke took part in the annual Taipo Dragon Boat Race, as one of a twenty-seven-man crew.

Journalists suggested that the one-year stint in Hong Kong was something of a respite from royal duties. Cathie Breslin, an American journalist based in Hong Kong, got hold of a

soi-disant friend who told her, 'It seems a great relief to them to be free of the London rat race. After two years in Hong Kong, it's back to London and into the royal harness for good.'[39]

Duke: When we went there in 1962, we had a quite small top-floor flat in a housing estate, pretty close to the sea, next door to Castle Peak. It was just a fishing village in those days but now it's a huge city. It was a lovely place to be. We looked across the sea to Lantau Island, where the airport now is, and saw the junks sailing by every day. Our son, George, was six months, and we had our Chinese amah, who came from the Shenzhen area – we just knew her as 'Armoi'. We had a brother officer from the Greys on the floor below us, and it was a lovely, happy, pretty well carefree existence.

The Duchess with Armoi, her amah, in Hong Kong on Christmas Day, 1962

189

Noël Coward must have written to us – anyway, we discovered he was visiting Hong Kong so we sent a message to the Peninsular Hotel and he duly came up for dinner. It couldn't have been more fun.

Noël Coward wrote, 'I had a meagre but agreeable lunch with Sir Robert and Lady Black at Government House . . . and a really enchanting evening with Prince Eddie and Kathy, who live in an ordinary officers'-issue flatlet in the New Territories and are as merry as grigs and having a lovely time untrammelled by royal pomposity. They really are a sweet couple and it is a pleasure to see two people so entirely happy with each other. I also saw George, who is thirteen months and blond and pink and smiling.'[40]

The Duchess of Kent: We had a wonderful year in Hong Kong, probably the best we had in our lives. We lived at Castle Peak. I rode a horse there, waterskied, and we made lots of friends. Noël Coward came to dinner one night. I remember him sitting by the water. It was wonderful having him. He certainly knew my mother-in-law well, and we were lucky enough to be edged in on that one.

Duke: The Governor, Sir Robert Black, was quite a dour character. He asked us out for a day on his yacht, a rather grand, old-fashioned vessel, which steamed about in the Hong Kong waters, and we all had to get dressed up. You couldn't just appear in a T-shirt and shorts on the Governor's yacht, far from it. Otherwise life there was pretty relaxed. We did a lot of sailing, explored the New Territories, which were then largely open country. They were so beautiful, and you could walk around the farms, with the rice farmers and pig farmers. It was China as it must once have been.

There were dragon-boat races. Quite often the crew floundered and ended up in the water but that was part of the fun.

Sam the tailor was a feature of Hong Kong life. I was a regular customer of his until quite recently as he used to come to London. He would get in touch, saying, 'I am here!' He was from Pakistan. He was a fine tailor and I still have garments he made me fifty years ago.

We were strictly forbidden to go into China. Oddly enough there was quite an incident because we had a tank squadron based at the Shek Kong airfield, which is in the New Territories, not very far from the frontier. At weekends we used to go out exploring and I drove along a lonely country road until I reached a barrier, with a notice that said: 'You are now leaving Hong Kong.' I went through the barrier and found myself in Shenzhen, which is now a huge industrial city but then was just a big village really. I was smartly told to go home. I could have been put away for years – I was lucky to get away with that.

Of course now the population of Hong Kong is about three times what it was in the early sixties or even more.

They flew home for Princess Alexandra's marriage to the Hon. Angus Ogilvy in Westminster Abbey in April 1963.

Duke: We came home for about a week and went to the ball the Queen gave at Windsor Castle. It's such an old-fashioned idea now. My sister's wedding was rather like Princess Margaret's. It was a big occasion. It was springtime so not too cold for the enormous crowds that had stayed up throughout the night before. It was my job to give her away, so we left Kensington Palace. The Queen loaned her best Rolls-Royce with the huge glass windows so that she could be seen. Because my mother

had so many royal relations in Europe, there was a large contingent of them, including King Olav of Norway, Queen Louise of Sweden, Queen Ena of Spain, Queen Ingrid of Denmark, Queen Frederika of Greece, Queen Helen of Romania – they were all there. Princess Anne was the head bridesmaid, her fourth such wedding, so she was very assured.

The reception was at St James's Palace.

The Duke and Duchess of Kent returned from Hong Kong in time for Christmas, with George, and Princess Marina was delighted to see her grandson growing up. Helen Habsburg remembered, 'George could walk, and my aunt was terribly excited that he would wear the proper clothes. She went out to buy a little blue coat, shoes and shirts. It was exciting.'

The Duke was immediately stationed in Germany. The Duchess remained at Coppins to give birth to her second child, Helen, who was born on 28 April 1964. Princess Marina was there and immediately telephoned the Duke in Germany.

Helen was christened in the private chapel at Windsor Castle in June. She commented: 'George lived in Hong Kong for the first year of his life. I was made in Hong Kong and born at Coppins. I lived in Germany for about the first year of my life.' Her brother George remembered his time there: 'I have some very faint memories of Germany as a very small boy. I remember being lifted into a tank at about three years old. And my father's Labrador.'

The Duchess of Kent: We spent a bit more than a year there. I loved the away times, being part of the community. In the army you certainly are, very much so.

Duke: The local Germans, on the whole, were very welcoming, and there were one or two families in particular who made a point of welcoming the British Army to emphasise their own pro-British connections. Reconciliation is so important.

Germany 1964–5

From 1964 the Duke was stationed at Fallingbostel, Germany, south of Hamburg, serving as Adjutant of the Royal Scots Greys. He was simultaneously preparing for the stiff exam, which consisted of six papers, in December to enter Staff College.

Duke: I was out in Germany still as Adjutant of my regiment when Winston Churchill died. I flew back with my brother Michael, who was then serving as a subaltern with the 11th Hussars. My mother and Katharine went to the lying-in-state in Westminster Hall. Four kings stayed at Buckingham Palace for the state funeral – Denmark, the Belgians, Norway, the Hellenes – and Queen Juliana of the Netherlands.

After the state funeral in St Paul's Cathedral, the coffin was transported up the river and I remember the cranes dipping in salute. It was a great and memorable occasion.

The Duke returned to Britain from West Germany in September 1965, and embarked on a missiles and rocketry course at Shrivenham Military College of Science. Following nine months at the Staff College, Camberley, at which he was described as 'one of our outstanding young officers', he took up a position at Headquarters Eastern Command in Hounslow.

During this time he and the Duchess still lived at Coppins, staying there until 1972.

The Duchess of Kent: I was extremely happy there. It was a very peaceful life.

Duke: We moved in and almost immediately went to Hong Kong, literally after three months. We spent a year there, then went to Germany. We finally left in '72.

The children loved it.

Earl of St Andrews: I've got memories of Coppins, which I loved as a boy. There was a large garden and a farm attached. When I had German measles I was off school and spent most of the time roaming around the farm, having great fun. I remember Agnes de Stoeckl and, of course, Zoia. I was too young to ask them about their memories of Poland, though I used to visit them for tea in their cottage. Coppins was fine, but it wasn't real country, I suppose.

Princess Marina with her grandson, George, in the garden at Coppins

The Duke and Duchess in Uganda for Independence in 1962

The Duke and Duchess with their new private secretary
Lt-Commander Richard Buckley

The Duke filming the celebrations
(above) and a photograph taken by
him on safari (below)

The Duke and Duchess dancing
at the Independence Ball

The Earl of St Andrews

Lady Helen Taylor

Lord Nicholas Windsor

The Duchess

The Duke with Frank Williams test driving a Williams Formula 1 car in 1983

The Duke in China. In 1979, he became the first member of the royal family to make an official visit to China

The Duke visiting factories. He was Vice Chairman of the Overseas Trade Board and later British Trade International from 1976 to 2001

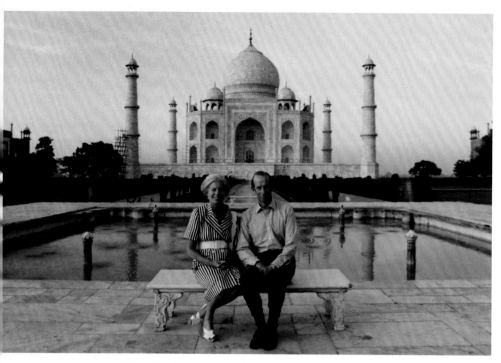

The Duke and Duchess at the Taj Mahal

The Duke and Duchess with King Tāufaʻāhau Tupou IV of Tonga
at the time of his Coronation in 1967

The Royal Colonels:
The Prince of Wales
(Welsh Guards),
The Duke of Edinburgh
(Grenadier Guards),
and The Duke of Kent
(Scots Guards)

The Duke and Duchess in a carriage on
their way to the Queen Mother's 80th
birthday service at St Paul's Cathedral

The Duke and Duchess
before the diplomatic
reception in 1986

The Duke taking the salute at the Colonel's Parade in 1986

The Duke back at Buckingham Palace with his grandson Lord Downpatrick.
His daughter-in-law, the Countess of St Andrews, looks on

The Duke of Kent and the Queen watch Andy Murray play against Jarkko Nieminen of Finland at the 2010 Wimbledon Lawn Tennis Championships. He was President of the All England Lawn Tennis Club from 1969 until 2021

The Duke with two of his grandchildren, Marina Charlotte and her baby sister Amelia

I used to go and see Amama [Princess Marina] in her house at Kensington Palace. I have distinct memories of her. She was very affectionate, but I was so young that I didn't have as close a relationship with her as I had with my mother's father. I remember talking to her elder sister, Auntie Olga, about her memories of staying at Pavlovsk before 1914 and of her cousins [the children of the Tsar]. Much later I was learning Russian and she was saying, 'I wouldn't bother learning Russian today. It's horrible and it isn't like the Russian they used to speak in my day.'

Uncle Paul [of Yugoslavia] was a lovely man. He took me to lunch at Prunier on St James's Street. I didn't have the chance to go to the Louvre with him. He used to take my father there, which he enjoyed very much. He was an immensely cultivated and intelligent man.

Lady Helen Taylor: I was at Coppins till I was about eight. It had a very nice, cosy atmosphere. I remember listening to *The Goon Show* on Sunday mornings on the radio. It was the days when children were brought down to the drawing room after baths when they were ready for bed.

My parents worked very hard, but the lives they led meant they were around for holidays. During term time they were away, and they travelled quite a bit, because they were going to far-flung places to give countries their independence and they'd be away for two or three weeks at a time. What an amazing thing to have done – and what fun it must have been.

I remember them working on speeches, just being aware of their public life and their sense of duty, and occasionally I'd get roped into things locally. My mother was Patron of the Not Forgotten Association, and there were homes for the elderly – I used to go with her to visit them.

I was four when Princess Marina died. I remember sitting next to her on the sofa at Coppins and her showing me the contents of her handbag. I wish I had known her later, though I think she would have been quite terrifying, very exacting.

14

PRINCESS MARINA 1964–8

Princess Marina – Cecil Beaton's 1964 photograph,
sent to friends after her death

Duke: My mother was living at Kensington Palace and she had a butler, William Corbett, a very upright, distinctly old-fashioned man, of the reserved, somewhat pompous variety. She liked him very much. He became a good friend of all the family.

Living at Kensington Palace, she often walked her dog in Kensington Gardens. There was a time when she was there and a man approached her with a camera, and she thought, Oh, this is a bore. I won't be able to walk here any more. Then he asked her to take a picture of *him* with his camera.

She was very busy in those last years. In September 1964 she went to Ottobeuren to hear Benjamin Britten's War Requiem. That was the first time any member of the family had made an official visit to Germany, a forerunner to the Queen's important visit the following year. Then we all went to Athens for my cousin Tino's wedding to Princess Anne-Marie of Denmark.* Hardly was my mother back than she made an official visit to Australia, which lasted thirteen days. It was hailed as a somewhat poignant visit, since my parents had been meant to go out there in 1938 for my father to be Governor General. Lord De L'Isle, the then Governor General and Sir Robert Menzies, the Prime Minister, looked after her. She told the waiting crowds, 'I am so glad to be in Australia at last.' In her first speech she said, 'Twenty-six years ago my husband and I were preparing to come and live among you – but God willed it otherwise. But for the tragedy of war – tragedy shared by so many Australian families – we would have become intimately familiar with this vast country and its people.'

Sir Robert Menzies was on form as ever when he spoke of the impact she had made on the Australians: 'Before you leave they will be just as much in love with you as I have been for many years.'

She visited the British Exhibition in Sydney, opened the headquarters of the Department of Defence, and the Gladesville Bridge across the Parramatta River. She spent four days in Malaysia on the way home. In November she came to stay with us in Germany for a few days.

She continued to represent the Queen. She did so at the funeral of Queen Elisabeth of the Belgians in November 1965.

* Crown Prince (later King) Constantine's wedding was on 18 September 1962.

She and my sister went to the wedding of the future Queen Beatrix of the Netherlands in March 1966.

One of her most important engagements was to give independence to Bechuanaland, which became Botswana, and to Basutoland, which became Lesotho that autumn. The fate of each country proved rather different.

Self-government was agreed for Botswana in London in February that year. The capital was moved to Gaborone, near the border with South Africa, and its first general election under universal suffrage was held. Sir Seretse Khama, a considerable figure in Africa, was elected as the first president. There was a lovely photograph of him and my mother driving together, and when I went to Botswana twenty years later, it was clear that they held her in very high regard. There is still a Princess Marina Hospital in Gaborone. My mother handed over the instruments of independence on 30 September.

The trip was not without incident. Seven armed Africans were arrested in the Chobe game reserve, which she was due to visit. When she got there, her arrival and departure were delayed by elephants! She would have enjoyed that.

At the time Botswana was the third poorest country in the world. It had only seven and a half miles of paved roads. Sir Seretse Khama proved to be an inspired leader of his country, establishing an economy based on the export of beef, copper and diamonds, recently discovered. He stamped out much corruption and upheld liberal democracy. As a result the economy grew in leaps and bounds. He was re-elected president three times. I represented the Queen at his funeral in 1980.

Basutoland was much trickier. It had been a British Crown Colony since 1884. The Paramount Chief, Moshoeshoe II, then the Queen's representative, decided he would tell my mother that the independence constitution was unsuitable

and unpopular and that it was being imposed on his people. This was surprising as the new constitution would establish him as constitutional monarch of Lesotho. He would have political power, but he also demanded control of defence, internal security and external affairs. In fact, under the new constitution, the rights of the King and the Prime Minister were very clearly defined. The King's demands confused the Basotho, who saw my mother hand over the constitutional instruments on 4 October. It was clear that the Prime Minister should not hand over responsibility for the army (then non-existent), the police, internal security and external affairs to the King. The Prime Minister consulted the King as head of the Chieftainship and Father of the Nation. It was pointed out that, rather than resorting to strong-arm tactics and clandestine alliances with political careerists, the King should use these consultations to influence government policy. There was plenty of confidence in Chief Leabua Jonathan, the Prime Minister.

In 1970 the Prime Minister drove the King into exile, and deposed him in 1990. Jonathan was pushed out in 1986, and the King returned briefly in 1995, but was killed in a car accident the next year.

My mother was proud to be made the first Chancellor of the University of Kent, and undertook many engagements for the RNLI. She invariably took a box of chocolates with her to give to the little boy or girl who presented her with flowers.

She was a popular attender at Wimbledon, giving the cups on the court at the end of the great matches, notably to Billie Jean King in three consecutive wins at Wimbledon singles. That did not stop a Labour backbencher called Alan Williams tabling a question in 1966 about how much it cost to convey the tennis results to Buckingham Palace and to my mother,

suggesting that police were called off normal duties to escort a messenger on his motorcycle. Alice Bacon, the minister of state, explained that a police escort had accompanied my mother's car to Wimbledon, but then an empty car had been hired and parked next to the royal entrance. It and the messenger were photographed together. No motorcyclists left the Wimbledon ground.

In 1967 a memorial was unveiled to Queen Mary in the wall at Marlborough House. This was the first time that both the Duke and Duchess of Windsor attended an event in public with the Royal Family. They came to lunch with my mother at Kensington Palace. I remember her saying, 'It might be nice if you bowed to him,' which was a typical thought of hers, so when I saw him off, I did bow.

In the last year of her life, she spent three weeks on safari with my brother Michael in Kenya, Tanzania and Uganda. That was in March 1968. In the summer she presented Sir Francis Chichester, the round-the-world yachtsman, with the Royal Geographical Society's top award. We all went to see Prince Charles installed as a Knight of the Garter in June, and as usual she presented the cups at Wimbledon. Her last public engagement was to confer degrees for the University of Kent at Canterbury on 12 July.

All was not well with Princess Marina, though neither she nor the world at large knew how seriously ill she was. Sir Charles Johnston left an account of Princess Marina's last summer in his diaries:

Her decline over June and July makes tragic telling.

In May she telegraphed to us before we left Canberra asking us to go with her to see *Hedda Gabler* two days after we arrived.

As it turned out, N.[Natasha] was in bed with a cold, but I went. The production with Gertrud Fridh* was a striking piece of Scandinavian Gothic. Peter Brook,† who put it on, came to supper at Kensington Palace afterwards and, with my new extrovert Australian approach to people whom I have previously found embarrassing, I rather warmed to him and felt I had never properly given him credit for his work as London's international impresario. Otherwise, alas, I remember nothing of the evening.

Next day, 8 June, was Trooping the Colour. Gerald Templer had sent us seats and as N. was still 'coldy' I took Joan Aly Khan. Even in the drizzle it had its unusual moments of emotion – the entry of the mounted band, coming round the corner of the Mall, with Alexander, the drum horse, in front and the kettles banging and the brass blowing and the hooves clopping, the deliberation, the neo-Roman majesty of the whole thing; then the Queen riding round, tiny and lonely, with three or four heraldic Shakespearian figures, like Kent and Beaufort, on horseback behind her. I felt for the first time how small and frail the whole set-up was. (Unfortunately the Shakespearian effect was a bit spoilt by Dickie Mountbatten who wore the helmet of the Life Guards at a groggy angle à la Admiral Beatty.)

Afterwards I dropped Joan in Eaton Square, picked up N., who was well enough to go out to lunch, on the steps of the Hyde Park Hotel, and raced to Kensington Palace in our usual fear of being late at that most punctual institution. Luckily Princess Marina, who had been watching the Trooping from the Horse Guards, had not been able to get away at once and was even later than us.

* Gertrud Fridh (1921–84), Swedish actress, described as the definitive Hedda Gabler.
† Peter Brook (born 1925), British theatre and film director.

It was fun being back again at Kensington Palace. Corbett, the tall spectacled butler, was on the doorstep. I washed in the gents' loo, on the right, with the coloured print of Wolfe landing at the heights of Abraham. Then along the passage between the tall bookcases, past de Laszlo's portrait of Ma'am's mother, Princess Nicholas of Greece, into the interior hall with the big round table in the middle and the doors opening off it – dining room, Philip Hay's office, staircase, Boss's office (Lady Rachel Davidson [Pepys] was lady-in-waiting), ladies' loo. Between Philip and the stairs is a passage with a marble table covered in bottles and glasses and ice-tins and biscuit tins, then beyond it the drawing room, looking out onto the privacy of the small walled garden, and always banked up with Windsor flowers. How often we used to sit in that room after dinner playing canasta and laughing and cursing our luck, until it was time for me to walk quickly down the private road to Kensington Gore, pick up a taxi and drive back in it to say good night to Ma'am and take Natoush home.

This time my friend Jones was there with the official Rolls and drove us all out to Richmond where we were lunching with the Ogilvys. The Beauforts were there and from having rather reacted against them when Princess Marina took us to dine with them at the White City last year and watch the jumping, I warmed to them this time. Angus had a bad cold but appeared in a dressing-gown to open the claret. Exquisite food, relaxed, Coppins-style custom of helping oneself from the sideboard so as to have no servants in the room, delightful gay self-debunking conversation – everything in fact in the Kent family tradition. What was particularly enjoyable was the touching relationship between mother and daughter and grandchildren.

Afterwards I wanted to go to the movies. N. didn't feel well enough, but I persuaded Princess Marina to go with me instead. We saw a rather macabre film called *No Way to Treat a Lady*,* which I enjoyed and I'm afraid the Princess didn't like at all. Afterwards in the taxi going home she suggested I should drop her off at the Hyde Park and let her go alone to K.P. As if I would, but it was typical of her sweetness and consideration.

She got us invited to Kitty Farrell's dance about two weeks later, and she and we dined first with Kitty's sister, Liz [von Hofmannsthal]. It was very gay and elegant, and crowded with young in all sorts of kit. There were lots of friends of our generation too, and we all wandered round, then met next door to the dancing downstairs and sat at a table with John and Liza Glendevon. Pss Marina was full of energy and outstayed us.

The same week she took John and Liza and N. and me with her to Wimbledon. We had an early lunch at K.P. first and a good afternoon of tennis, especially Pasarell vs. Rosewall:† the clash of opposites, the beefy young American amateur against the wiry little oldish Australian pro. Rosewall won, but only by calling on all the resources of his professionalism in terms of guts and determination. Princess Marina enjoyed this, and as always was completely at home at Wimbledon and on her usual easy joking terms with the tennis officials and their wives.

The same evening Princess Marina, N. and I dined with Cecil Beaton in his exquisite little house in Pelham Place and went to the Mermaid to see *Hadrian the Seventh* – a good dramatisation of poor Corvo's Walter-Mitty-dream novel, very moving until he

* *No Way to Treat a Lady*, a black comedy thriller in which Rod Steiger assumes various disguises in order to murder unsuspecting elderly ladies.
† Charles Pasarell, Jr (b. 1944), Puerto Rican tennis player, and Ken Rosewall (b. 1934), Australian.

becomes Pope but losing in credibility thereafter. In the interval we went upstairs to the bar looking over the river, and Princess Marina talked a long time to McCowen* who played the part of Hadrian.

Everything so far completely happy and active and normal. Alas, it was the last time we saw her so. For about two weeks we didn't meet at all. Princess M. had functions during the week and at the weekends we were away. On 9 July we dined at K.P. with Diana Daly making a fourth, and played canasta. Princess M. seemed to me tired and only partly with us. She enjoyed winning – as she and N. did – as endearingly as ever, but instead of wanting us to go on playing until all hours she sent us home early. We were to give her dinner at La Fontana in Soho, where we had taken her last year, and then go to the theatre. It was to be our last outing with her before N. and I left the following Monday. A day or two beforehand it was cancelled. Ma'am had had to go into hospital for a few days.[41]

On 17 July Princess Marina was admitted to the Hospital for Nervous Diseases in Bloomsbury, for examination of recurring weakness in her left leg. She came home to rest at Kensington Palace on 21 July. Meanwhile she cancelled all her engagements.

Sir Charles continued:

The day we left, Monday 22 July, she was out of hospital again and we went to say goodbye to her at Kensington Palace. We found her sitting up in bed looking as beautiful and elegant as ever, but also somehow vague and abstracted. *'Eh bien, mes enfants,'* she said, but that look in her eye that told you she was thinking of something else.

* Alec McCowen (1925–2017), actor. This was his career breakthrough.

We were to have a quick lunch with Sheila and Dmitri* [of Russia] in Wilton Street before leaving to catch our aircraft. We stayed too long upstairs with Ma'am and had to hurry away. As we came down, Philip Hay was standing in the door of his office and I sensed that he wanted to talk to me, but there was no time for anything but goodbye and away.

Not too good, we said to each other in the taxi, but had no idea that in just over a month darling Ma'am would be dead and all this world blown to smithereens . . .

We had just arrived in Perth for our yearly visit [August 1968] and were installed in provincial comfort at the Esplanade Hotel, in a suite banked with vases of Kangaroo paws, when a telegram arrived from England: 'Fear news may be very bad, Eddie'. Cryptic but, alas, unmistakable in its meaning, this message prepared us humanely for the shock headline next morning: PRINCESS MARINA DIES OF A BRAIN TUMOUR.

For us both the message cast a shadow over the luscious spring landscape and dimmed the Milky Way West Australian light and made the Kangaroo paw look an insensitive fleshy monstrosity. We simply couldn't believe that the main focus of our lives ever since we married could be so abruptly removed.[42]

Duke: At the end of July 1968, I remember going into her room. Everything was very hush-hush: in those days cancer was a word that nobody wanted to use, and nobody wanted to say she had cancer. We did know she was having tests. And I remember in late July she'd been in to have a scan, which had shown up some pretty undesirable things – I remember hearing that. Then we went on holiday to Sardinia to stay with some friends [the

* Prince Dmitri of Russia (1901–80), nephew of Tsar Nicholas II, and his wife Sheila Milbanke (1895–1969).

Poklewskis] and later up to Scotland. When we came back to London and saw her, she was saying, 'It's such a bore,' because she never knew how ill she was, she just knew something was wrong, and the one thing she dreaded against all else was that her sister should learn she had cancer, as it was always regarded, probably rightly at that date, as a death sentence. We all had to be frightfully circumspect in how we talked about it. And we saw her in London, perfectly cheerful and in her sitting room, doing a crossword.

Then we went off and stayed with Johnny Dalkeith [later Duke of Buccleuch] to shoot and we'd only been there a day when we got a message to come back straight away. And by the time we got back, she'd gone, I'm afraid. It was all very quick. It was only about a month from the time we learned there was something amiss that she died, really no time at all.

Princess Marina's nieces were also upset by her death.

Princess Elizabeth of Yugoslavia: Once I was standing with her in the entrance of Kensington Palace and she slipped and said, 'Oh dear! That was my leg,' because one leg was a bit shorter than the other. In fact it wasn't, it was a mini stroke. And that is what at the end killed her. She died much too young.

Helen Habsburg: When my Aunt Marina died, for us it was terrible. And for Princess Alexandra – they got on very well, as mother and daughter. She was a wonderful mother because she never interfered or asked too many questions, quite different from Princess Olga who didn't get on with her daughter at all, and was always criticising. She was like a friend with us too. She would sit down and talk about her youth, and the boyfriends she'd had, and unheard of things. She was very good at that.

Princess Alexandra wrote from Balmoral to describe the last days of her mother's life to Natasha Johnston, then in Australia where her husband, Sir Charles, was High Commissioner:

The shock for you must have been immense. Thank God Darling Min was spared all suffering & fear. Her passing was so peaceful & blessed that I thank for this every day in my prayers. Knowing that she is happy with Papa and A. Woolly is an immense comfort.

Sorrow is bewildering and the missing of a loved one's presence is at times acute. But for her it was a merciful thing. She only had 6 or 7 months to live – so to go in 5 weeks was in a way a miracle. She had no pain. Her only trouble was the acute uselessness of her left leg & during the last 10 days her left arm had become very weak.

The Friday before she went she spent 2½ hours with me in the garden at T.H.L. The nurse & Jones bringing her down, and she lying on my garden chair, one of which I gave her to use at K.P. She found it very comfortable. Hot day – we stayed outside talking all the time.

Sunday 25th – 2 days later – Angus & I lunched with her & Zoia, who had stayed at K.P. with her to keep her company, on & off. She looked lovely & so young. After lunch we sat in the garden, she & I alone, talking. Eventually we left around 2.30 & that was the last time we said goodbye to each other. I have a vivid memory of that sunny day in her garden sitting near that flowing green tree.

We children had been told around the middle of July that all was not well. We *knew* only – so she was saved from so much . . .

Beloved Min – she never wanted to grow old – & she used to make faces at me as she disliked being dependent on others! How we used to laugh together. She was brave – she used to say to me quite casually, 'Of course, all my left side is becoming atrophied.' God was merciful and loving to take her so swiftly.

Monday 26th – Zoia rang to say Min had had a black out the night before. In effect a spasm in the head. By 9 a.m. on Monday morning she fell into a gentle, natural sleep – and never awoke. Tuesday the 27th – 11.40 – Min finally passed on. But her spirit had left on Monday evening. I feel sure Papa came to fetch her.

It seems extraordinary to be writing all this. I feel my scribble is illegible.

The funeral at St George's Chapel – very serene, full of gay flowers, which would have suited her. But somehow all this was too earthbound – I am conscious of her spirit, which is free & joyous. And is around me at times. I hope all this helps a little. I know how deeply fond you were of each other. And being so far away – a great strain.

The burial at Frogmore was very moving. Papa's grave had been moved down there the night before – with Eddie & Maou [Prince Michael] in attendance. So they are together under a magnificent plane tree . . .[43]

The Duke wrote to George Galitzine:

There is not much that can comfort me at such a horrible time, but if anything can, it is the knowledge of how much genuine love and admiration existed for her and in particular the tributes of her direct and dearest friends.[44]

Princess Olga also wrote:

> You know how closely united we were & that life with-
> out her can never be the same for me . . . All that matters
> is that thank God she went in peace without suffering &
> without even knowing the cause of her illness.[45]

Prince Paul and Princess Olga had been at Pratolino during
the summer. On 9 August Princess Marina had telephoned to
say she would not be able to make her habitual summer visit
for the foreseeable future. Princess Olga had not been told
how ill Princess Marina was for fear of Princess Marina
finding out. She arrived from Milan on 26 August with her
daughter, Elizabeth, and rose at 4 a.m. to take up her vigil
beside her sister's bed.

The private funeral took place at St George's Chapel on
30 August, the Queen flying down from Balmoral, with
Prince Philip, the Queen Mother, Prince Charles and
Princess Anne. The Duke of Windsor flew from Paris for
the day. The service was conducted by the Dean of Windsor
and the Archbishop of Canterbury; the Greek Archimandrite
also took part.

At the funeral Princess Olga wore Princess Marina's black
coat, hat and veil as she had no mourning clothes of her own.
When she left on 7 September, Princess Marina's dog, Chin,
was brought in to say goodbye. Lady Rachel Pepys, one of
Princess Marina's ladies-in-waiting, gave Chin a home.

Prince Michael: When my mama died, I went and stayed with
them at Coppins for about six weeks. I always regarded Coppins
as a home from home. It looms large in my list by any
calculation.

210

Princess Marina's funeral at Windsor, 1968. The Duke
and Duchess, Prince Paul of Yugoslavia, Princess Alexandra,
Angus Ogilvy and Prince Michael. In the background
the Queen Mother, the Queen and Prince Philip.
Princess Olga is hidden behind the Duke

Sir Charles Johnston assessed Princess Marina:

One of their nieces* used to call Princess Marina and her sisters 'the Fabergé Aunts', a very good compendium name. All three had the same mosaic-like brilliance, the glitter of Byzantine empresses. They had an extreme neatness. And, above all, they had an absolutely

* In fact, Prince Michael of Greece, who applied the term to the many Greek cousins, such as Queen Helen of Romania and Princess Irene, Duchess of Aosta, all of whom looked somewhat similar.

unshakeable elegance. Whatever the circumstances, whether it was in her fishing clothes at Birkhall, or wearing my mackintosh and Homburg hat in a charade, Princess M. was a figure of tremendous chic and panache. And with it all, a certain ease and naturalness in these strange get-ups, as if she had never worn anything else. Always the same stunning effect of effortlessness, whether in silk or an old housecoat or a tweed suit with a tall cornflower in sapphires and diamonds pinned on the lapel as if it had grown there. One was exposed to an inbred unconscious distinction and finesse, which made other Royals look chunky and homespun by comparison: the extraordinary cachet of the Romanovs, inherited from her mother, a quality transmitted (like haemophilia) through the women and reaching back through St Petersburg and Moscow to Byzantium.

With this went a strong taste for mimicry and slapstick comedy. Suddenly one would see the beautiful empress-face distorted into a lopsided leer. This was the imitation of an old gaga pony that had once existed at Sandringham. Projected in a flash across the most solemn dining table, it never failed to induce hysterics in Princess M.'s sisters or in N. (The act was firmly believed by its performer to be quite invisible to anyone else.) In fact the sisters and cousins spent a lot of time in an esoteric *fou rire*, which could be disconcerting for those not on the wave-length. There was a good-natured mockery of certain British institutions like the Ascot picture-hat worn '*à propos de rien*'. A certain ultra-British way of talking was much mimicked, preferably in the most incongruous connections. Bad hands at canasta would be grumbled about in French, and then at some particularly unfortunate [point] in the game out

would come, in a Poona-colonel voice, 'Oh murdy-wurdy.' Princess M. loved the public-school way of ending words and proper names in '-ers'. From Chassy, N.'s name for me, I became Chassers. Chin, the one-eyed Pekinese at Kensington Palace, became Chinners-old-top. Sometimes he was called Chassers by mistake.

Princess Marina had the strong and admirable sense of duty that characterised the Romanov women. She carried out a heavy public programme with typically effortless ease. Close though we were to her, she never spoke a word to us about this side of her life – not a complaint, not a joke, not a shadow of a comic description such as she was always pulling out of her unofficial life for our entertainment. The official part of her existence was a closed book. In the 1920-ish slang of her family, a public function was 'a stunt' – and that was all one heard about it. Having seen her for years at Wimbledon, I can imagine that she got a good deal of satisfaction out of her duties. She certainly carried them out with incomparable grace.

She brought her children up to the same high standard of public obligation, and to her daughter she transmitted the extra gift of turning duty into elegance and fun. It was a delight to see such a happy and united family.

She had a rare capacity for loyalty and friendship. Entirely thanks to N., I was enabled to experience the strength and sweetness of this. Consulting her in time of adversity, I could feel a rocklike strength, which came from the firmness of her inherited faith. Also I knew I could depend on an absolute, sepulchral discretion. There was common sense and great warm-heartedness – though none of N.'s flashing Georgian intelligence and instantaneous grasp of a situation. In the last

conversation she had with her, the day we left London in July, Pss Marina was expressing her worry about what I would do when I retired. 'If only he could get some tremendous great plum.' Like what? 'Like, say, Cairns's job.' Cairns's job – Marshal of the Diplomatic Corps – my idea of a total nightmare! 'Well, you see,' rejoined N. mildly, 'he's not really a courtier.'[46]

The nation mourned the loss of Princess Marina from afar, *The Times* producing a leading article:

From the day of her marriage thirty-four years ago Princess Marina had been one of the most popular members of the Royal Family. Her good looks, her ease of manner, and the tragedy of her early widowhood are sufficient explanation of that. But she achieved something more than simple popularity. She made a distinctive contribution to the evolution of that subtle relationship between the Royal Family and the British public. That is not so easily explained of someone of foreign birth, who was widowed after only eight years of marriage, and who thereafter brought up her children as much as possible away from the public gaze and in circumstances of limited affluence.

Despite, or perhaps even to some extent because of, these hardships she was able to respond particularly well to the need for some adjustment of attitude by royalty at a time of rapid social change. She could react warmly to public interest and attention without any loss of dignity. Her presentation of prizes at Wimbledon each year was a case in point. She became in a personal sense part of a

great popular occasion but remained as gracious as ever. It was this capacity to meet in substance both the old and the new demands upon royalty that won a depth of respect and affection among the British public.[47]

Cecil Beaton wrote a fine appreciation of her for the *Sunday Times*. Privately he recorded his deep shock: 'Dreadfully sad. A blow that came very near . . . for people of my age the loss is great for she was so much part of an era, and she added so much to the early days. She was always so vividly around, even until now, so that with her going she leaves a very great gap.'[48]

And Kenneth Rose wrote a tribute, which ended: 'The most adoring of mothers, she watched over her children with a fidelity that was not wholly maternal. She taught them that their lives belong as much to their country as to themselves.'[49]

15

CYPRUS AND
NORTHERN IRELAND

The Duke had a spell in Cyprus, where his squadron of the Greys was part of the United Nations peace-keeping force.

Duke: We were in Cyprus as part of the UN contingent there, which continues to this day and which had started after the EOKA uprising in 1955 – bombing attacks in Nicosia, which caused the then Governor, Field Marshal Lord Harding of Petherton, to declare a state of emergency. Archbishop Makarios was exiled, and the trouble continued until an agreement was reached making Cyprus an independent republic. We decided to send a force to contribute to it. We had a squadron, a small unit, equipped with armoured cars. They were actually scout cars, little things called Ferrets, quite fast and nippy, but they did carry a gun. We had about twenty of these things and we were to cover the whole island of Cyprus, going to visit villages as much as we could, showing ourselves to prove to the local community that the UN were on their side and they'd better behave them-selves, because there was communal friction, which continues today. The Greeks and the Turks actually detested each other intensely. We didn't encounter any particular trouble. Certain villages were notoriously Greek nationalist and others were notoriously Turkish nationalist. You always had to be aware of that and careful of them.

On 25 July 1970, the Duchess of Kent gave birth to her third child, Lord Nicholas Windsor.

Duke: My squadron were out there unaccompanied, but my wife was allowed to come out for a week or so. At one point I was allowed to go home because my youngest, Nicholas, arrived about halfway through our tour.

One incident of that tour left a deep impression on me – the Turks garrisoned the north of Cyprus with quite a lot of troops, so about once a year a ship would arrive with about a thousand Turkish troops and we had to go and protect all this to make sure the Greeks didn't throw bombs at them. It was known as the Turkish rotation. It was a well-polished routine. We were responsible for seeing everything went smoothly and there was no interference. Otherwise it was fairly peaceful. Everybody enjoyed themselves and there was waterskiing and fun, a lot of flying too. It's a lovely island.

The Duke's regiment then moved to Edinburgh. On 4 February 1971 Lord Carrington, the then defence secretary, told the cabinet he would be sending an additional battalion of troops and a squadron of armoured cars to the province, following trouble provoked by army searches of Catholic homes in Belfast. On 5 February the Duke's squadron was sent from Edinburgh to Belfast. This happened shortly after Gunner Robert Curtis was shot dead in the New Lodge Road. He was the first soldier to die during the disturbances.

Duke: We'd been in Cyprus, and were brought back and stationed in Edinburgh. Quite early one morning in February 1971 I was woken by my commanding officer and told, 'You're

off to Northern Ireland,' literally at six o'clock in the morning. There was quite a rush. I had my squadron – 120 men – and we had to get ready in very short order. We drove across, got onto a ferry with all our kit and armoured cars, and went to Omagh, where there was a frightful attack some years later. This was very early on in the campaign. There had been a few isolated incidents, but we used to drive around in ordinary Land Rovers. I was given a revolver as my protection. A year or two later, such a lack of precaution would have been unthinkable. We were brought back after three weeks

I never had that fully explained to me, but it's possible that they thought of me as a target. The whole of my squadron were sent back. I did hear later that Lord Carrington, who was then Secretary of State, was quite upset when he discovered my squadron had been sent and nobody had referred it to him.

We didn't actually do much. We sat about in our barracks, drove around a bit, and I saw a few friends. Then we came back. I suppose I could at least say I'd been in Northern Ireland.

The Duke was photographed commanding an armoured squadron on border patrol in County Tyrone. Concern grew after riots in which a soldier and three civilians were killed. Finally he boarded a vessel at Larne, Co. Antrim after three weeks' border control duty.

Sir Richard Buckley: Spearhead was a squadron on standby to go anywhere in the world at short notice, up in Edinburgh, and he was there. He rang me at two or three o'clock in the morning and said, 'I'm going to Northern Ireland. I want you to know, but don't tell anybody else.' Now, come on! I rang the Queen's

private secretary, Michael Adeane, then Carrington and the whole thing was a great harouche,* I can tell you.

He was there a shortish time, quite sensible, but one general did say to me, 'It's not quite our only worry that the Duke might get killed. We are also afraid that the Duke might have to order people from his squadron to shoot a British citizen, which would be a major disaster.' True or false, that's what the general said to me, and I think a much better reason for leaving, than being got out of the way.

Government papers give the timeline that Commander Buckley telephoned Buckingham Palace to ask if the Queen knew that her cousin was in Ulster. She did not. Neither did senior courtiers nor the cabinet. Five days later Sir Michael Adeane, the Queen's private secretary, lunched with Lord O'Neill, former Prime Minister of Northern Ireland. He then wrote a report for Sir Robert Armstrong, the cabinet secretary, for him to give to the Prime Minister, Edward Heath. Adeane's letter included a warning: '[Lord O'Neill] noted that if any means could be found . . . of sending the Duke of Kent elsewhere before the beginning of March or even sooner it should be taken.' At the Queen's request, the Duke was kept away from the Belfast trouble spots and undertook border patrols instead.

Sir Robert Armstrong highlighted the problem in his reply to Adeane:

In one sense it is admirable and right that the Duke of Kent should be regarded in exactly the same light as any other

* Harouche: a colonial word indicating a bureaucratic disturbance, in which a culprit was often sought.

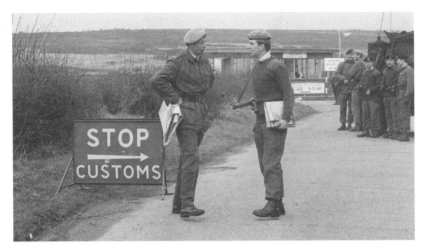

The Duke on border control in Northern Ireland in 1971

officer. But that is to take too limited a view. We accept that orders to him to go to Northern Ireland should not have been given without prior consultation. We are all sorry that this was not done and the Defence Secretary is taking steps to see that it will not happen again.

Sir Richard Buckley: You can see how the pattern of his life was changed by the Northern Ireland problem. The generals were very keen on saying, 'He's such a good army officer we don't want to lose him,' which was very nice, but it was edging up to a new style. He started to take an interest in mechanics and electronics, which had not been his scene.

HV: Richard said that the generals were terribly keen to keep you in the army as long as possible. He remembered that. And obviously Northern Ireland made it all a bit complicated.

Duke: Peter Carrington, who was then defence secretary, discovered I had gone – he hadn't known! My squadron had been the

standby squadron to go. And evidently no one had informed the Ministry of Defence. And he was apparently furious and said that we must come back. This wasn't particularly alarm over danger to me but the fear that I might be captured, I suppose, by the IRA.

HV: Oh, that is interesting because Richard also said it might have been that you would have had to order the squadron to fire . . .

Duke: Well, that is also a possibility, but I think the trouble was the same as that facing my poor cousin Harry in Afghanistan. I think he was pulled out for very similar reasons – there was worry about the possibility of him being captured, which is quite understandable.

Of course I wanted to be treated exactly the same as everyone else. It was still quite an early stage in the emergency. In fact, it was quite difficult to tell that there was an emergency going on. There were very few incidents and it was almost peaceful but I don't think that lasted very long.

I remember giving an interview to somebody in the media at quite an early stage when I got out there.

The Duke and his squadron returned to Edinburgh, where Philip Norman interviewed him about his life and he was photographed by the well-known war photographer Don McCullin. That took place on 16 March 1971 as part of a series showing a day in the life of all members of the Royal Family.

Duke: I was photographed at Redford Barracks in Edinburgh. My black Labrador, Flint, was there. Flint wasn't a great success.

The trouble was that he was fine with me and he wasn't a bad gun dog but he was vicious with other dogs. He attacked a lot of them so I had to get rid of him, which was a great pity. He didn't last very long, poor old thing.

The article stated that the regiment ate their meals under a portrait of a previous honorary colonel, Tsar Nicholas II. In the summer the Royal Scots Greys were to amalgamate with the Third Carabiniers to form the Royal Scots Dragoon Guards. The Duke regretted the loss of berets, which represented the grey chargers of his regiment at Waterloo and Balaclava, and that the Carabiniers would lose their identity altogether. (The grey berets were reinstated four years later.) The squadron was just back from Northern Ireland. Some of the men were on leave and others had already been posted to Germany. The barracks 'with their faint odours of polish and cooked cabbage had some of the mournfulness of school in the holidays'.[50] The Duke's recreations were a record player, reading Sir Basil Liddell Hart on the Second World War, and novels by Evelyn Waugh and Anthony Powell.

Duke: The amalgamation happened a couple of months later, at the beginning of July. The Queen came to a ball at Preston Hall, just outside Edinburgh. I went to Edinburgh for the fiftieth anniversary of the amalgamation in September 2021.

Following his peremptory return to Edinburgh, there was not much going on so the Duke was glad to have some days' hunting.

On 20 March, he was hunting with Lord Dalkeith, heir to the Duke of Buccleuch near Hawick. Lord Dalkeith's horse failed to take a drystone dyke and fell on him. He

was paralysed from the chest downwards, with a fractured
spine.

Duke: He was a good friend and he knew that I liked hunting so
he very kindly said, 'Well, come and hunt with us one day and
I'll find you a nice horse.' I went over there and we went off on a
bitterly cold day, up in the hills of Dumfriesshire. Out hunting
there can be quite long pauses when nothing much happens.
And we had lost sight of the hunt, so Johnny said, 'You wait
here.' We were on the edge of a wood. 'I'll meet you on the other
side. I'm just going round to see where the hounds have got to.'
Ten to fifteen minutes later I rode round the wood and found a
woman holding Johnny's horse. And I said to her, 'Isn't that his
horse?' She said, 'Yes, it is and he's had a very bad fall. He's just
over there.' I went across and there he was, lying on the ground,
quite inert. His horse had fallen and flung him off over its head
and he had broken his spine, the poor man.

It woke me up to the extraordinary unreality of the hunting
world. Of course there was no doctor or on-site ambulance so it
took *ages* for any sort of medical attention. Finally somebody
appeared in a Land Rover and poor Johnny was lifted off the
ground in great pain, shoved into the back and taken off to
hospital.

It was an absolutely ghastly day. I will never forget it. He was
paralysed from then on.

Afterwards he was totally positive. He told his mother that
even as he lay there on the moors he had realised he would
probably never walk again, but that a kind of calm and serenity
had come over him and he had determined that he could live a
worthwhile life. When she went to see him in hospital, he said
how lucky he was that he could still move his arms. I was very
fond of him – he was a remarkable man.

Lord Dalkeith stayed in hospital in early September 1971, and spent the rest of his life in a wheelchair. He was the first MP since the Second World War to enter the chamber of the House of Commons in a wheelchair. The Prime Minister, Harold Wilson, crossed the floor to shake his hand.

In 1972 the Kents put Coppins on the market and the Queen offered them Anmer Hall, near Sandringham.

Duke: We finally got out of Coppins in 1972. It was in very nice country before the war, but by the 1960s and 1970s it was becoming very grimy and the traffic was appalling, so we had set our hearts on something a bit further away in real country. We were lucky enough to be offered a house at Sandringham. We had to find a buyer for Coppins and, fortunately, we did. We were quite sure we would have to keep a foothold in London so we were offered an apartment, York House, at St James's Palace. It had two reception rooms and five bedrooms and housed our Household office alongside. It was a small part of York House, which had been the Prince of Wales's in the twenties and thirties. My father shared it with him before he was married, not the part we had, but it was very close. At that time in the seventies there were still sentries marching up and down in the courtyard, which became intolerable because it went on all night. Thump! Thump! Thump! Thump! Crash! Eventually my wife and I decided we couldn't stand that any longer and we complained and they shifted the sentry a bit. It was a huge thing to move the sentry, but they did, thank God! We were in that house for certainly twenty years, probably more.

We were so pleased to be offered Anmer Hall. Anmer was occupied but we were taken to have a look – we saw two or three

Anmer Hall, Norfolk

places, and Anmer was by far the nicest. The family who were living in it were quietly encouraged to move out and were very nice about it. They had their own house anyway not very far away.

We were at Anmer longer than we were at Coppins. It was a lovely house, a perfect family home. It was too big really, but it was ideal for three children – it had a lot of space, a lovely garden, and it sits in quite a large park. The children could run around with the ponies or their bicycles. Also a great many people lived nearby who became friends and we were not far from the sea. It had every advantage. I regret ever having left it.

The Duchess of Kent: We absolutely loved it. It was close to the beach at Brancaster.

Earl of St Andrews: Anmer was on the Sandringham estate: we could go out rabbiting with the keeper, the sea was nearby and Brancaster. Anmer was a lovely house, plenty of space, very quiet, peaceful, dark skies at night and no traffic noise whatsoever. We were there for nearly twenty years, I suppose. We left Anmer in 1990.

We were in London a bit too. We had York House from 1972 until 1997 or 1998. We were very lucky to have that house in St James's Palace. It didn't have a garden but it had a lot of history and it was fun to walk up St James's Street and explore that bit of London. It was a great London base.

When we first went there the place was still open to the public, and people would stare through the dining-room window. It was only two or three years later that the security was stepped up a bit. I remember that we were there when the bomb went off at the Carlton Club. It was really quite close, and shook the house.

Lord Nicholas Windsor: I was sitting with my father and we both heard this powerful thud that could only be one thing, and went outside to have a look and then were chivvied back indoors. It was very close. In those days there were always two armed soldiers in their fatigues going around at night. That was before anyone got used to seeing armed police.

My father was very much a countryman at heart. His bedroom looked more or less up St James's Street and at night there was a thing that large unladen lorries were allowed to drive down through central London but only at night, and they made this particular noise, as they used to clatter round the corner and up the hill (I can hear it now) and I know it didn't improve his sleep. So he couldn't wait to get up to Norfolk. Total quiet!

Every Friday night we'd bundle into a train, my mother and me, because my siblings were at boarding school, and every Sunday night we'd come back late in my father's car. And the journeys were not so short in those days. He'd make a big effort to get up there.

When we first lived there, Ambassador's Court, the inner courtyard, was completely open to traffic and it was a favourite rat run for taxis. At a certain point they closed it to cars but pedestrians were still allowed through, and people used to come in and peer in at us having breakfast and perhaps other meals as well, because the dining room was on the ground floor but then they built a rather feeble set of railings outside the window.

Duke: We moved into York House at about the same time as moving from Coppins to Anmer, which was quite ambitious. We wanted to be near the office, which was also in York House. I can't pretend I was ever very fond of it as a home. Ambassador's Court was completely open and a lot of people used to come in there.

Lady Helen Taylor: There was a year between Coppins and Anmer, and we were at York House, which is now the Prince of Wales's office, and I don't think anyone liked that house. We called it 'the workhouse'. We loved Anmer deeply. I was at school in London and we used to get the train up to Norfolk on Friday night. Those were the days where there were compartments and stewards would bring hot buttered Chelsea buns so we ate the whole way. Anmer was heaven to grow up in, so I'm glad it's in good hands now. We were very lucky to live there.

Although Christmas had been celebrated at Sandringham at the beginning of the Queen's reign, the Queen would give Christmas parties at Windsor Castle for the extended Royal Family, which continued until 1987. At that point the castle was to be rewired and the Queen, with her immediate family, returned to Sandringham for Christmas.

Duke: By the time we were at Windsor for Christmas the family was quite large, certainly twenty or more with all the children. It was quite exciting. The Queen would go to the room where the presents were and she would open the doors. The children would run in and see the Christmas tree and then the lights would be turned on and the rest of us were allowed to follow.

Earl of St Andrews: Christmases at Windsor were really special. We did that till I was twenty-five. It really left a great impression, staying in a place like that, having the chance to look at the pictures on the Long Corridor, then the library, a couple of days' shooting after Christmas and seeing the castle from the Long Walk, lit up in front – that was magical. There were one or two pedal cars and, as children, we used to ride up and down the Long Corridor – and roller-skated in St George's Hall and the Waterloo Chamber. I hope we did not do too much damage!

Lady Helen Taylor: We spent Christmas at Windsor every year, and we had to have many changes of clothes. My poor mother! When I think of having to dress my four children for four days at Windsor, where you change before every meal – I'd have to sell the house! But we absolutely loved it. Each family had its own nursery, with a sitting room, and bedrooms and a footman to look after us. We didn't join the grown-ups in the dining room until we were about thirteen, so there were nursery teas,

228

lunches and suppers, and we joined in the nursery dining room with the cousins. We all spent a lot of time together as children. Edward, Sarah, James* and I we were all the same age. There is a lovely photograph of the 1963 Christmas, with the four expectant mothers, all wearing their beautiful Dior evening dresses. Tony Snowdon decided to dress up as Cecil Beaton and in the manner of Beaton took photographs of the expectant mothers. Then the following Christmas he took photographs of the four mothers with their babies.

Christmas at Windsor Castle: the Queen, the Earl of Ulster and the Duke of Gloucester.

The Duke was promoted to Lieutenant Colonel on 30 June 1973. He retired from the army on 15 April 1976. (He was promoted to Major General on 11 June 1983 and to Field Marshal on 11 June 1993.)

* Prince Edward, Lady Sarah Armstrong-Jones and James Ogilvy.

From 1971 to 1975 the Duke had a job in the department of the Deputy Master General of the Ordnance.

Duke: The department was responsible for procuring weaponry and equipment, and I was working in the Ministry of Defence. After my regiment was amalgamated, I did two jobs involved with equipment. I remember sitting in a dingy little office somewhere in Hounslow. That wasn't much fun but the tactical management of the project was interesting. I did that for a year, perhaps eighteen months.

Then I worked in the main Ministry of Defence building, occupying a room whose windows were on Horse Guards Avenue. Outside, there are two huge figures, *Earth and Water*, by Sir Charles Wheeler, and between them a balcony with a big terrace. That was my office, looking out between those gargantuan figures.

The Ministry of Defence job involved working on a collaborative project. It was an Anglo-Belgian deal involving the production of 2,700 vehicles for the British and Belgian armies, in the hope that Britain's incorporation into Europe would increase employment chances for British workers.

At that time I did very few royal engagements as I had a job but gradually the engagements increased.

The Duke left the army partly because his service was restricted – he was not allowed to serve in politically sensitive areas such as Northern Ireland. But he also wanted to move forward. He had become interested in promoting the drive in the nation's overseas trade.

16

CIVILIAN LIFE

After leaving the army, the Duke's working life can be divided into three different elements with a certain amount of cross-over: his work for the nation; work with his charities, taken on as a member of the Royal Family; and the royal duties he undertook directly in support of the Queen. He threw himself into it all with enthusiasm.

Duke: I finished at the Ministry of Defence in 1975. I had been looking for something else and in 1973 we had been to Japan, which showed me what I would like to do as an alternative to the army. I joined the British Overseas Trade Board later in 1975. I was not paid for this work.

Sir Richard Buckley: He was setting up a different life, while he was still in the army. He did some quite interesting foreign visits, a few visits at home, looking at things like electronics. He had a great friend in George Edwards, who was at the British end of Concorde.

When he retired from the army, I was really quite worried about what he was going to do. The Royal Family don't do proper jobs. I took out a copy of *Whitaker's Almanack*, went through it and found a section on government offices. I looked down them, and up came the British Overseas Trade Board. The Duke had always been interested in overseas trade. It was cleared through the Queen's private secretary and then the

Prime Minister, Mrs Thatcher, at Number 10. He had his own office and was vice-chairman for several years. That's why he went to China, Korea, Japan and other places, and it generated new interests, more foreign visits, which were right up his street.

The Duke at the wheel of a Rolls-Royce

Duke: At that time the British Overseas Trade Board existed to promote overseas trade and, above all, to persuade companies that weren't doing much about exports to try to enter that field. It was amazing to discover how many businesses had never considered exporting. The Board had a lot to offer, a wide range of different forms of help, with schemes to enable people to get into exporting at minimal cost.

Sir Frederick Catherwood was chairman from 1975 to 1979 and I became his deputy. He had a reputation as an economist.

He was a slightly odd choice for that job because he'd never had any experience as an exporter or a businessman, so many were rather surprised by his appointment, but he was effective. Then there was Lord Limerick, and in 1983 he was followed by the lively Lord Jellicoe who had a great war record, awarded every sort of decoration. He'd founded the Special Boat Service and had done daring and risky things during the war, mostly in the Balkans. He was running one of the big engineering companies. George and I got on extremely well, and I liked him enormously. The job involved a good deal of travelling and I went with George all around the world, particularly to West Africa and the Far East.

Sir Derek Hornby took over from George – his son is the well-known novelist Nick Hornby. He ran London and Continental Railways and believed that big business should benefit society as a whole. He was highly respected internationally as a businessman, known for oiling the wheels and getting things done.

In 1979 I went to China, a fascinating visit at the beginning of the opening up of China. Mao Zedong was dead, and Deng Xiaoping was reforming China. It was now that the great range of radical economic measures was announced.

The British government decided to put on a major British exhibition in Beijing. Around three hundred firms took part, all big names, most of which have now disappeared.

The point was that it was a British exhibition. It showcased what British industry could do, which was quite a lot, and the Chinese welcomed it with dinners and receptions. That was my first visit to China, and we went to see the Great Wall, of course. At that time the country was still in a fairly primitive state. There were no private cars, just a great many bicycles and large trucks, but I saw some of old Peking in the Forbidden City.

When I returned to China twenty years later, the changes were enormous.

Later on I was able to visit other parts of China. We spent a night in Shanghai – the ambassador, Percy Cradock, was a renowned sinologist and fought for the Hong Kong agreement. We also went to Xi'an to see the Terracotta Warriors.

When the Duke left the army, there was an intervention from Lord Mountbatten.

Duke: When I came out of the army, I was looking for something to do, and wanted to become involved in industry and Dickie Mountbatten suggested the National Electronics Council, a rather high-flown title. It had been a brainchild of his in 1963, and I suspect that one or two friends of his in industry had said to him, 'You could do something to advance our interests,' and, with his lively imagination, perhaps he said, 'We'll set up a body to do it.' So he invited me to join the Council – 'Be my vice-chairman, and eventually you could take it over.' I did so and I found it interesting.*

He had managed to get all the big names of our electronics industry, like Weinstock, Plessey, GEC and Ferranti, to come in, and they did because they all had such regard for him. I'm not sure they thought it would do anything particularly valuable, but they were willing to support it. Then, sadly, he stepped down and handed it to me. After that the major players were much less interested in coming to meetings but it continued

* Mountbatten had founded the National Electronics (Research) Council 'to make sure Britain did not neglect the key to the future – electronics'. In April 1977 he became president and the Duke took over as chairman. 'Over the last five or six years I have been training Eddie to take my place as chairman and he has been my deputy, getting better and better all the time,' he wrote in his diary.

until at least the late seventies. John White, who worked with me, had been in the telephone side of the Post Office and understood the technical side of the industry. He was my main point of contact, a wise and intelligent man.

The great discussion at the time was about a strange new means of communication. It hadn't even got a name but, of course, it turned into the internet. At that time no one could have foreseen what it would become.

The Duke and Duchess at the International Exhibition in Japan in 1973

Sir Frederick Catherwood announced that at the British Overseas Trade Board the Duke would take charge of the sixteen committees responsible for exports in different areas. Alongside this, he would undertake certain royal engagements. The job was unpaid.

Peter Shore, the Labour trade secretary, asked why the Duke had been appointed instead of an 'experienced

businessman'. He was told that, while there were plenty of experienced businessmen, to have the Queen's cousin added tremendous prestige.

In 1975 the Duke went to Tehran to attend the International Trade Fair.

Duke: The Shah was still in place. In 1971 he had put on a wild extravaganza at Persepolis to celebrate two thousand years of the monarchy. We didn't go to that event, but Prince Philip and Princess Anne did. There were many sniping comments about the extravagance of the whole occasion. We had wildly ambitious ideas about selling huge quantities of things to the Shah. He wanted to buy Concordes, and it wouldn't have been one or two, it would have been at least a dozen, and a lot of weapons. Luckily, in the end, it never came to anything.

At the trade fair there were groups from the British Steel Corporation, General Electric and others, and the Shah came to look round.

I had travelled on Concorde as a prototype before it went into service. I also travelled on Concorde on its very last flight. George Edwards, of what was then called the British Aircraft Corporation, had become a friend and he arranged that. I was connected and much involved with aerospace for many years.

Our ambassador was Sir Anthony Parsons and he became a good friend. We didn't realise at the time that within three years the Shah would have been overthrown. We hadn't realised how precarious the situation was, although the ambassador hinted at it. We were told to to be very careful about what we said, and that the secret police (Savak) were always watching and listening. But it was a fascinating and beautiful country – we went to Persepolis, Shiraz, and several such places.

Quite early on I visited more than fifty factories in the UK, from British Leyland to a fifty-man company on Humberside selling oils to the Middle East. There were lots of regional exporting conferences as well as tours to Europe, the Middle East, Far East and the Americas. As a nation we are pretty good at exporting. In the late 1970s we were selling about £2,500 million worth of goods each month in visibles alone, which was no small figure. We also managed to grab back an increasing share of total world trade from our rivals. Volume rose by 10 per cent. Even so, three-quarters of our exports were made from a few hundred companies. I was keen to encourage those firms that did not export at all to have a go. Some were probably put off by perceived difficulties and they did not seem to appreciate how many comprehensive government services existed to help small, first time exporters. The target was to get even ten per cent of these firms into the export market, which would make a huge difference.

When I started out, I soon became aware that Britain's best opportunity was selling high-tech goods to newly rich and less traditional markets.

In 1977 R. H. Greenfield wrote in the *Sunday Telegraph*: 'The British are still not very good at selling things, especially to foreigners, at getting onto the customer's doorstep, and staying there until he has placed an order. So, with an inspired illogicality that is typically British, we picked a royal duke out of a cavalry regiment to do it for us, and persuade our industrialists to do likewise. Progressives were suitably outraged, our foreign competitors were duly amused . . . and His Royal Highness the Duke of Kent was astonishingly successful . . . Those maddeningly incomprehensible British

had once again popped an anachronism into the hat, and pulled out a winner.'[51]

In June 1976 the Duke was appointed Chancellor of Surrey University.

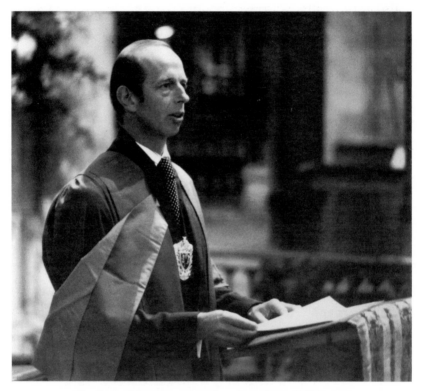

The Duke delivering a speech as President of the British Association for the Advancement of Science, at their 150th anniversary meeting at York Minster in 1981

Duke: Forty-five years later I am still in post, which I value highly. It has been fascinating to watch the development of the university, especially as I didn't go to university. We had some very strong and determined vice-chancellors leading the place.

Professor Max Lu, from Shanghai, has been my vice-chancellor for about five years. He used to be at the University of Queensland, Australia and specialises in nanomaterials. Surrey University is an excellent institution, and thriving.

They emerged from Battersea College of Technology. So they have that basis. Now they are much wider in scope. They have also a strong link with the aero industry and indeed George Edwards who became the chairman of the British Aircraft Corporation was their Pro Chancellor. It was he who first approached me in the 1970s and so I considered becoming Chancellor because I loved the idea. Wonderful. George was there at my right hand when I had become Chancellor. An excellent man and a great friend. They have their degree ceremonies out in the cathedral at Guildford as well, right on top of the hill.

Another key organisation, of which the Duke is still Patron to this day, was the Edge Foundation.

Duke: The Foundation offers British technical education, culminating in a BTech, and I became associated with it around forty years ago. I was always interested in educating young people in some form of trade – I felt it was important that people should learn how to do things – in connection with my particular interest in promoting export trade. In Britain we had slipped behind as manufacturers, although we had often been the first to manufacture certain products, because we were weak in educating people in particular skills. We had been left behind largely by the Germans and Japanese. That was where Edge started life.

And presently he became involved with BICC.

Duke: As the name suggests, British Insulated Callender's Cables

were cable manufacturers basically. They asked me to become a non-executive director in the early eighties, and I accepted. I wanted to gain some experience in the way industry worked, which turned out to be significantly valuable. BICC had started out in 1870 and manufactured insulated cables on their site near the Thames. They were much involved in creating the British National Grid. They went into power cables, telecommunications, and metals, exporting into the Commonwealth during the 1980s.

Shortly after that Vickers, originally an aerospace company, invited me to become a non-executive director. David Plastow had rescued Rolls-Royce when it got into trouble, and became chairman in 1972. Three years later he became a director of Vickers. Again, I accepted. What I learned there was useful in what I did with the Overseas Trade Board.

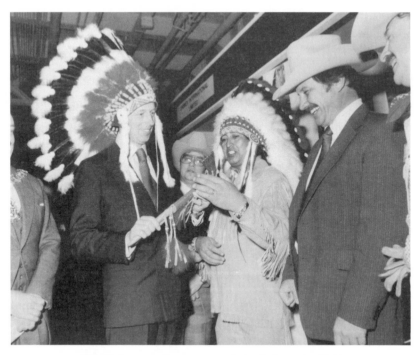

The Duke attending a stampede in Calgary in 1968

The Duke retired from the British Overseas Trade Board in 2001.

I went to Pakistan, India and around the Far East: Singapore, Malaysia, Thailand. I have visited most of the Commonwealth, never for trade purposes. Sometimes HMY *Britannia* was involved for entertaining, and proved to be a huge attraction, giving a magnificent impression. I have been to Russia twice. I stayed briefly in Moscow, and on my second visit in 2000 or thereabouts, I went to St Petersburg, which, of course, is filled with family associations. I had been invited to a conference, which was taking place in the former house of my great-grand-parents, Grand Duke Vladimir and Maria Pavlovna. Remarkably, their home was still in the condition that they had left it. A picture of my grandmother hung on the wall, and my grand-father's desk was still there. It is a very grand house, a proper palace and was astonishingly well preserved.

My great-grandfather died in the 1900s and the Grand Duchess went to live in the South of France. She had a lucky escape. My mother knew her as a child. Of course Princess Olga went to Russia often as a child with her mother, and she knew all of the Imperial cousins who were murdered: at the time they were killed in 1918 she would have been about fifteen.

17

PERSONAL ROYAL DUTIES

Until he returned from Hong Kong and Germany, the Duke's life had been primarily military, with the occasional summons to a royal engagement. Gradually the emphasis changed and he was called on to undertake more prominent royal duties.

During these years there was a balance between his role as Special Representative for International Trade and Investment and his royal duties and patronages.

Duke: Even before my mother died, there weren't so many members of the family available for royal duties. In 1965 the Duke of Windsor, my uncle, was in the London Clinic recovering from an operation for a retinal detachment, and my mother was one of the members of the family to visit him, spending an hour with him and his wife in March. This was a moment of reconciliation: the Queen went to see them twice. My Aunt Mary, the Princess Royal, visited them just ten days before she died suddenly of a heart attack. We all flew up to Yeadon, near Leeds, to attend her funeral at Harewood House. Rather touchingly, the coffin was taken on a tractor-drawn farm cart to the Church of All Saints for her funeral.

The Queen Mother did a number of tours during these years. My cousin Princess Margaret had a young family, and Charles and Anne were still too young.

Having lost the Princess Royal, we soon also lost the Duke of Gloucester, whose health went into decline in 1965. He was unable

to ride in Trooping the Colour that June, and though he continued to undertake engagements, he made limited appearances after the summer of 1966. He'd had a bad car crash driving back to Barnwell from Winston Churchill's funeral. By the summer of 1968, he was suffering from circulatory trouble and dropped out of royal engagements. A series of strokes eventually deprived him of speech and he spent his last years in retirement at Barnwell. It was very sad for him and my Aunt Alice that their son William was killed taking part in an air race in 1972. Uncle Harry died in 1974.

In 1970 Prince Henry, Duke of Gloucester, had resigned as President of the Commonwealth War Graves Commission, due to ill health. He had served for thirty-three years.

Duke: In 1970 I became President of the Commonwealth War Graves Commission. There was a reception to mark this at Canada House in March 2020, coinciding with the seven-hundredth full meeting of the Commission in London. Each visit to the final resting place of those who gave their lives for us is as profoundly moving as the first.

I make a point if ever I go abroad and I can find a war cemetery of going to see it. It adds up to quite a number. I have seen the graves on Ascension Island. Of the 1.7 million of the war dead, very nearly a third have no grave, so although it's called the War Graves Commission, it is actually the War Dead Commission. They don't like to use that word. The remains of soldiers killed during the two world wars are still being found, particularly in Northern Europe. I've been to some of the re-interments, which are very moving. The remains can almost always be identified, thanks to modern science, DNA and so on. Occasionally you come across a headstone with the inscription 'Known only unto God'

because no one has been able to establish the soldier's identity, but that is rare.

The Commonwealth War Graves Commission was founded in the First World War by Sir Fabian Ware. He had wanted to join the army in 1914, but was too old. Instead he commanded a mobile ambulance unit, and took to marking the graves of the war dead. In 1917 as the casualty numbers in France mounted and became increasingly substantial, he said, 'We must lay them in proper sites, and the form of commemoration should be completely uniform, whatever rank they were.' People disagreed. In 1919 the idea that a general should be buried next to a private soldier was anathema. But Sir Fabian won. My uncle David, then Prince of Wales, gave him great encouragement and became the first President.

The Duke, as Colonel-in-Chief of the Royal Regiment of Fusiliers, after presenting new Colours to the 6th Volunteer Battalion at Alnwick Castle on 6 October 1978. The Duke of Northumberland is on the left. On the right is Lieutenant-General Sir James Wilson, the Regimental Colonel

Those lovely memorial crosses and the headstones that you see at the war graves were designed by Lutyens, Herbert Baker and Reginald Bloomfield. Rudyard Kipling came up with the inscription to appear on the memorials: 'Their name liveth for ever more.' It's so evocative of that time. I am very proud to have been connected with the organisation for fifty years.

The Duke balanced this work with travelling for the nation.

Duke: I was able to combine visits for my trade work with War Graves. Quite often a visit overseas for a trade event could incorporate other things as well.

In 1982 my cousin Philip got me involved with the Duke of Edinburgh's Commonwealth Study Conferences (UK Fund), making me a Trustee that year, and Chairman after Edward Guinness retired in 1986. These conferences were originally inspired by Sir Harold Hartley in 1956, Prince Philip being aware that the living conditions of people working in factories were often lacking in facilities, so he was keen to get people to examine 'the tensions, problems and opportunities created by this dichotomy between industrial enterprise and community development.' He convened people locally to address this, right across the Commonwealth, helped by good men such as Sir James Dunnett and Sir Peter Parker.

Besides meetings in in Britain, I went with Prince Philip to the 6th conference in Bombay in May 1986, and on to more sessions in Australia afterwards. We both spent several days at sessions in Oxford for the 7th conference in July 1992, which ended with a banquet at Blenheim Palace. I also took part in Mont Tremblant, Quebec in September 1998, and New Delhi in March 2007. Around 1998 Princess Anne became involved and she took over as Chairman in 2011.

18

SERVING THE QUEEN

There is no defined age for a member of the Royal Family to undertake royal duties. Often they begin gradually, appearing as a page or bridesmaid, perhaps handing out a cup at the Royal Windsor Horse Show. The Duke had walked in the funeral processions of King George VI and Queen Mary, played a prominent part at the Coronation and presided over independence ceremonies. He and his sister, Princess Alexandra, were much called upon in their twenties.

There was no specific training: they had to learn as they went along. A classic case occurred on 21 February 1967 when the Duke was called on to take an investiture at Buckingham Palace. The Queen was ill, Prince Philip was travelling to Australia, the Queen Mother was recovering from a recent operation, Princess Margaret had a chill and the Duke of Gloucester was on a recuperative holiday in Jamaica.

Duke: There were definitely times when I felt I was being thrown in at the deep end, with little warning or the chance to prepare. Doing an investiture was one example.

I did two investitures for the Queen. I was in a staff job in Hounslow, very close to Heathrow, and had just got to my desk when I was rung up and told, 'You'll have to come to London immediately, because there's an investiture starting in two hours' time and you're going to represent the Queen. You have to be in uniform.'

Luckily I had someone at Iver who could collect my uniform, come up to London and meet me at the Palace. There was every chance that it could go wrong but it worked. It's quite a thing to do an investiture. I did another a year or two later. The first was nerve-racking. I'd had no time to read through all the hundreds of names and see what they'd all done and who they were. I remember saying to someone afterwards, 'Well, that didn't take very long,' and he said, 'When Her Majesty does it, she talks to them,' and I hadn't. Of course I hadn't seen it. The second time I did it, I got it right.

The Duke and Duchess of Kent also attended the State Opening of Parliament unless he was stationed overseas.

Duke: Until the hereditary peers were dropped, I used to attend the State Opening. We used to go and sit there in our parliamentary robes with the collar of the senior order we belonged to – GCVO, GCMG or Garter. There was a Royal Family procession through the Royal Gallery before the Queen's procession.

I had taken my seat in December 1959. Then for each session you had to sign on. When a new peer is introduced into the Lords he chooses two sponsors to escort him in. I was going to be one of Prince Charles's, along with the Duke of Beaufort when he took his seat in February 1970. I remember coming down from Edinburgh in 1970 to get to the House of Lords. It was all a bit of a rush. I hadn't a driver so someone had to meet me and get me to the House of Lords for six o'clock – a week before Prince Charles's ceremony of introduction.

Unlike some members of my family, Prince Charles, my cousin Richard Gloucester and Tony Snowdon, I never spoke in

the Chamber. In fact, I was preparing to speak when, along with most of the hereditary peers, I lost my seat in 1999! My particular interests at that time were all to do with youth training and young people's experiences, especially training. I had my speech ready but the system changed and I never had my chance. The current Duke of Gloucester delivered a speech about smoking. Snowdon spoke on disabled issues.

Inevitably politicians came into my life. I met Alec Douglas-Home* a number of times, a delightful man. James Callaghan was a fellow Garter Knight† – he was very agreeable. He had to come rushing back from Guadeloupe in January 1979, in the middle of the 'Winter of Discontent', denying that people out in the world considered Britain to be in a state of mounting chaos. This inspired a tabloid heading: 'Crisis. What crisis?'

I found myself seated next to Margaret Thatcher at events such as state banquets, of which there were quite a number in those days. A conversation with her tended to be one-sided. She would almost deliver an address to one. Denis, her husband, was very nice, very relaxed. We were both members of Buck's Club, and I remember being there once at lunch time when Denis was alone. 'Have a gin and tonic, old boy,' he said. He was very chatty and good fun.

Most orders of chivalry have a royal Grand Master. The Order of the Bath had the Duke of Gloucester, the Royal Victorian Order had the Queen Mother, and the Order of the British Empire had the Duke of Edinburgh.

* Sir Alec Douglas-Home (1903–95), Conservative Prime Minister 1963–4.
† The Duke was appointed in 1985 (see page 258), and Lord Callaghan of Cardiff in 1987.

On 12 October 1967, the Duke was given the Grand Cross of the Order of St Michael and St George (GCMG). This was the colonial order, founded in 1818 by Lieutenant General the Honourable Sir Thomas Maitland. In 1957 the Earl of Athlone, its Grand Master, died, and the officers of the order began to look for a successor. At twenty-one, the Duke was thought too young, so various other candidates were considered. The officers failed to find a royal Grand Master so they opted for an 'exalted personage' as a stopgap. They chose the Earl of Halifax, and after his death in 1959, Field Marshal Earl Alexander of Tunis took over. He considered himself another stopgap, waiting for a time when the Duke was old enough to take it on.

Duke: It was a great honour to be appointed Grand Master of the Order of St Michael and St George, and quite unexpected. There was an annual service at St Paul's but it now takes place every second or third year. When I took over from Earl Alexander, it was a big order, about 1,400 strong, but now it is a good deal smaller because fewer people are being given it. Everyone used to turn out for the service and the big reception afterwards. I can't pretend it was an onerous burden. Some very distinguished people, largely from the diplomatic world, were and are members, senior ambassadors such as Charles Johnston, Nico Henderson, who has been ambassador in almost capital you could think of, and Ewen Fergusson*, ambassador in Paris. Some from Africa and the Commonwealth used to come over for the service.

* Sir Nicholas Henderson (1919–2009), ambassador to West Germany, France and the USA; and Sir Ewen Fergusson (1932–2017), ambassador to France 1987–92.

In 1966 the Queen had appointed the Duke a personal ADC, an honour then only held by the Duke of Edinburgh, the Duke of Gloucester and Earl Mountbatten of Burma. ADCs are chosen to be of particular help to the Sovereign, though it is an honorary appointment reserved for close members of the Royal Family. They wear aiguillettes on their uniforms.

The Duke first rode in the Birthday Parade on 10 June 1967 in his capacity as personal ADC. The Duke of Gloucester had not been well enough to ride in the parade since 1964.

Duke: I was still serving in the Scots Greys and the regiment found me a grey horse. He was a police horse. Police horses are very well trained. They have to be. Finding a suitable *grey* police horse wasn't always easy.

Then someone had to find me the right full dress uniform: the army no longer wore full dress, other than the Household troops. Until the war, it was quite often worn, so it existed, as did the the special swords, spears, and the several ornaments that are needed. It was uncomfortable, especially the bearskin, but I've done it for many years now so I'm used to it.

I hadn't always been a rider. I'd been to that riding school with my sister when we were both quite small but I had never taken to it. When I joined a cavalry regiment, the Greys, my commanding officer said, 'All my officers must learn to ride, so you will go on a riding course,' which I did. I was very grateful that I had. It stood me in good stead.

I had to practise quite a bit before Trooping the Colour. I had to get used to the horse and he had to get used to me. Even though he was a police horse he was quite nervous, and so was I. Afterwards, as we came back to the Palace he was suddenly

bucking and jumping about. Luckily we were coming through the arch into the quadrangle – my bearskin had fallen over my eyes and I couldn't see anything. Later, someone suggested my horse might have been stung by a wasp.

The Major General's Review takes place two Saturdays before Trooping the Colour, and on the Saturday, there is the Colonel's Review. I have ridden in the Colonel's Review – it was considered good practice for the Birthday Parade.

Before I became Colonel of the Scots Guards, I took part as a personal ADC. We rode immediately behind the Queen on the way down but further back on the return as only the Colonels follow her closely and she is always at the front.

The day before the Trooping, at the senior colonels' conference at Buckingham Palace we discuss matters of mutual interest, such as what all the regiments have been doing, where they have been, how their recruiting has been going. Then we have dinner together.

I became Colonel of the Scots Guards in 1975 after my uncle, Harry, Duke of Gloucester, died. That was a tremendous honour.

Every year the Duke rode down the Mall to Horse Guards Parade as Colonel of the Scots Guards. On 13 June 1981, two months before Prince Charles married Lady Diana Spencer, he was again on parade. On this occasion there was a major incident. The Queen was riding Burmese and as the procession turned into Horse Guards Avenue, shots were fired.

Duke: I was right behind the Queen, then Prince Philip and Prince Charles. As we came round the corner from the Mall to go down to Horse Guards, shots were fired. You can imagine the

startled horror. We and the police were rushing about, but the Queen carried on imperturbably. Her horse never batted an eyelid.

HV: Interestingly, it was hardly mentioned at all in the broadcast commentary so it wasn't until the news at one o'clock that I heard anything about it. Then, of course, the Queen rode back past the same spot.

Duke: In that procession the Queen would have had two close escorts. One rode up to tell her everything was under control. There must have been a moment when she wondered whether one of us had been shot behind her.

The culprit was jumped upon by one of the street liner troops, a Scots Guardsman, who became a bit of a hero.

HV: There was also the time in 1974 when Princess Anne was stopped in the Mall.

Duke: She had to sit with the potential kidnapper in the back of the car. Luckily she had an intrepid policeman with her who was quite badly wounded. He was given the George Cross afterwards.

HV: I suppose after that they increased security generally, didn't they?

Duke: Oh, yes. Inevitably security was considerably increased after those incidents.

I remembered something Sir Richard Buckley had told me.

HV: Richard mentioned you might have become Governor General of New Zealand.

Duke: That must have been at least thirty years ago. We still had Anmer Hall in Norfolk. I remember Richard telling me that the idea had come up and, of course, it was very tempting. I would have loved to go there as I'm very fond of New Zealand. But I had young children and it just wasn't practical for me to be twelve thousand miles away with them at school in England.

Representing the Queen also became more of a feature. On 7 November 1967 the Duke represented her at the memorial service for the former Labour Prime Minister, Earl Attlee. The Duke was meant to visit Swaziland soon after his mother's death, but this was cancelled due to him being in mourning – a Swaziland tradition.

Duke: I had laid my first wreath at the Cenotaph in 1961 and continued to do so if I was in the United Kingdom. In 1968 the Queen and Prince Philip were in Brazil so it fell to me to lay her wreath at the Cenotaph. My brother Michael also laid one. We were the only two members of the Royal Family laying wreaths that day. The other royal wreaths were laid by representatives.

Members of the Royal Family died in the older generation, the Duke of Windsor in Paris in 1972 and the Duke of Gloucester at his home, Barnwell, in 1974.

Duke: When the Duke of Windsor died, Katharine and I went to RAF Benson to meet his coffin. There was a funeral in St George's Chapel, attended by family, friends and government representatives, then burial at Frogmore, not far from my parents. Frogmore is very peaceful. I've been inside the Mausoleum, next door. Queen Victoria treated it as a shrine.

My Uncle Harry was accorded a full military funeral at Windsor, with a procession through the town, some of us following the gun carriage. He was buried at Frogmore next to his son William.

In the 1970s Prince Charles and Princess Anne were old enough to undertake royal duties and inevitably the focus fell on them. They both married, Princess Anne to Captain Mark Phillips in 1973 and Prince Charles to Lady Diana Spencer in 1981; the Duke's son, Nicholas, was a page at the latter wedding in St Paul's Cathedral.

Lord Nicholas Windsor: The entire route from the Palace to St Paul's was lined by foot soldiers, but also very thick crowds all the way, and we, the page boys and bridesmaids, went along that route and it was quite an astonishing thing to see. It's a long way! It's unimaginable we'll ever see anything like that again.

With younger members of the Royal Family taking a more prominent role in public life, the world focused less on the other members of the family, though they still undertook an enormous number of engagements at home and abroad to support the Queen.

The Queen's Silver Jubilee was an important milestone, marking the first twenty-five years of her reign. It was widely celebrated across Britain and in the Commonwealth.

Duke: It is extraordinary to think it is now forty-five years ago. Few monarchs have achieved that. I had been born at the end of the Silver Jubilee year of my grandfather, George V, in 1935. 1977 was a very busy year for the Queen, who made extensive

tours of the Commonwealth, away for seven weeks early in the year, and also went to the major cities in the United Kingdom, including a ground-breaking visit to Northern Ireland. A cartoon in one of the newspapers showed the Queen being given the Victoria Cross for valour on account of that visit.

That year started busily for me. In my new role, I opened the Wembley Conference Centre, Britain's first purpose-built conference centre, with seating for some 2,700 people. It was all very high tech. As I spoke, I was magnified on to a giant four-colour video apparatus behind my podium. It was encouraging to know that the organisers already had bookings well into the early 1980s.

A few days later I was installed as Chancellor of Surrey University. I conferred an honorary degree on Lord Robens of Woldingham, the outgoing Chancellor. There was a service at Westminster Abbey to mark another anniversary – the Diamond Jubilee Service of Combined Women's Services, at which Katharine was Controller Commandant of the WRAC, Princess Anne as Chief Commandant of the WRNS, and my Aunt Alice, Duchess of Gloucester as Chief Commandant of the WRAF.

On 30 May, with the rest of the Royal Family, we attended the Silver Jubilee Gala at Covent Garden. I suppose this was one of the last evenings when the Royal Opera House abounded with guests in white tie and decorations, and ladies in full evening dress and tiaras. Yeomen of the Guard were lining the staircase, and the performance opened with a fanfare from Kneller Hall trumpeters. The programme was partly opera and partly ballet, which included a *pas de deux* to music by Liszt, danced by Rudolf Nureyev and Dame Margot Fonteyn. At the end of the evening, hundreds of tiny silver discs were released into the auditorium.

We had our own semi-state landau to take us, with the three children, to St Paul's Cathedral for the Thanksgiving Service for the reign. This was one of those rare occasions called a 'collar day' so I wore the riband of the GCVO and the collar of my senior order, GCMG. The press caught Nicholas, then aged six, yawning in the front row of the cathedral, where we sat along-side the Queen Mother, Princess Margaret and her children, Dickie Mountbatten, old Princess Alice of Athlone and her daughter May, with husband Sir Henry Abel Smith. The Commonwealth heads of government conference was being held in London, so behind us were Commonwealth leaders, including Archbishop Makarios of Cyprus who, having survived four assassination attempts, died in August that year aged sixty-three.

At the Guildhall, the Queen made her famous speech: 'When I was twenty-one I pledged my life to the service of our people and I asked for God's help to make good that vow. Although that vow was made in my salad days when I was green in judgement, I do not regret or retract one word of it.'

A few days later there was a river pageant, and in the evening we went to the twenty-fourth floor of the Shell Building on the South Bank of the Thames for a cold buffet, to watch a fireworks display over the Thames, which was impressive despite the rain. There were simultaneous fireworks at Alexandra Palace, Crystal Palace, and at Richmond and Greenwich. We all went back to Buckingham Palace in a carriage procession at 11 p.m., and that night the Queen gave Katharine the Grand Cross of the Royal Victorian Order, as a reward for all her work over the last fifteen years. She was able to wear it for the State Opening of Parliament later in the year.

I was also on HMY *Britannia* for the Spithead review of the fleet.

The other great anniversary that year was the centenary of Wimbledon tennis. The Queen joined us for the women's final, won by Virginia Wade. On one day of the tournament some fifty heroes and heroines of the game, who had triumphed in singles since 1877, came to Wimbledon to receive commemorative awards. The two great doubles players Jacques 'Toto' Brugnon and Elizabeth 'Bunny' Ryan got the biggest cheer of the day.

Royal engagements often produce surprises. On one such, Katharine met a boy with a teddy bear called 'Gladly'. She thought that was a curious name and asked him about it, only to be told that he was 'Gladly, my cross-eyed bear', a misunderstanding of the hymn 'Gladly, My Cross I'd Bear.' It has become a family joke, fondly remembered by both of us to this day.

Earl of St Andrews: The Silver Jubilee was wonderful. I remember going in the open carriage to St Paul's, and coming back from the fireworks in a closed carriage at night. That was magical.

George was occasionally drawn into other engagements:

I was my mother's page one year when she was Chancellor of Leeds University – and I remember Edward Boyle, who was vice-chancellor at the time, and meeting some interesting characters at the university. One was Mongolian Shema, who also a historian and he had been brought up in Mongolia.

I went to Trooping the Colour, to Sandhurst for a passing-out parade, and I was lucky enough to go to Wimbledon quite often, and occasionally to the Cup Final when my father still did that.

In October 1985 the Duke turned fifty, and the Queen appointed him a Knight of the Garter. The order is the most prestigious in the world, having been founded by Edward III in 1348. Originally it included the King, the Prince of Wales and twenty-four Knights. They would meet at Windsor for feasting, jousting and a religious service.

Foreign sovereigns were first appointed to the order in the reign of Henry IV. King George III extended membership to include sons of the Sovereign in addition to the twenty-four Knights. In 1805 it was further extended to lineal descendants of George I, who were elected. In 1821 George IV described these as Extra Knights. Queen Victoria gave the Garter to many foreign sovereigns, and at one time Edward VII had as many foreign Knights as English.

When the Queen succeeded George VI in 1952, there were a number of foreign kings and queens, and in the British Royal Family, the Duke of Windsor, the Duke of Gloucester and the Duke of Edinburgh. The Queen had been appointed as Princess Elizabeth in 1947 and there were two Ladies of the Garter, Queen Mary and Queen Elizabeth the Queen Mother.

Prince Charles automatically became a Knight of the Garter when he was created Prince of Wales in 1958. He was installed ten years later. The Queen's other royal appointments have been the Duke of Kent in 1985, the Princess Royal in 1994, the Duke of Gloucester in 1997, Princess Alexandra in 2003, the Duke of York and the Earl of Wessex in 2006, the Duke of Cambridge in 2008, and the Duchess of Cornwall in 2022.

Duke: The Order of the Garter came out of the blue. The Queen sent me a personal letter saying, 'I'm appointing you to be a KG,'

which arrived on the day before my fiftieth birthday. It was so thoughtful of her to have planned it like that. They found my father's Garter star for me – all of the insignia has to go back on the death of the holder. I have got two Garter stars, one was his, and the other was issued to me.

I had to be invested twice. In 1986, there was some fault in the Service of Investiture, which happened in the Garter Throne Room at Windsor with a set of injunctions to the new Knight – although I was given a copy of the New Testament as is the practice at these ceremonies. It had to be done again so I've got two New Testaments signed by the Dean. As supporters, I had Prince Philip and Prince Charles.

Windsor had played a part in the Duke's life from his earliest days, when he was sent there during the war, and went to see the housekeeper during his Eton days, and he had attended many services in St George's Chapel, the most poignant the funeral of his mother in 1968.

A happier occasion occurred in 1992, when his daughter Helen married Timothy Taylor in the chapel.

Duke: The wedding was in the summer. It was lovely to be able to have it in St George's Chapel, which is so special.

Soon afterwards, Windsor Castle was the focus of national interest for a very different reason. The castle caught fire on 20 November. We were driving and saw the fire blazing in the distance hours later. The restoration was extraordinary, so striking and beautiful. It was brilliantly done. It wasn't a matter of putting things back as they had been. I think whoever designed it was determined that they would improve it and the result was highly successful.

Another supreme honour had come on 11 June 1993 when the Queen promoted the Duke to be a Field Marshal in the British Army. Today he is one of five living Field Marshals: he is the senior one, then Lord Inge, the Prince of Wales, Lord Guthrie of Craigiebank, and Lord Walker of Aldringham.

19

FOREIGN TRAVEL

There were several independence ceremonies in quick succession, this being a feature of the Queen's reign as one former empire country after another achieved independence, particularly the African nations, but later several in the Caribbean. An independence ceremony marked the change from British rule to home rule. It was not appropriate for the Queen or the Queen Mother to preside over this, though the Duke of Edinburgh, the Duke of Gloucester and the Princess Royal (Princess Mary), did so. It was a moment of transition. The Queen was most keen that these countries and islands remained as part of the Commonwealth, so it was a dignified transition. Sometimes, though not always, the Queen remained as head of state.

Duke: Soon after Sir Winston Churchill's funeral we left for The Gambia [in February 1965] for independence celebrations. The Gambia was a tiny place in the middle of Senegal. It was the oldest of the British colonies in West Africa, the British ruling there for three hundred years. In my speech in Sierra Leone, I joked that my mother having done the independence ceremony in Ghana and Princess Alexandra in Nigeria, my brother Michael might do The Gambia at some time in the future, but I was sent. We flew in a Britannia aircraft and arrived on 15 February. We were met by the Governor, Sir John Paul, and his wife, and by the Prime Minister, Dawda Kairaba Jawara, previously a

261

veterinary surgeon, who had formed the People's Progressive Party in 1960.

Hardly had we touched down than we were driven to Bathurst, beneath ceremonial arches declaring 'Independence 1965', and gave it a Royal Charter.

There would normally be a twenty-one-gun salute from cannons, but the cannons at the airport did not work, so the operators lit thunder-flashes and threw them into the barrels.

The next day state delegates were presented and in the evening after dinner we watched a procession of traditional lanterns. The Wednesday was a public holiday, during which representatives of the six area councils were presented and then all the district head chiefs. The Royal Marines were on parade for the tattoo and flag-raising ceremony that night in MacCarthy Square followed by fireworks. On Independence Day the Governor was sworn in as Governor General, and I read out a message from the Queen, then handed the constitutional instruments to the Prime Minister. Afterwards schoolchildren sang traditional songs, and in the evening there was a state ball at Government House. On the last day there was a State Opening of Parliament. I read the speech the Prime Minister had given me and he replied. Before we left, the Prime Minister renamed Clifton Road. It became Independence Drive.

Cledwyn Hughes and Lord and Lady Milverton were with us from the British government, and The Gambia became the twenty-first member of the Commonwealth.

On the same day as independence, 18 February, my mother represented the Queen at a Thanksgiving Service in Westminster Abbey to mark the occasion. In 1970, after a second referendum, the country became a republic, with Sir Dawda Kairaba Jawara its president. He was re-elected five times.

In May 1966, the Duke and Duchess flew to British Guiana
for the independence ceremonies, and then in October 1966
to Barbados.

Duke: British Guiana became Guyana following independence,
granted in May 1966. The country had been under British rule
for 135 years since 1831. The ceremony took place in Queen
Elizabeth Park, immediately renamed National Park. There was
a tremendous water pageant on Demerara River and dancing to
steel bands long before the midnight flag-raising. Guyana
became a republic in 1970.

We went to Barbados later that year. English settlers had
arrived there as long ago as 1627. It was very much a plantation
economy and enslaved Africans worked on the plantations until
slavery was abolished in 1807. Barbados remained a colony until
it became an independent state in the Commonwealth, the
Queen remaining as head of state. Recently, on 30 November 2021,
the fifty-fifth anniversary of independence, the country became a
republic with a president. The Queen sent a message to say that
it was 'a source of great satisfaction that Barbados remains an
active participant within the Commonwealth' and looked
forward 'to the continuation of the friendship' between Britain
and the Barbadians. She sent Prince Charles to ensure a smooth
and amicable transition.

For independence in 1966 we stayed at Government House.
On that night, Errol Barrow, the Prime Minister, was jubilant as
the new flag of Barbados was raised on the parade ground.

It is also traditional to send a member of the Royal Family to
attend coronations overseas on behalf of the Queen. The
well-loved Queen of Tonga, Queen Salote, had died in 1965.
Her son's Coronation took place two years later in June 1967.

Duke: The Coronation of the King of Tonga – King Tāufa'āhau Tupou IV – in June 1967 was a very grand occasion in the equivalent of the cathedral in Nuku'alofa, the country's capital, a fine white building with mahogany panelling inside. Tonga has 169 islands in all, though only thirty-six are inhabited. Nuku'alofa is on the main island, Tongatapu. Keith Holyoake, Prime Minister of New Zealand, was among the guests, and the King's children were flown in from school in New Zealand. When we arrived, there was a guard of honour for me, in tropical uniform, to inspect. The King wore red velvet and ermine, rather like a peer's robes, with a long train carried by two pages. The Queen was identically dressed. We watched from our positions on the right-hand side as they were crowned, kneeling side by side. People had come from far and wide, and the noise outside was almost deafening as twelve thousand children cheered their new King.

For weeks pigs and chickens had been fattened for the Coronation feast and brought in from the neighbouring villages. We sat cross-legged in a tent and ate spit-roast pork with our fingers from banana-leaf baskets, while singers and dancers entertained us.

On a visit to Britain, the King came to see us at Coppins. He was a big man, and I'm sorry to say he broke one of our chairs, which wasn't up to Tongan weight standards. We should have built a special one for him.

After Tonga, we visited the Cook Islands, then as now under New Zealand administration. There were marvellous flower festoons to greet us. We were certainly the first members of the Royal Family to go there. We went on to Western Samoa and to Fiji.

In April 1969 I was sent to represent the Queen at Queen Ena's funeral in Lausanne. She had been so kind to me when I was at

Le Rosey. When President Husain of India died suddenly the next month, I was sent out for the funeral, staying only a day or two. It was a huge affair, rather disorganised, very noisy. He was the first Indian president to die in office. I was given twenty-four hours' warning that I had to go. He was buried on the campus of Jamia Millia Islamia in New Delhi.

The Duke and Duchess visited Australia in 1969, going to Canberra and Darwin (for its centenary), then toured the north, south and west.

Duke: Later in the year we went to Australia for a long tour. It was my first visit. We went all over the country and were lent the Australian equivalent of the Queen's Flight aircraft to move us around. The distances are enormous. Sir Paul Hasluck was the Governor General and we stayed with him in Government House at Yarralumla, just outside Canberra. It was especially interesting for me to stay in that house because that was where my father was to have been at the beginning of the Second World War. His appointment was cancelled in July 1939. He had planned much of the décor — such as the curtains and carpets – but he never saw them in place. Lady Hasluck pointed them out to me: 'They were all chosen by your father.'*

I couldn't help thinking that, had things turned out differently, my siblings and I might have spent our childhood there. There's so much to see and the Australians are so welcoming and

* Prince George selected curtains with interlinings, linings and furniture covers costing £1,212, carpet costing £1,109, dressing-tables and mirrors at £60 and Celanese net voile at £260, at the expense of the Australian government. This was all thought to be expensive and there were fears in Canberra lest this might provoke criticism that would prove embarrassing to Prince George and Princess Marina, in light of the heavy Defence programme under way in 1939.

friendly. We admired a lovely concert hall in Melbourne, and the Sydney Opera House is spectacular. We went to nearly every state, north, south and west, to Adelaide, Perth, and Darwin for its centenary. We've been there a number of times since and on that particular trip we covered most of the country. I developed an affection for it that has never left me. It is a wonderful place and I would love to go back.

On a later trip I went to the Australian War Memorial, one of the great features of Canberra. It was opened in 1941 as a memorial to all the Australians killed in the First World War. Later it was extended to take in all conflicts in which Australians had died – in the Sudan, the Boxer Rebellion, the Boer War, right up to the Malayan Emergency and Vietnam. The Australians have their own unknown soldier from the First World War, and I went to the ceremony that took place when he was brought back to Australia. He was buried there on Remembrance Day, 1993. More than 102,000 Australians died fighting in wars overseas.

The Kents also visited Papua New Guinea, the British Solomon Islands and the New Hebrides.

Duke: Papua New Guinea was very special. We went to the opening of the Third South Pacific Games. The Sing Sing sticks in my mind: it was a huge gathering of thousands of people, who were half naked. They covered their bodies with mud, painted their faces in dramatic colours, wore vast feather head-dresses, and their costumes were a mixture of grass skirts, ferns, other greenery and colourful cloth, a truly memorable sight. We felt completely out of place in our European clothes.

Of course, it isn't always so peaceful there. New Guinea is known for its tribal fighting, mercenaries becoming central

figures in Enga warfare. The Enga occupy mountainous regions and are gardeners growing sweet potatoes. There are numerous wars. I read that between 1991 and 2006 there were more than 340 wars, in which 3,800 people were killed, with three million kina and sixty thousand pigs handed over in compensation. Notices were put up, urging the hill tribes not to fight but to resolve their differences in local courts. They addressed issues concerning the killing of women, burning of women's houses, mutilation of corpses, finishing off the wounded, killing in cold blood, taking revenge after peace had been declared, fighting in the wars of others, killing the enemy outside the battle area, or on the lands of other clans in the high forest, or at major rituals, or Tee exchanges.*

The ones we met were very charming people, and they did wonderful dancing and singing. We were very honoured to see that. That all happened as an adjunct to the Games.

In 1986 the Duke went to Botswana for the twentieth anniversary of independence. He took his son George with him.

Duke: I remember going with my son George and a group to Botswana in 1986.

Earl of St Andrews: It was a wonderful trip. We flew down there in stages. I think we picked up a Queen's Flight plane in Dar Es Salaam and went on from there. It was the twentieth anniversary of independence so we were at the official events, the parades and ceremonies, and then a few days at the

* Tee exchanges integrate a system of economic barter in which pigs, shells, and other valuables are exchanged in a formal and ordered fashion.

Okavango Delta – I think de Beers arranged it – and saw many birds and animals. On the way back we stopped at Zimbabwe and went to Victoria Falls, then stopped at Harare and Khartoum. I was twenty-four, and had come down from Cambridge the year before.

Duke: We also went to places like Gabon and Cameroon. They were way off the beaten track and hardly visited at all.

In the 1990s and through to the present day, the Duke's royal duties continued. From time to time he travelled in HMY *Britannia*. He was present at the decommissioning ceremony at Portsmouth in December 1997.

Duke: That was sad. I had been on board her several times because she was used frequently when trade missions came to the UK or even for purely diplomatic purposes. She was a wonderful place for parties. I undertook a voyage in Portugal from Faro to Lisbon in her, and later, in 1995, the Kiel Canal. I also did a tour of Britain in her just before she was decommissioned. Princess Alexandra and I boarded in Liverpool. It was always so special sailing on her.

The Duke continues to represent the Queen at home and abroad.

In the 1990s, the Duke and Duchess gave up Anmer Hall.

Duke: We moved to Wren House in the nineties, which suited us very well, although it was quite small. After we left Anmer, we bought Crocker End, near Henley. I think that after Anmer anything else would have been a bit of a disappointment, which

Crocker End was. It had its points, including a nice garden, but we stayed there for only a short time. It never came close to Anmer in our affections.

Earl of St Andrews: We weren't at Crocker End for long. We made some good friends and got to know that corner of the Chilterns quite well. I think my father may have regretted giving up Anmer. Those years we had we enjoyed.

The Queen had celebrated her Silver Jubilee in 1977. Since then there have been two more: the Golden Jubilee of 2002 and the Diamond Jubilee of 2012.

Duke: At the beginning of 2002, my cousin Princess Margaret died, after a long illness, on 9 February. She had been our neighbour at Kensington Palace and on the Monday evening, we all came out to follow her coffin to the advance gates, the hearse piped by two pipers. Her son David had put candles in all the palace windows and it was very moving. My Aunt Alice, Duchess of Gloucester, then aged 100, sat in her porch, to watch it go by. Katharine and I attended the funeral in St George's Chapel with all our children, and the Queen Mother flew down from Sandringham for the service. She died a few weeks later on Easter Saturday at the age of 101.

Walking in the processions for my Aunt Elizabeth, we were moved by the touching response of the general public, who came out to pay their respects. Particularly interesting was the diversity of ages of those who had travelled miles to see the funeral procession, or to queue for the impressive lying-in-state. It took us twenty-eight minutes to process from Marlborough Road to Westminster Hall.

The year of the Golden Jubilee began with sadness for the family, and in a sense this set the tone for the year: support for the Queen, arising from sympathy towards her in the loss of her mother, and the sister who had been her childhood companion. As with the Silver Jubilee, she travelled to many parts of Britain and the Commonwealth, and the affection and respect in which she was personally held was almost tangible.

In the summer there were the usual celebrations, this time highlighted by a classical concert in the grounds of Buckingham Palace and the famous pop concert with Brian May playing 'God Save The Queen' on the roof of the Palace. Then, as in 1977, the Gold State Coach made a rare appearance, bringing the Queen and Prince Philip to St Paul's Cathedral for the Thanksgiving Service.

In a year of some 231 engagements, some were specifically related to the Jubilee – I opened an exhibition of royal vehicles over the previous half-century, 'Royals on the Road', at the Heritage Motor Centre in Gaydon, Warwickshire, in March, and a Jubilee Roller Coaster in Lincolnshire in May, then went to Belfast for a Jubilee Thanksgiving Service in June.

There was some independent overseas travel. In May I paid a short official visit to Mongolia to strengthen Anglo-Mongolian relations and in June, with the RNLI, to Galway. In July work with the Commonwealth War Graves Commission found me at the Archangelsk and Vaenga cemeteries in northern Russia. I was hardly back than I was off to the Menin Gate at Ypres. Especially memorable was the Garter ceremony in June at which five European sovereigns walked in the procession. On that day the Queen installed King Harald of Norway.

On 18 October I flew to Egypt for the sixtieth anniversary of the Battle of El Alamein, recognising this alongside President Ciampi of Italy. I showed President George Bush round the

American Air Museum at Duxford at its re-dedication, with
Prince Charles present.

By the time of the Diamond Jubilee, ten years later in 2012,
the Queen was eighty-five and Prince Philip ninety-one, so the
world came to them rather than them travelling to far-off places
in the Commonwealth. As much as possible the Royal Family
undertook the travelling for them. Prince Philip missed most of
the main celebrations, as he was hospitalised with pneumonia,
following the river pageant.

On 30 March 2012 there was a fine memorial service in
St George's Chapel for the Queen Mother and Princess Margaret,
to mark the tenth anniversary of their deaths. In April I repre-
sented the Queen at the Sovereign's Parade at Sandhurst, which
was also the two-hundredth anniversary of the Academy's
foundation.

During that year, I visited Melbourne, Australia, for a raft of
different engagements, including Commonwealth War Graves,
the ladies' singles tennis finals in the Australian Open, and the
Australian British Chamber of Commerce, and went to a naval
shipyard in Adelaide before flying home. In July there was a
Commonwealth War Graves visit to Greece.

The Queen gave a lunch for sovereign monarchs from all
over the world at Windsor Castle on 18 May. I also went to
Prince Charles's dinner for them at Buckingham Palace. The
Diamond Jubilee was further commemorated with an Armed
Forces Parade and Muster at the castle, an arts evening at the
Royal Academy, the flotilla on the Thames, the Diamond
Jubilee concert at the Victoria Memorial and the traditional
Thanksgiving Service at St Paul's. London hosted the Olym-
pic Games and I went to the opening ceremony on
27 July, and then greatly enjoyed attending a number of
the events.

I went to Uganda for the fiftieth anniversary of independence, and to the Falkland Islands for the thirtieth anniversary of the war, attending their Remembrance Day commemoration in the cathedral. Meanwhile my brother Michael laid a wreath on my behalf at the Cenotaph in London. I travelled via Ascension Island, where I visited the Jubilee Island View Picnic Site.

It was a memorable year.

The Duke with a local yak herder in Mongolia,
enjoying time off during his overseas travels

20

THE PRESENT DAY

The Duke continues to undertake numerous royal duties. A number of his charities and organisations have family connections, just as he has a strong emotional bond with the county of Kent, from which his title derives. He became president of the Royal National Lifeboat Institution in 1969, after Princess Marina's death.

Duke: The RNLI is very close to my heart because I inherited that from my mother, who had been their president since my father's death in 1942. I've done it now for over fifty years and of course I have the highest regard, respect and affection for it as a body and individually. Lifeboat crews are nearly all local people who live around the coast. They might be shop keepers or farm managers – they have other jobs. They all carry a little alarm in their pockets – it used to be known as a pager – which rings if they're needed. Then, if they're not a hundred miles away, they drop everything and rush to be in the lifeboat to take part in the rescue.

It may be the rescue of a ship or a boat, or people, sometimes even a dog stuck on a cliff. It doesn't matter what it is. They turn out to save a life. The weather is very often dark, foul, but out they go.

After fifty-two years I have got round many of the lifeboat stations and hope to visit more.

Nick Turnbull: The Duke is Patron of the Polish Hearth Club. He is very proud of his Polish links, which connect him directly to his father. The Polish clearly think of him as theirs. Then there are the Freemasons, another family thing, as his father and before him the Duke of Connaught were involved. They value their relationship with him. For him, it evokes service, charitable giving, brotherhood. He feels connected.

In December 1963, the Duke became a Freemason, joining the Royal Alpha Lodge, No. 16, which was founded in 1722. The Royal Family had been associated with Freemasonry since Prince Frederick Louis, father of George III, was initiated in 1737. The Duke's father had been initiated into the Navy Lodge in 1928, succeeding the Duke of Connaught in 1939, and Prince Philip joined the Navy Lodge in 1952. In 1966 the Duke became Senior Grand Warden and the following year Grand Master.

Duke: I was first approached about becoming a mason while we were in Hong Kong or soon afterwards, in the early sixties. I agreed. Of course, all the people involved at the top level were many years older than I was. I wasn't even thirty, I suppose. Eventually it became clear that they had an idea of me becoming Grand Master, the top person. In the end I agreed to that. It was all very much accelerated. Normally you would wait for years to go to that sort of position. In my case, I became Grand Master about three and a half years after I joined. I wasn't very well prepared, but it has been a great source of interest, fascination and satisfaction for a long time. And now it's been fifty-four years since I became Grand Master.

My father had been Grand Master before the war, but sadly for only three years, and they definitely wanted another member of the family. There hadn't been a Grand Master who wasn't a member of

the family for many, many years. Lord Harewood, husband of my Aunt Mary, had followed my father for five years or so. Then Lord Scarbrough – and I followed him. The Duke of Connaught held the record for the longest service, but I have overtaken him.

The Grand Lodge was formed in 1717 of four London lodges. They, the Irish and Scottish lodges all subscribe to the same basic principles of brotherly love, relief and truth. I have always seen Freemasonry as a way to contribute in a practical way to improving the world, and alleviating suffering and distress.

There is much more openness about Freemasonry now. Freemasons have frequently been accused of being a secret society but they rebuff that: 'We are not a secret society at all. We are a society of people who know one another, and we share a few secrets simply as a matter of privacy, but there is nothing secret, and still less anything sinister.' They list the kind of things they do – the old people's homes they run – and they raise an enormous amount of money every year for good works.

One of the things I've been trying to do in the last fifty years is to make Freemasonry more open so that people understand there is nothing secret about belonging to or the activities of Freemasons.

The Duke had never been to a Masonic meeting in another country until his cousin Princess Elizabeth of Yugoslavia organised a visit to celebrate the centenary of the Grand Lodge of Serbs, Croats and Slovenes in Belgrade. Freemasonry had been renewed in Serbia in 1876 and the Grand Lodge established on 9 June 1919. At that time the Lodge defined their focus as contributing to a better and more humane world, with humanitarian missions, seeking a balance between the cosmopolitan and the local, striving for the modernisation and Europeanisation of Serbia and Yugoslavia, building and

democratising society. They were particularly committed to maintaining peace in the Balkans and in Europe. The visit took several months to plan. The Duke was present at the fiftieth annual assembly in Belgrade on 22 June 2019.

The Duke of his visit to the Freemasons in Serbia in June 2019. Left to right: Dr Lukas Rasulić, Grand Master of the Regular Grand Lodge of Serbia, Denis Keefe, British Ambassador to Serbia, the Duke and his cousin, Princess Elizabeth

Princess Elizabeth: One great thing we did was to bring Eddie here two years ago because he is the head of the Masons in the UK. They bent over backwards to give him a good time. Here the head of the Masons was a remarkable neuro-surgeon in Belgrade, and they entertained Eddie at a huge banquet with a thousand people. They were so happy to have him there. Later, at the British Embassy, there was a ceremony for Novak Djokovic, who came to open the tennis court there. That was when I first met Djokovic, an absolute delight. Eddie came to that.

The Duke made a speech in which he hailed Freemasonry as 'the calm centre' in a challenging world. He said:

Your history has not been an easy one. Despite attacks from government and your being driven underground for long periods, there were those among your Brethren who were willing to face the ultimate sacrifice to keep the light of Freemasonry burning. We should today remember them with pride.

Today we live in a world in which the principles of Freemasonry still have a major part to play. They are as relevant in our time as they were when Freemasonry was organising itself more than three hundred years ago. We have a duty to preserve them and to pass them on to our successors.[52]

In 1995 the Duke paid the first of several visits to Dresden. The city had been bombed by the RAF and the US Allied Forces between 13 and 15 February 1945. The Duke became Patron of the British Dresden Trust in 1994. The Queen had visited in 1992 with President Richard von Weizsäcker as part of her state visit to honour the civilian victims. On that occasion, she was booed and eggs were thrown. Banners protested about the actions of 'Bomber' Harris.

The Duke holding hands with President Frank-Walter Steinmeir of Germany and his wife, Elke Büdenbender, in a human chain in Dresden in 2020, respecting the 75th anniversary of the bombing in 1945.

Earl of St Andrews: His engagement with Dresden means a lot to him. He was quite involved in the Dresden Trust, which helped raise money for the reconstruction of the Frauenkirche, in particular the cupola with the golden cross, and was present when it was lowered onto the dome. I was talking to another cousin, Princess Gisela of Saxony, who was there when that happened and she told me that the whole city fell silent. The bells rang. The circle had turned.

Duke: Apart from the Queen's visit, there had been no official contact for fifty years and then somebody invited me through our embassy to go for the fiftieth anniversary of the bombing, in 1995. There was a ceremony at the cemetery with solemn speeches and I went in uniform. Our chief of defence staff was there, and the ambassador, and then they invited me to come for a further visit. Shortly after that they announced they were going to rebuild the great cathedral, the Frauenkirche, which had been totally destroyed. I saw it in ruins. The Communists had wanted to keep it as a pile of ruins to act as a kind of shrine, and it was quite controversial. In fact they were outnumbered and it was decided to go ahead. It cost a great deal, of course, and with typical German thoroughness, they'd gone through the pile of ruins, and sorted it all out and had numbered every single piece of stone, shard of glass and wood, and it was all in huge sheds, carefully numbered, all over the square. I came back at least once while the rebuilding was going on.

When I first went in 1995, the Bishop of Coventry, Simon Barrington-Ward, came and preached. Coventry was twinned with Dresden. Coventry Cathedral had been bombed at the very beginning of the war. But the destruction in Coventry was on a lesser scale than it had been in Dresden.

The trouble was that Sir Arthur 'Bomber' Harris had taken the raids to extremes. Churchill and the cabinet wanted the RAF to bomb military targets as far as possible – aircraft factories, ammunition – but Harris said, 'No, it's much more important to kill civilians. We shall destroy their morale.' People argued, 'Why should we destroy their morale? They haven't destroyed ours.'

Alan Smith, whose father had been a Lancaster bomber pilot and had taken part in the raids, was a silversmith and he, with a few others, made a replica of the orb and cross, which now sit on the cathedral's cupola.

I handed over the cross in the freezing cold of a snowstorm in 2000. In June 2004, when the cathedral restoration was finished, we saw it hoisted up and lifted onto the top of the spire. When the cathedral had been rebuilt, we saw it had been restored in every detail to what it was – an elaborate baroque interior.

The only thing that suggests the new building is not the original is the exterior stonework, which varies in colour. The masons used as many of the original pieces of stone as they could, alongside new, so much of it is very dark as it bears burn marks. But it's been beautifully done.

I went back early in 2020 for the seventy-fifth anniversary of the bombing. We stood and joined hands. I held hands with the President [of Germany] and we sang psalms. I met a woman who had been a child at the time of the bombing, and she told me a moving story of how she and her family had run to the river and jumped into the water while the air raid was in progress. They thought it would be the only safe way to survive, and they did – she was there to tell the tale. It was so terrifying, she said, because there were burning people everywhere.

I have read a lot about the actual bombing, which is controversial still. I don't think it would have been at the time since it was just part of our campaign to try to eliminate Germany from

the war. Admittedly it occurred very late on, but at that date there were few scruples about killing innocent civilians. That came much later.

Dresden was quite close to Russia and there were a lot of munitions stored there. In February 1945, the Russians were getting very close. A lot of German reservists were there, and they were willing to do anything to slow the Russian advance. The first time I went to Dresden I attended a service in the Kreuzkirche. As we walked across to the service, one or two voices shouted, 'Murderer,' but on the whole I found most people friendly, and glad that I'd come. They seemed to appreciate the gesture. The whole point was for everyone to reach out the hand of friendship and solidarity.

Nick Turnbull: The affection they have for him in Dresden is tangible. He is somewhat embarrassed by it. As a symbol of reconciliation, he held the hand of the President of Germany, in front of the Frauenkirche, It was one of those moments that was truly important. Dresden has been an extraordinary experience for him.

The Duke himself was honoured with the Dresden Peace Prize on 14 February 2015 for his contribution to the reconciliation of Great Britain and Germany especially with his patronage of the Dresden Trust. He was asked to present the same award on the 75th anniversary of the bombing on 14 February 2019, to Kim Phúc Phan Thi, who was the young Vietnamese girl famously photographed following the napalm attack in Vietnam.

Duke: A photograph was taken in 1972, at the latter end of the Vietnam conflict, that became famous. It showed a naked child running, screaming, away from the enemy, severely burned on her back. The South Vietnamese Air Force had dropped a napalm bomb on the town of Trảng Bàng. The picture won the Pulitzer Prize in 1973. She was called Kim Phúc Phan Thi, and I

met her forty-seven years later. She gave me a book she'd written, and she became a friend. She'd gone to live in Canada and founded an organisation supporting international groups providing free medical assistance to children who were victims of war and terrorism. She was also a UNESCO goodwill ambassador for peace. I gave her the prize at the opera in Dresden in 2019.

That 1972 photograph showed the world the full horror of that conflict.

The Duke's private secretary outlined other key charities with which the Duke is most actively involved, including Blood Cancer UK, and he is President of the King Edward VII's Hospital.

Duke: I went the other day to see a new gallery at the main museum in Lambeth – a gallery devoted entirely to the Holocaust. It's intensely moving.

The Duke had been President of the Stroke Association since 1977. In March 2013, he himself suffered a mild stroke.

Lady Helen Taylor: He went to say goodnight to my mother and tried to lift his arm to turn off the light switch and said, 'That's very odd. I can't lift my arm.' She jumped and said, 'Can you really not? I think you might be having a stroke.' He said: 'Don't be so ridiculous.' My mother followed her instinct and immediately called an ambulance. A woman's intuition should never be disregarded and she was spot on. He was lucky. It was a mild one.

Duke: I was all for doing nothing till the day after but Katharine said, 'No, I'm going to call the doctor now,' and did so, and the ambulance came very quickly. In the case of a stroke, it's

important to catch it as soon as possible. At that time I was, and still am, President of the Stroke Association. It was rather appropriate that I should have direct experience. I drew from that connection how important it was to act quickly.

A more serious incident occurred in Scotland in April 2015, when he dislocated his hip.

Duke: I'd had a hip replacement several years previously, and Helen and I were out walking. I don't know if I put my foot in a rabbit hole, but I fell over very awkwardly and knew as I was crashing to the ground that my hip was dislocated. I could feel it. It was always a risk. I thought it had been long enough since the operation to settle down, but it can pop out years later. It's a very disagreeable experience. I was lying there in the heather with my dog beside me, and Helen summoned an ambulance. I was whisked off to Aberdeen, where they dealt with it.

Lady Helen Taylor: It was much more frightening when he dislocated his hip. He was staying with us at Craigowan, up at Balmoral, and he needed to do up his shoelace. He put his foot up on a rock and his false hip popped out. He collapsed on the ground in agony, screaming blue murder, and there was no phone signal. His dog stayed with him, so sweet, and I had to run until I got a phone signal. Luckily the Prince of Wales was staying at Birkhall. I rang Birkhall and their team came up in a Land Rover to the site. They called in a mountain-rescue helicopter, which went off to Aberdeen Royal Infirmary with him in it.

Manoeuvring him into the helicopter was awful to watch because he was in so much pain. He had to have an operation right away. Apparently any other dislocation you can replace manually. A hip has to be done under general anaesthetic but he

was out of hospital the next morning. I went in to pick him up. Apparently Matron had gone in to ask him what he'd like for lunch and he'd thought he could order anything he liked, so he'd said, 'What I'd really like is some cheese.' Someone had had to go to the local delicatessen in Aberdeen and get him the cheese platter with grapes.

And then they said to him: 'But, Your Royal Highness, you'll be needing a stick.' And he said: 'I don't need a stick. Absolutely not.'

As we walked through the ward, it was full of people of his age, seventy-nine, and he said, 'You know, there are a lot of very old people in here.'

Obviously thought is given to transition as far as the charities and organisations are concerned. The Duke stepped down as President of the All England Lawn Tennis Club in July 2021 after an exciting season. He had been president since 1969. It was one of the times when he and the Duchess were most prominently seen by the world.

Duke: Wimbledon had a strong connection with the Kent family, because my father became president in 1929, following the Prince of Wales, and continued up to his death. Then my mother took it over. Of course there wasn't any Wimbledon during the war, so it was effectively from the end of that time. And I followed from her in 1969. So in my case it was fifty-two years, quite a long run for any presidency. It's a great event and a marvellous institution. It's certainly the envy of the world of tennis. All of the leading players and organisers readily acknowledge that Wimbledon is their model. It's the one big event they all look up to, and it's the one all the players want to win. I hope it will always continue. They started covering number one court

about fifteen years ago. For a long time they said, 'You can't cover the court. You must leave it open to the sun and the rain. It's all part of the natural process. Anyway, it's too expensive.' Eventually they were forced to do it by the TV people: 'We can't have that. We can't put up with having no tennis,' they said. And as the broadcasters pay a lot of money, Wimbledon's arm was twisted. Now the other courts are being done. It's expensive covering a court that's already in existence. If you do it from the beginning, it isn't as bad.

HV: I remember that if Queen Mary decided she'd like to go and have a cup of tea, and some chocolate cake, she would rise and the game had to stop.

Duke: Queen Mary didn't like sitting in the sun so if the sun came onto the Royal Box, she would move back a row or two, which also displaced everybody, but that was before my time.

There has always been something rather special about Wimbledon. Even after more than five decades I'm as struck by the electricity in the air I was at my first visit. It changes, but in many ways it is the same. Apart from when I was serving overseas, I have never missed a single Wimbledon.

I have seen many changes over the years – new courts, two new roofs, a museum, and more screens – but the familiar staples remain: the whites, the strawberries and the high standards. The game itself gets more exciting every year, as players reach ever higher levels of excellence and embrace the new technology – even the Hawk-Eye, on which so much can now hinge. For Katharine and me to have shared in even a small part of the highs and lows has been a privilege.

As president, I know that every point won is worthy of recognition, but as a fan, I have my tournament highlights. The first

trophy I ever presented as president was to Rod Laver after his astonishing win in 1969, securing his fourth Wimbledon title. Since then, there have been many edge-of-seat moments. In 2007 the then four-time defending champion Roger Federer took on Rafael Nadal: that was some of the best tennis I've ever seen.

In 2021 there were some shocks. We were disappointed to see Federer apparently wiped out very easily by a Polish player of whom we had never heard. I was there for seven days, rather more than I would normally have been, this being my last year. They presented me with a half-size replica of the men's trophy. It is a beautiful object. The chairman was kind enough to say, 'Please let us know when you next want to come. We hope to see you here in the future.' So I hope to attend from time to time.

Wimbledon always had the Queen as their Patron. I am delighted that the Duchess of Cambridge, who is passionate about tennis, has become their new Patron.

Nick Turnbull: Wimbledon connects with Princess Marina, and I think the Duke has always sensed a very strong familial connection. The Duchess of Cambridge taking over as Patron from the Queen was quite a significant moment. The Duke made the decision this year to withdraw as President of the All England Tennis Club. He may have thought that this was the time to move on.

He is also President of the Scout Association, another passion of his, and I was approached by the Scouts, who described the Duchess of Cambridge's long-standing involvement with the Scouts and wondered what the future might bring. We concluded rather neatly that she and the Duke will be joint Presidents of the Scout Association. The young Scouts have said

they would like to achieve better connectivity with older members of society so,with the Duke of Kent and the Duchess, they have the best of both worlds. I think it achieves quite a lot for an organisation like the Scouts and the principals. I can't imagine we'll be able to achieve the same thing with other patronages, but with the Scouts we've done it and with Wimbledon. We have managed to move rather neatly into the challenging space of succession.

Duke: It's a bit early to say with the Scout Association. The Queen's Scouts, who have achieved various qualifications, have a parade at Windsor Castle in the Quadrangle. They parade first, then go to St George's Chapel. I may be doing that in a few months' time. We'll probably take it in turns.

Music has played a large part in the lives of both the Duke and Duchess of Kent. For many years the Duchess has supported the charity Future Talent.

Lady Helen Taylor: There were many areas that my mother was passionate about, and she really gave them her all, but she particularly loved any music charities. As well as having a strong singing voice (she was in the Bach choir for many years) she's also a really fine pianist, virtually concert-hall level, so that was what she went back to when she gave up royal duties. She went to teach at a primary school in Hull as Miss Katharine and just got on with it. From that she created the charity Future Talent. It just shows it's never too late to find your purpose in life.

Nick Turnbull: The Duchess was determined to do her own thing, go to Hull and be a teacher, have an identity that was distinct, yet she did not want to cut across the institution.

Future Talent is really a fantastic achievement for the Duchess and Nick Robinson, with whom she created it.

The Duchess of Kent: I had been teaching for about ten years in a primary school in Hull, and one of the main things I realised was that so many children from certain areas of the inner cities were never going to get music teaching. I think it all stemmed from that – that there were children who weren't getting music in their lives. Then somebody wrote to me, saying, 'I would like to come and work for you.' Now I have twenty trustees and it's going well. We don't buy many musical instruments – other charities do that. We provide music education. We start them young – the younger the better. We can get music into their bodies and then it just flows. Some are as young as three or four. We started off with three local ones and now they are writing to us for guidance. We have wonderful supporters who come to our events. Nick Robinson, who was headmaster of King's College, Cambridge, is my chairman. That's why we met.

Our vision is to support talented young musicians from every corner of the country and in every genre of music. We hope to break down barriers, enhance opportunities and make a career in music an equal reality for all, as well as to capture the power of music as a force for change that can improve young people's lives.

On 25 October 2021, on her behalf, the Duke accepted the APKM UK medal 'Pro Tuitio Fidei Et Obsequium Pauperum' from the Polish Knights of Malta. In thanking them for the great honour, he said: 'What you have said has reminded me of my wife's interests over the years, especially her interest in music, which has been an abiding thing throughout her life, and still is.'

The Duke's greatest love in music is Wagner.

Earl of St Andrews: My father has a great love of opera and has been to the Bayreuth Festival [celebrating Wagner]. I went with him a couple of times, the first time with Paul Channon, who of course was a lifelong friend, and his wife, Ingrid. That was the memorable Chéreau production of 1980, with Pierre Boulez conducting. I remember that we met Wolfgang Wagner, the composer's grandson.

Duke: It started with Kenneth [Rose] and Giles St Aubyn. They were both keen Wagner lovers, and I remember they said, 'Let's all go off together to Bayreuth.' So we did, and this was in the early 1950s. I was only eighteen, having just left school, and at Sandhurst. I knew nothing about Wagner as there were very few recordings in those days. I had no idea what was going on – I hadn't even read the stories – and I was completely captured by those extraordinary operas.

Some people hate them and find them pompous and over-bearing, but I love them. They tend to be considerably longer than most. Some of the *Ring* operas last four hours. You need a bit of stamina, and the language can be largely incomprehensible to most English speakers – it certainly was to me. It gets into your system eventually and then becomes an enthusiasm that doesn't go away.

Nick Turnbull: The Duke's sense of service is very real, but I think he feels his passion for music lies beyond service. I see more of 'the man' through his affection for music than I do of anything else.

Duke: My interest in music goes beyond Wagner. It started

early and intensified later. At school and Sandhurst, I developed a love of jazz, which I shared with my cousin, Gerald Lascelles. Classical music came later and there is a wide stretch of composers, certainly the seventeenth- and mid-eighteenth-century ones. I am less good on the modern ones. My love of Chopin was inspired by Zoia Poklewska during the war. Then in 1977 Gerald's elder brother, George Harewood, started Opera North, which is an offshoot of the English National Opera, and got me involved with that. They have their base at the Leeds Grand Theatre, and there are performances in Yorkshire, Nottingham and Newcastle, and even sometimes in London.

The Widor Toccata, the final movement of the 5th Organ Symphony, was first played at Princess Margaret's wedding in 1960 and became even more popular when it was played at ours by York Minster's organist, Francis Jackson, who lived to be 104 and only died lately. He was still playing the organ at the age of 100. It was also played at my sister's and at the Cambridge wedding in 2011, and at many weddings both in Britain and abroad.

My music patronages cover a broad spectrum: Trinity Laban Conservatoire of Music and Dance in Lewisham, the International Music Seminars Prussia Cove, which was founded by the Hungarian violinist, Sándor Végh, in 1972. It is based in Cornwall. He was visiting the county and thought it would be an inspiring place to hold masterclasses. Then there are the Royal Choral Society, the Hanover Band (a small orchestra with no state funding), the Newbury Spring Festival, and the King's Lynn Festival. George and Valerie Solti persuaded me to become Patron of the London Philharmonic Orchestra. He had been their chief conductor for some years.

I was going to the Wigmore Hall a lot before I became Patron.

I'm very fond of that place. In the last few years, until the pandemic, I had been going there regularly. The concerts are all on quite a full scale and of very high quality, mostly chamber music. It is something of a spiritual home.

It was music that led to a visit to Grenfell Tower. After the terrible fire at Grenfell Tower in 2017 in which seventy-three people died, my wife went to teach at Holland Park Primary School where a number of the children who had lived there were studying. And on the anniversary, a year after the tragedy, we both went to the Remembering Together Event at the Tower, where I laid a wreath. That was a moving occasion.

The Duke and his maternal cousins: Prince Alexander of Yugoslavia, Princess Alexandra, Helen Habsburg, the Duke and Hans Veit Toerring at York House, St James's Palace.

The Duke remains in close touch with his maternal cousins. In about 2019 Princess Elizabeth of Yugoslavia wanted to talk to Prince Philip about the paintings of her grandfather, Prince

Nicholas of Greece, so she and the Duke drove down to
Windsor Castle together.

Princess Elizabeth: We sat there for an hour chatting to him.
He was very articulate, beautifully dressed in a tweed jacket and
looked really handsome. We talked about my grandfather's
paintings and I said I wanted to do an exhibition. And he said,
'Well, I have two of them here.' He showed me the paintings and
then he sent me two photographs and I had permission to put
on a show of my grandfather's work because he was a brilliant
artist. Cartoonist, artist, portrait painter, and he taught all his
daughters to paint, I think especially Marina. She was a very
good artist. And when I had my exhibition in Belgrade, I exhib-
ited some of his art work.

They took the opportunity to visit the graves of Prince George
and Princess Marina at Frogmore.

By that time Prince Philip had retired from public life. He
died at Windsor Castle on 9 April 2021, at the age of ninety-
nine. Because of the pandemic, only thirty members of the
Royal Family, including some of Prince Philip's own relations,
were able to attend the funeral service at St George's Chapel.
The Duke was driven down with his cousin and neighbour, the
Duke of Gloucester. They sat in the Quire, socially distanced,
which produced the poignant image of the Queen sitting alone.
The numbers were so restricted that, of his immediate family,
only the Duke and Princess Alexandra were present. Prince
Michael, a page at the wedding in 1947, could not be included.

Duke: I did find that moving, and particularly, of course, the
sight of the Queen sitting there on her own in the corner of the
front row. And Prince Philip's descent into the Royal Vault. It

was dramatic, and made me think of my own father who was lowered into that vault in 1942. He remained there until my mother died when they were buried together at Frogmore.

It's a superb place. I love that chapel. Prince Philip's funeral had been pared down to the minimum, as he would have wished.

It was extraordinary to gather in the antechamber, so recently opened up with the ceremonial staircase once more in use, and also to have that view of the Long Walk, and the troops and others gathered in the Quadrangle. Many of the family had not seen each other for months due to Covid restrictions. We wore morning dress with Garter stars and medals.

I thought back to the young Prince who came so often to Coppins as a naval officer on leave from Far Eastern waters in the mid-1940s, how kind he was to me, taking me to Sweden with him for the Olympic Games in 1952 and steering me into the army when I consulted him about my future. My mother was very fond of him, and we saw a great deal of him over the years. He did not boast of his achievements and so many people were surprised to learn of the extent of his work after he died.

I was aware that he had chosen every detail of the service. There were the lay clerks and a soprano who sang so beautifully, and there was something especially moving about going out into the nave when it was completely empty as I had never seen it before. St George's Chapel has been the scene of so many important events in my life – the funerals of the King and of Queen Mary, and the hauntingly beautiful service for my mother in 1968, then the happier times, such as my daughter Helen's wedding on a lovely summer day in 1992.

I felt privileged to have been one of the thirty in the chapel that April day.

The life of the Queen and of my cousin Philip set such a remarkable example for all of us – the essence of royal service, which my mother taught me, my brother and sister, and which it has been a privilege and a joy to follow all my life.

21

FINALE

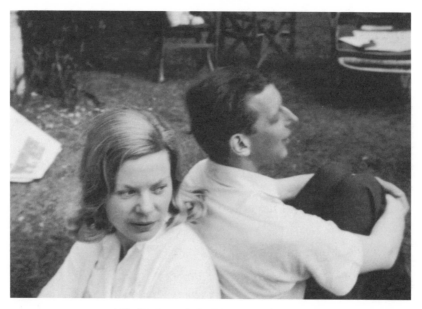

The Duke and the Duchess at Coppins

One day while I was working on this project the Duchess of
Kent invited me to come for a chat. I went to Wren House,
and the Duke took me to her, and left us together. So many
people had asked after her when they knew I was working on
this book. It was good to talk to her too.

The Duchess of Kent: What made you decide to do this?

HV: When the Duke was being christened, there were hundreds
of people in Belgrave Square, watching him come out from the

house, hundreds, and now he can walk along Kensington High Street and people probably don't know who he is.

Duchess: No. They really don't.

HV: I know he would never say so, but it's a pity.

Duchess: It is a pity, but it is completely true. It's not rude in any sense, just the way of life nowadays.

HV: I was in a documentary about Princess Alexandra and one thing I found myself saying in that was that the best members of the family are those who support the Queen and don't compete with her. He's always done that.

Duchess: So right. I never thought of that. It's so true.

HV: I asked him and he said that in the back of his mind he would always look to find a way to lighten the Queen's burden. She can't do everything and he's always been there to help. That's the message I want to get across.

Duchess: Well, that's absolutely perfect. Exactly what he does. Exactly.

British and Danish Family Trees

KING CHRISTIAN IX OF DENMARK
(1818–1906)
=
Princess Louise of Hesse-Cassel
(1817–98)

King George I
of Greece
(1845–1913)
=
Grand Duchess Olga
of Russia
(1851–1926)

Princess Alexandra = King Edward VII
(1844–1925) (1841–1910)

Prince Arthur
Duke of Connaught
(1850–1942)
=
Princess Louise of
Prussia
(1860–1917)

Prince Nicholas
(1872–1938)
=
Grand Duchess Helen
(1882–1957)

King George V
(1865–1936)
=
Princess Victoria Mary
of Teck
(1867–1953)

Princess Louise
The Princess Royal
(1867–1931)
=
Duke of Fife
(1849–1912)

Princess Alexandra = Prince Arthur
Duchess of Fife of Connaught
(1891–1959) (1883–1938)

Princess Marina = Prince George
(1906–68) Duke of Kent
 (1902–42)

Prince Edward
Duke of Windsor
(1894–1972)
=
Mrs Wallis Warfield
(1896–1986)

Princess Mary
The Princess Royal
(1897–1965)
=
Earl of Harewood
(1882–1947)

**Prince Edward
Duke of Kent**
(b. 1935)
=
Katharine Worsley
(b. 1933)

Princess Alexandra
(b. 1936)
=
Rt Hon Sir Angus Ogilvy
(1928–2004)

Prince Michael
(b. 1942)
=
Baroness Marie-Christine
von Reibnitz
(b. 1945)

George
Earl of Harewood
(1923–2011)

Hon Gerald Lascelles
(1924–98)

George
Earl of St Andrews
(b. 1962)
= Sylvana Tomaselli
(b. 1957)

Helen
(b. 1964)
=
Timothy Taylor
(b. 1963)

Nicholas
(b. 1970)
=
Princess Paola Francopan
(b. 1969)

QUEEN VICTORIA = Prince Albert of Saxe-Coburg
(1819–1901) (1819–61)

Princess Alice
(1843–78)
=
Grand Duke Ludwig IV
of Hesse
(1837–92)

Princess Helena
(1846–1923)
=
Prince Christian
of Schleswig-Holstein
(1866–1917)

Prince Leopold,
Duke of Albany
(1853–84)
=
Princess Helen of
Waldeck
(1861–1922)

Princess Beatrice
(1857–1944)
=
Prince Henry
of Battenberg
(1858–96)

Princess Victoria
(1863–1950)
=
Prince Louis
of Battenberg
(1854–1921)

Princess Marie Louise
(1872–1956)

Princess Alice
(1883–1981)
=
Earl of Athlone
(1874–1957)

Princess Victoria Eugenie
(Ena)
(1887–1969)
=
King Alfonso XIII
of Spain
(1886–1941)

Louis, Earl Mountbatten
of Burma
(1900–79)

Princess Alice
(1885–1969)
=
Prince Andrew
of Greece
(1882–1944)

Prince Henry
Duke of Gloucester
(1900–74)
=
Lady Alice
Montagu-Douglas-Scott
(1901–2004)

King George VI
(1895–1952)
=
Lady Elizabeth Bowes-Lyon
(1900–2002)

Prince William
(1941–72)

Prince Richard
Duke of Gloucester
(b. 1944)
= Birgitte van Deurs
(b. 1946)

Princess Margaret
(1930–2002)
=
Antony
Earl of Snowdon
(1930–2017)

Queen Elizabeth II
(b. 1926)

= Prince Philip
of Greece
Duke of
Edinburgh
(1921–2021)

Charles
Prince of Wales
(b. 1948)

Princess Anne
The Princess Royal
(b. 1950)

Prince Andrew
Duke of York
(b. 1960)

Prince Edward
Earl of Wessex
(b. 1964)

Russian and Greek Family Tree

TSAR NICHOLAS I of RUSSIA = Princess Charlotte
(1796–1855) of Prussia
(1798–1860)

Tsar Alexander II = Princess Marie
(1818–81) of Hesse
(1824–80)

Grand Duke Vladimir = Princess Marie of
(1847–1909) Mecklenburg-Schwerin
(1854–1920)

Grand Duchess Helen = Prince Nicholas King Constantine I = Princess Sophie
(1882–1957) of Greece (1868–1923) of Prussia
 (1872–1938) (1870–1932)

Princess Olga Princess Elisabeth Princess Marina Princess Helen
(1903–97) (1904–55) (1906–68) (1896–1982)
= = = =
Prince Paul Count Carl Theodor Prince George King Carol II
of Yugoslavia zu Toerring-Jettenbach Duke of Kent of Romania
(1893–1976) (1900–67) (1902–42) (1893–1953)

Prince Alexander Count Hans Veit Countess Helen
(1924–2016) zu Toerring–Jettenbach zu Toerring-Jettenbach
 (b. 1935) (b. 1937)
 =
 Archduke Ferdinand
Prince Nicholas of Austria
(1928–54) (1928–2004)

Princess Elizabeth
of Yugoslavia
(b. 1936)

Grand Duke Constantine = Princess Alexandra
(1827–92) of Saxe-Altenburg
 (1830–1911)

Grand Duchess Olga = King George I of Greece Grand Duke Constantine = Princess Elizabeth
(1851–1926) (1845–1913) (1858–1915) of Saxe-Altenburg
 (1865–1927)

Prince Andrew = Princess Alice Princess Tatiana = Prince Constantin
(1882–1944) of Battenberg Mother Tamara Bagration-Mukhtransky
 (1885–1969) (1890–1979) (1889–1915)

King Paul I Princess Irene Prince Philip Princess Natasha
(1901–64) (1904–74) Duke of Edinburgh Bagration-Mukhransky
= = (1921–2021) (1914–84)
Princess Frederika Aimone = =
of Prussia Duke of Aosta Queen Elizabeth II Sir Charles Johnston
(1917–81) (1900–48) (b. 1926) (1912–86)

Prince Edward, Duke of Kent King Constantine II
(b. 1935) (b. 1940)
 =
 Princess Anne-Marie
 of Denmark
 (b. 1946)

Source Notes

1 Tribute by M.H. [Sir Michael Hawkins], *The Times*, 15 June 1974.

2 Simon Heffer (ed.), *The Diaries of 'Chips' Channon*, 9 October 1935 (Hutchinson, 2021), p. 476.

3 *The Times*, 10 October 1935.

4 *The Times*, 21 January 1936.

5 Queen Mary's diary, 28 January 1936, quoted in James Pope-Hennessy, *Queen Mary* (George Allen & Unwin, 1959), p. 562.

6 Simon Heffer (ed.), *The Diaries of 'Chips' Channon*, 14 May 1936, (Hutchinson, 2021), p. 513.

7 Simon Heffer (ed.), *The Diaries of 'Chips' Channon*, 1 November 1936, (Hutchinson, 2021), p. 576.

8 W. Macqueen-Pope, *St James's, Theatre of Distinction* (W. H. Allen, 1958), p. 40.

9 *Country Life*, 24 September 1938, p. 300.

10 Agnes de Stoeckl, *My Dear Marquis* (John Murray, 1952), p. 205.

11 *Country Life*, 24 September 1938, p. 305.

12 Agnes de Stoeckl, *Not All Vanity* (John Murray, 1950), p. 95.

13 Agnes de Stoeckl, *Not All Vanity* (John Murray, 1950), p. 96.

14 Agnes de Stoeckl, *My Dear Marquis* (John Murray, 1952), pp 205–7.

15 Agnes de Stoeckl, *Not All Vanity* (John Murray, 1950), p. 239.

16 Horace Smith, *A Horseman Through Six Reigns* (Odhams Press, 1955), p. 152.

17 Agnes de Stoeckl, *Not All Vanity* (John Murray, 1950), p. 240.

18 Agnes de Stoeckl, *Not All Vanity* (John Murray, 1950), p. 243.

19 Agnes de Stoeckl, *Not All Vanity* (John Murray, 1950), p. 246.

20 Unpublished diary of Sir Charles Johnston, 8 September 1968.

21 'Marina', Cecil Beaton, *Sunday Times*, 1 September 1968.

22 *The Times*, 10 July 1952.

23 Bryan Cannon, *Beverley Nichols – A Life* (Constable, 1991), p. 236.

24 *The Times*, 30 September 1952.

25 *The Times*, 10 October 1952.

26 Miscellaneous press cutting – headed 'Week-end Abroad I' (possibly *Daily Express*), 19 October 1952.

27 HRH Princess Marina to Natasha Johnston, Singapore, 10 October 1952.

28 *The Times*, 18 October 1952.

29 *The Times*, 17 December 1952.

30 *The Times*, 28 July 1953.

31 *Daily Mirror*, 28 July 1953.

32 *Daily Express*, June 1956.

33 Sir Maurice Dorman to the secretary of state for the colonies, 24 April 1961 [CO554/2529 – National Archives, Kew].

34 Ibid., 26 April 1961 (CO554/2529 – National Archives, Kew).

35 Cecil Beaton's unpublished diary, 9 June 1962 (Cecil Beaton papers, St John's College, Cambridge).

36 *Daily Mail*, 30 May 1962.

37 Secretary of state for the colonies to Sir Walter Coutts, 11 May 1962 (CO 822/2963 – National Archives, Kew).

38 *Daily Telegraph*, October 1962.

39 *Star Weekly*, 2 November 1963.

40 Graham Payn and Sheridan Morley (eds), *The Noël Coward Diaries* (Weidenfeld & Nicolson, 1982), p. 534 (entry for 19 May 1963).

41 Unpublished diary of Sir Charles Johnston, 1 September 1968.

42 Ibid.

43 HRH Princess Alexandra to Natasha Johnston, Balmoral (undated) September 1968.

44 HRH The Duke of Kent to Prince George Galitzine, Coppins, 31 August 1968.

45 HRH Princess Paul of Yugoslavia to Prince George Galitzine, Kensington Palace, 4 September 1968.

46 Unpublished diary of Sir Charles Johnston, 8 September 1968.

47 *The Times*, August 1968.

48 Cecil Beaton private diary, August 1968, quoted in Hugo Vickers (ed), *Beaton in the Sixties* (Weidenfeld & Nicolson, 2003), pp. 260–1.

49 'The World of Princess Marina', *Sunday Telegraph*, 1 September 1968.

50 'A Day in the Family, 16 March 1971', *Sunday Times Colour Supplement*, July 1971.

51 'Royal Salesman turns out to be a winner', *Sunday Telegraph*, 1977.

52 *Ars Regia 1919–2019*, example 056 of 500 (not for sale), privately printed in Belgrade.

Picture Acknowledgements

Integrated Images

Page 2: © REUTERS/Arthur Edwards/POOL

Page 5: © Max Mumby/Indigo/Getty Images

Page 7: © PA Images/Alamy Stock Photo

Page 22 – Page 84: HRH The Duke of Kent's private collection

Page 86: HRH The Duke of Kent's private collection © Hay Wrightson

Page 89 – Page 119: HRH The Duke of Kent's private collection

Page 122: © Hulton Archive/Getty Images

Page 127: © Popperfoto via Getty Images/Getty Images

Page 133 – Page 141: HRH The Duke of Kent's private collection

Page 144: © TopFoto

Page 154: © Illustrated London News/Mary Evans

Page 162: © Cecil Beaton. Courtesy of the Victoria and Albert Museum, London

Page 170: Hugo Vickers' private collection © Cecil Beaton Courtesy of the Victoria and Albert Museum, London

Page 172: Courtesy of the Buckley Family's private collection

Page 177 – Page 194: HRH The Duke of Kent's private collection

Page 197: HRH The Duke of Kent's private collection © Cecil Beaton. Courtesy of the Victoria and Albert Museum, London

Page 211: Hugo Vickers private collection
Page 220: © PA Images/Alamy Stock Photo
Page 225 – Page 272: HRH The Duke of Kent's private collection
Page 276: Courtesy of HRH Princess Elizabeth of Yugoslavia's private collection
Page 277: © DPA Picture Alliance/Alamy Stock Photo
Page 290 – Page 294: HRH The Duke of Kent's private collection

Inset Images
Inset 1

Pages 1–4: HRH The Duke of Kent's private collection
Page 5, top: © PA Images/Alamy Stock Photo
Page 5, bottom: HRH The Duke of Kent's private collection
Page 6, top: © Cecil Beaton. Courtesy of the Victoria and Albert Museum, London
Page 6, bottom: © Keystone-France/Gamma-Rapho via Getty Images
Pages 7–8: HRH The Duke of Kent's private collection

Inset 2

Pages 1–6: HRH The Duke of Kent's private collection
Page 7, top left and right: © Hugo Vickers
Page 7, bottom: HRH The Duke of Kent's private collection
Page 8, top: © Oli Scarff/WPA Pool/Getty Images
Page 8, bottom: HRH The Duke of Kent's private collection

Text Permissions

The following unpublished writings are copyright and published with permission:

Letters of HRH The Duke of Kent © HRH The Duke of Kent

Letter of HRH Princess Alexandra © HRH Princess Alexandra, The Hon Lady Ogilvy

Letters of HRH Princess Marina, Duchess of Kent © HRH The Duke of Kent

Letter of HRH Princess Paul of Yugoslavia © HRH Princess Elizabeth of Yugoslavia

Diary of Sir Cecil Beaton © The Literary Executor of the late Sir Cecil Beaton – Hugo Vickers

Diary of Sir Charles Johnston © The Literary Executor of the late Sir Charles Johnston – Hugo Vickers

Index